# Learning UML 2.0

# Other resources from O'Reilly

# Learning UML 2.0

*Russ Miles and Kim Hamilton*

O'REILLY®

Beijing · Cambridge · Farnham · Köln · Sebastopol · Taipei · Tokyo

**Learning UML 2.0**
by Russ Miles and Kim Hamilton

Copyright © 2006 O'Reilly Media, Inc. All rights reserved.
Printed in the United States of America.

Published by O'Reilly Media, Inc., 1005 Gravenstein Highway North, Sebastopol, CA 95472.

O'Reilly books may be purchased for educational, business, or sales promotional use. Online editions are also available for most titles (*safari.oreilly.com*). For more information, contact our corporate/institutional sales department: (800) 998-9938 or *corporate@oreilly.com*.

| | |
|---|---|
| **Editors:** Brett McLaughlin and Mary T. O'Brien | **Cover Designer:** Karen Montgomery |
| **Production Editor:** Laurel R.T. Ruma | **Interior Designer:** David Futato |
| **Copyeditor:** Laurel R.T. Ruma | **Cover Illustrator:** Karen Montgomery |
| **Proofreader:** Reba Libby | **Illustrators:** Robert Romano, Jessamyn Read, and Lesley Borash |
| **Indexer:** Angela Howard | |

**Printing History:**

April 2006:          First Edition.

 This book uses RepKover™, a durable and flexible lay-flat binding.

ISBN: 978-0-596-00982-3
[M] 42.5#

# Table of Contents

# Preface

The Unified Modeling Language (UML) is the standard way to model systems, particularly software systems. If you are working on a system beyond "Hello, World," then having UML in your toolbox of skills is a must, and that's where *Learning UML 2.0* comes in.

*Learning UML 2.0* is about coming to grips with UML quickly, easily, and practically. Along with a thorough set of tutorials on each of the different UML diagram types, this book gives you the tools to use UML effectively when designing, implementing, and deploying systems. The topics covered include:

- A brief overview of why it is helpful to model systems
- How to capture high-level requirements in your model to help ensure the system meets users' needs
- How to model the parts that make up your system
- How to model the behavior and interactions between parts when the system is running
- How to move from the model into the real world by capturing how your system is deployed
- How to create custom UML profiles to accurately model different system domains

## Audience

*Learning UML 2.0* is for anyone interested in learning about UML, but it is helpful to have some exposure to object-oriented (OO) design and some familiarity with Java. However, even if you have only a small amount of experience with object orientation, *Learning UML 2.0* will improve and extend your knowledge of OO concepts and give you a comprehensive set of tools to work with UML.

Although this book is intended to take you through each subject on the path to learning UML, some UML modeling subjects, such as use cases and activity diagrams, are self-explanatory, which means you can dive right into them.

# About This Book

*Learning UML 2.0* aims to answer the "what," "how," and "why should I care?" for every aspect of UML. Each chapter picks one subject from UML and explains it based on these questions.

Since not everyone is new to UML, there are two main routes through this book. If you're new to UML as a subject and want to get an overview of where the modeling language came from, then you should start with Chapter 1. However, if you want to get your hands dirty as quickly as possible, then you can either skip the introduction chapter to delve directly into use cases or jump to the chapter that describes the UML diagram in which you are most interested.

Now you know what *Learning UML 2.0* is about, it should be explained what this book is not about. This book is not about any one particular modeling tool or implementation language. However, some tools have their own way of doing things, and some implementation languages do not support everything you can legally model in UML. Wherever appropriate, we have tried to point out where UML tools or implementation languages deviate from or follow the UML standard.

Lastly, because of the large variation in software development processes, this book is not about any particular process or methodology. Instead, it focuses on modeling and provides guidelines about appropriate levels of modeling that can be applied in the context of your software development process. Since this book adheres to the UML 2.0 standard, it works alongside any process or methodology you use.

## Assumptions This Book Makes

The following general assumptions are made as to the reader's knowledge and experience:

- An understanding of object orientation
- Knowledge of the Java™ language for some of the examples

## Conventions Used in This Book

The following typographical conventions are used in this book:

*Italic*
> Indicates new terms, URLs, email addresses, filenames, file extensions, pathnames, directories, and Unix utilities.

`Constant width`
> Indicates commands, options, switches, variables, attributes, keys, functions, types, classes, namespaces, methods, modules, properties, parameters, values, objects, events, event handlers, XML tags, HTML tags, macros, the contents of files, or the output from commands.

**Constant width bold**

Shows commands or other text that should be typed literally by the user.

*Constant width italic*

Shows text that should be replaced with user-supplied values.

This icon signifies a tip, suggestion, or general note.

This icon indicates a warning or caution.

# Using Code Examples

This book is here to help you get your job done. In general, you may use the code in this book in your programs and documentation. You do not need to contact us for permission unless you're reproducing a significant portion of the code. For example, writing a program that uses several chunks of code from this book does not require permission. Selling or distributing a CD-ROM of examples from O'Reilly books *does* require permission. Answering a question by citing this book and quoting example code does not require permission. Incorporating a significant amount of example code from this book into your product's documentation *does* require permission.

We appreciate, but do not require, attribution. An attribution usually includes the title, author, publisher, and ISBN. For example: "*Learning UML 2.0*, by Russ Miles and Kim Hamilton. Copyright 2006 O'Reilly Media, Inc., 0-596-00982-8."

If you feel your use of code examples falls outside fair use or the permission given above, feel free to contact us at *permissions@oreilly.com*.

# Safari® Enabled

**Safari**
BOOKS ONLINE
ENABLED
When you see a Safari® Enabled icon on the cover of your favorite technology book, that means the book is available online through the O'Reilly Network Safari Bookshelf.

Safari offers a solution that's better than e-books. It's a virtual library that lets you easily search thousands of top tech books, cut and paste code samples, download chapters, and find quick answers when you need the most accurate, current information. Try it for free at *http://safari.oreilly.com*.

# How to Contact Us

Everything has been done to ensure that the examples within this book are accurate, tested, and verified to the best of the authors' ability. However, even though UML is a standard modeling language, the best practices as to its usage may change with time and this may have an impact on this book's contents. If so, please address comments and questions concerning this book to the publisher:

O'Reilly Media, Inc.
1005 Gravenstein Highway North
Sebastopol, CA 95472
(800) 998-9938 (in the United States or Canada)
(707) 829-0515 (international or local)
(707) 829-0104 (fax)

There is a web page for this book where you can find errata, examples, and any additional information. You can access this page at:

*http://www.oreilly.com/catalog/learnuml2*

To comment or ask technical questions about this book, email:

*bookquestions@oreilly.com*

For more information about our books, conferences, Resource Centers, and the O'Reilly Network, see our web site:

*http://www.oreilly.com*

Additional information about this topic, including exercises, can be found at:

*http://www.learninguml2.com*

# Acknowledgments

## From the Authors

Thanks to Brett and Mary, our ace editors. We are indebted to Brett for providing valuable guidance throughout, and to Mary for her UML expertise, her amazing work bringing this book to completion, and her ability to line up an outstanding team of reviewers.

We'd also like to thank all the kind individuals who put in the hours to provide such excellent technical feedback on this book. Thanks to Ed Chou, Glen Ford, Stephen Mellor, Eric Naiburg, Adewale Oshineye, Dan Pilone and Neil Pitman, and Richard Mark Soley (the history of UML would not have been nearly as interesting without your help).

## From Russ Miles

First and foremost, my thanks go to my family and friends: Mum, Dad, Bobbie, Rich, Ad, Corinne (thanks for all your help through the last hectic stages, you're one in a million!), Martin and Sam, Jason and Kerry, and Aimee (wonder dog!). You are always there for me 100 percent and, as a bonus, have the uncanny but very useful ability to get me away from the Mac once in a while when I really need it.

I'd also like to take this opportunity to thank my uncle, Bruce Sargent. You got me started on the first steps in this career and for that I am, and always will be, very grateful!

I'd like to thank all my proofreaders, including Rob Wilson, Laura Paterson, and Grant Tarrant-Fisher. You've been great proofreaders, tech reviewers and, most of all, friends. With your comments this a much better book than anything I could have put together on my own. Also, a special thanks to Rachel "Kong" Stevens for being the unwitting inspiration for the front cover—we love ya!

A big thanks must go to M. David Peterson (*http://www.xsltblog.com*) and Sylvain Hellegouarch (*http://www.defuze.org*) for all their help and inspiration with the CMS example that is used throughout this book. You're both top bloggers, developers, and friends and I want to say thanks to you and all the LLUP hackers (*http://www. x2x2x.org/projects/wiki*) for making my coding life that much more interesting, cheers!

Last, but not least—with what is quickly becoming a standard catch-all—thanks to everyone who has helped me out while writing this book. I haven't forgotten your help and I know I owe you all a beer or two!

## From Kim Hamilton

Thanks again to Ed Chou for his gaming expertise that helped create the FPS example (among his many other excellent contributions!) and for the long hours spent reviewing this book at every phase. A big thanks goes to my reviewers: Frank Chiu, Albert Chu, Yu-Li Lin, Justin Lomheim, Samarth Pal, Leland So, and Delson Ting. You were great at everything—from providing technical feedback to pointing out the humor in the word OMG. Thanks to John Arcos, Ben Faul, Mike Klug, Dwight Yorke, and Paul Yuenger, whose support helped me get this book out the door. Also, thanks to Thomas Chen for his CMS help!

Most of all, thanks to my wonderful family and friends—Mom, Dad, Ron, Mark, Grandma and Ed, Grandpa (in loving memory), Aunt Gene, Anne Marie, Kim, Ed C, Sokun, and Tien—who have all been so supportive this past year. Special thanks to my Mom and Dad: my Mom keeps me going with her love, friendship, and phone calls; and my Dad has always been my number one technical mentor.

# CHAPTER 1

# Introduction

The Unified Modeling Language (UML) is *the* standard modeling language for software and systems development. This statement alone is a pretty conclusive argument for making UML part of your software repertoire, however it leaves some questions unanswered. Why is UML unified? What can be modeled? How is UML a language? And, probably most importantly, why should you care?

Systems design on any reasonably large scale is difficult. Anything from a simple desktop application to a full multi-tier enterprise scale system can be made up of hundreds—and potentially thousands—of software and hardware components. How do you (and your team) keep track of which components are needed, what their jobs are, and how they meet your customers' requirements? Furthermore, how do you share your design with your colleagues to ensure the pieces work together? There are just too many details that can be misinterpreted or forgotten when developing a complex system without some help. This is where modeling—and of course UML—comes in.

In systems design, you model for one important reason: to manage complexity. Modeling helps you see the forest for the trees, allowing you to focus on, capture, document, and communicate the important aspects of your system's design.

A model is an *abstraction* of the real thing. When you model a system, you abstract away any details that are irrelevant or potentially confusing. Your model is a *simplification* of the real system, so it allows the design and viability of a system to be understood, evaluated, and criticized quicker than if you had to dig through the actual system itself. Even better, with a formal modeling language, the language is abstract yet just as precise as a programming language. This precision allows a language to be machine-readable, so it can be interpreted, executed, and transformed between systems.

To effectively model a system, you need one very important thing: a language with which the model can be described. And here's where UML comes in.

# What's in a Modeling Language?

A modeling language can be made up of pseudo-code, actual code, pictures, diagrams, or long passages of description; in fact, it's pretty much anything that helps you describe your system. The elements that make up a modeling language are called its *notation*. Figure 1-1 shows an example of a piece of UML notation.

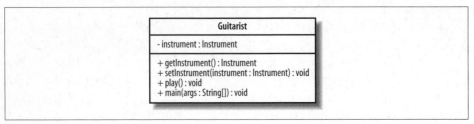

*Figure 1-1. A class declaration as it can be shown using UML notation*

 There are references to the UML meta-model and profiles throughout this book. A more complete description of what the UML meta-model contains and why it is useful is available in Appendix B, but for now, just think of the UML meta-model as the description of what each element of notation means and a profile as a customization of that description for a specific domain (i.e., banking).

However, notation is not the whole story. Without being told that one of the boxes in Figure 1-1 represents a class, you wouldn't necessarily know what it is, even though you might be able to guess. The descriptions of what the notation means are called the *semantics* of the language and are captured in a language's meta-model.

A modeling language can be anything that contains a notation (a way of expressing the model) and a description of what that notation means (a meta-model). But why should you consider using UML when there are so many different ways of modeling, including many you could make up on your own?

Every approach to modeling has different advantages and disadvantages, but UML has six main advantages:

*It's a formal language*
Each element of the language has a strongly defined meaning, so you can be confident that when you model a particular facet of your system it will not be misunderstood.

*It's concise*
The entire language is made up of simple and straightforward notation.

*It's comprehensive*
It describes all important aspects of a system.

*It's scaleable*
> Where needed, the language is formal enough to handle massive system modeling projects, but it also scales down to small projects, avoiding overkill.

*It's built on lessons learned*
> UML is the culmination of best practices in the object-oriented community during the past 15 years.

*It's the standard*
> UML is controlled by an open standards group with active contributions from a worldwide group of vendors and academics, which fends off "vendor lock-in." The standard ensures UML's transformability and interoperability, which means you aren't tied to a particular product.

## Detail Overload: Modeling with Code

Software code is an example of a potential modeling language where none of the detail has been abstracted away. Every line of code *is* the detail of how your software is intended to work. Example 1-1 shows a very simple class in Java, yet there are many details in this declaration.

*Example 1-1. Even in a simple Java class, there can be a lot of detail to navigate through*

```
package org.oreilly.learningUML2.ch01.codemodel;

public class Guitarist extends Person implements MusicPlayer {

    Guitar favoriteGuitar;

    public Guitarist (String name) {
        super(name);
    }

    // A couple of local methods for accessing the class's properties
    public void setInstrument(Instrument instrument ) {
        if (instrument instanceof Guitar) {
            this.favoriteGuitar = (Guitar) instrument;
        }
        else {
            System.out.println("I'm not playing that thing!");
        }
    }

     public Instrument getInstrument() {
        return this.favoriteGuitar;
    }

    // Better implement this method as MusicPlayer requires it
    public void play() {
        System.out.println(super.getName() + "is going to do play the guitar now ...");

        if (this.favoriteGuitar != null) {
```

*Example 1-1. Even in a simple Java class, there can be a lot of detail to navigate through (continued)*

```java
        for (int strum = 1; strum < 500; strum++) {
            this.favoriteGuitar.strum( );
        }
        System.out.println("Phew! Finished all that hard playing");
    }
    else {
        System.out.println("You haven't given me a guitar yet!");
    }
}

// I'm a main program so need to implement this as well
public static void main(String[] args) {
    MusicPlayer player = new Guitarist("Russ");
    player.setInstrument(new Guitar("Burns Brian May Signature"));
    player.play( );
}
}
```

Example 1-1 shows all of the information about the Guitar class, including inheritance relationships to other classes, member variables involving other classes, and even implementation details for the methods themselves.

What's wrong with using software source code as your model? All of the details are there, every element of the language's notation has meaning to the compiler, and with some effective code-level comments, such as JavaDoc, you have an accurate representation of your software system, don't you?

The truth is that you haven't actually modeled anything other than the software implementation. The source code focuses only on the software itself and ignores the rest of the system. Even though the code is a complete and (generally) unambiguous definition of what the software will do, the source code alone simply cannot tell you how the software is to be used and by whom, nor how it is to be deployed; the bigger picture is missing entirely if all you have is the source code.

As well as ignoring the bigger picture of your system, software code presents a problem in that you need to use other techniques to explain your system to other people. You have to understand code to read code, but source code is the language for software developers and is not for other stakeholders, such as customers and system designers. Those people will want to focus just on requirements or perhaps see how the components of your system work together to fulfill those requirements. Because source code is buried in the details of how the software works, it cannot provide the higher level abstract views of your system that are suitable for these types of stakeholders.

Now imagine that you have implemented your system using a variety of software languages. The problem just gets worse. It is simply impractical to ask all the stakeholders in your system to learn each of these implementation languages before they can understand your system.

Finally, if your design is modeled as code, you also lose out when it comes to reuse because design is often reusable whereas code may not be. For example, reimplementing a Java Swing application in HTML or .NET is much simpler if the design is modeled rather than reverse engineering the code. (Reverse engineering is extracting the design of a system from its implementation.)

All of these problems boil down to the fact that source code provides only one level of abstraction: the software implementation level. Unfortunately, this root problem makes software source code a poor modeling language.

## Verbosity, Ambiguity, Confusion: Modeling with Informal Languages

At the opposite end of the spectrum from complete and precise source code models are informal languages. *Informal languages* do not have a formally defined notation; there are no hard and fast rules as to what a particular notation can mean, although sometimes there are guidelines.

A good example of an informal language is natural language. Natural language—the language that you're reading in this book—is notoriously ambiguous in its meaning. To accurately express something so that everyone understands what you are saying is at best a challenge and at worst flat-out impossible. Natural language is flexible and verbose, which happens to be great for conversation but is a real problem when it comes to systems modeling.

The following is a *slightly* exaggerated but technically accurate natural language model of Example 1-1:

> Guitarist is a class that contains six members: one static and five non-static. Guitarist uses, and so needs an instance of, Guitar; however, since this might be shared with other classes in its package, the Guitar instance variable, called favoriteGuitar, is declared as default.
>
> Five of the members within Guitarist are methods. Four are not static. One of these methods is a constructor that takes one argument, and instances of String are called name, which removes the default constructor.
>
> Three regular methods are then provided. The first is called setInstrument, and it takes one parameter, an instance of Instrument called instrument, and has no return type. The second is called getInstrument and it has no parameters, but its return type is Instrument. The final method is called play. The play method is actually enforced by the MusicPlayer interface that the Guitarist class implements. The play method takes no parameters, and its return type is void.
>
> Finally, Guitarist is also a runable program. It contains a method that meets the Java specification for a main method for this reason.

If you take a hard look at this definition, you can see problems everywhere, almost all resulting from ambiguity in the language. This ambiguity tends to result in the, "No, that's not what I meant!" syndrome, where you've described something as clearly as possible, but the person that you are conveying the design to has misunderstood your meaning (see Figure 1-2).

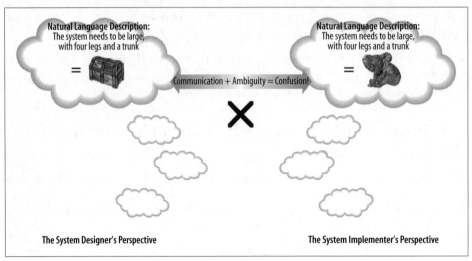

Figure 1-2. *Even a simple natural language sentence can be interpreted differently by different stakeholders in the system*

The problems with informal languages are by no means restricted to written languages. The same description of Guitarist might be presented as a picture like that shown in Figure 1-3.

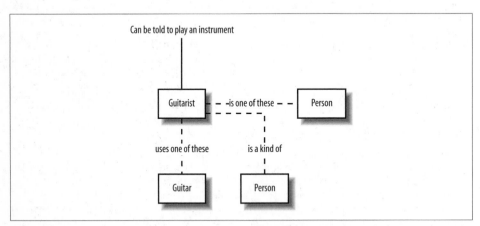

Figure 1-3. *Informal notation can be confusing; even though my intentions with this diagram might appear obvious, you really can't be sure unless I also tell you what the notation means*

Figure 1-3 is another example of an informal language, and it happens to be a notation that I just made up. It makes perfect sense to me, but you could easily misinterpret my intentions.

As with the natural language model, all of the details are present in Figure 1-3's picture, but without a definition of what the boxes, connections, and labels mean, you can't be sure about your interpretation (or mine!).

 So, why does any of this matter if your team has a home-grown modeling technique it's been using for years and you all understand what each other means? If you ever have to show your design to external stakeholders, they might become frustrated trying to understand your home-grown symbols, when you could have used a standard notation they already know. It also means you don't have to learn a new modeling technique every time you switch jobs!

The basic problem with informal languages is that they don't have exact rules for their notation. In the natural language example, the meanings of the model's sentences were obscured by the ambiguity and verbosity of the English language. The picture in Figure 1-3 may not have suffered from quite the same verbosity problems, but without knowing what the boxes and lines represent, the meaning of the model was left largely to guesswork.

Because informal languages are not precise, they can't be transformed into code as a formal language can. Imagine if Figure 1-3 had a set of formal rules; then you could generate code that implemented the classes for Guitarist, Person, and so on. But this is impossible without understanding the rules. Unfortunately, informal languages will always suffer from the dual problem of verbosity and ambiguity, and this is why they are a poor—and sometimes extremely dangerous—technique for modeling systems, as shown in Figure 1-4.

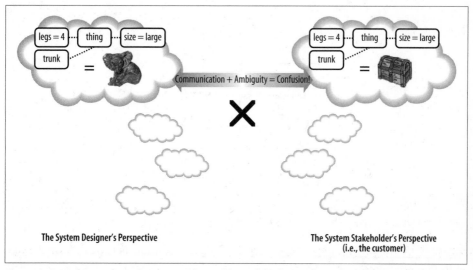

*Figure 1-4. With an informal notation, the problem of confusion through ambiguity still exists*

Although natural language is dangerously ambiguous, it is still one of the best techniques for capturing requirements, as you will see when you learn about use cases in Chapter 2.

## Getting the Balance Right: Formal Languages

You've now seen some of the pitfalls of using a too-detailed language for modeling (source code) and a too-verbose and ambiguous language for modeling (natural language). To effectively model a system—avoiding verbosity, confusion, ambiguity, and unnecessary details—you need a *formal modeling language*.

Ideally, a formal modeling language has a simple notation whose meaning is well-defined. The modeling language's notation should be small enough to be learned easily and must have an unambiguous definition of the notation's meaning. UML is just such a formal modeling language.

Figure 1-5 shows how the code structure in Example 1-1 can be expressed in UML. For now, don't worry too much about the notation or its meaning; at this point, the UML diagram is meant to be used only as a comparison to the informal pictorial and natural language models shown previously.

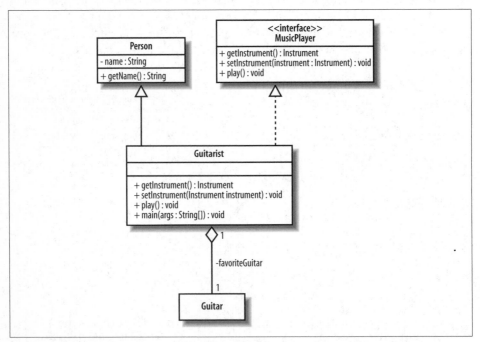

*Figure 1-5. Expressing the static structure of the Guitarist class structure in formal UML notation*

Even if you don't yet understand all of the notation used in Figure 1-5, you can probably start to grasp that there are some details present in the code—see Example 1-1—that are not modeled here. For example, the specific implementation of the play( ) method has been abstracted away, allowing you to visualize the code's structure without excess clutter.

The best thing about having modeled the system using UML is that the notation in Figure 1-5 has a specific and defined meaning. If you were to take this diagram to any other stakeholder in your system, provided he knows UML, the design would be clearly understood. This is the advantage of using formal languages for modeling as shown in Figure 1-6.

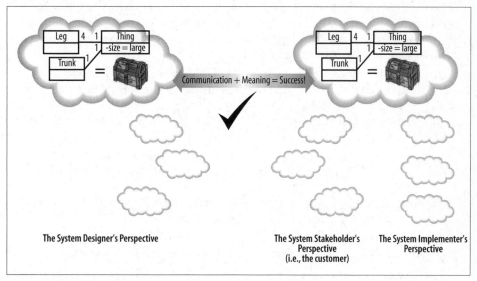

*Figure 1-6. With a modeling language that has a formally defined meaning, you can ensure that everyone is reading the picture the same way*

## Why UML 2.0?

The first version of UML allowed people to communicate designs unambiguously, convey the essence of a design, and even capture and map functional requirements to their software solutions. However, the world changed more fundamentally with the recognition that systems modeling, rather than just software modeling, could also benefit from a unified language such as UML.

The driving factors of component-oriented software development, model-driven architectures, executable UML, and the need to share models between different tools placed demands on UML that it had not originally been designed to meet.

Also, UML 1.x and all of its previous revisions were designed as a unified language for *humans*. When it became important for models to be shared between *machines*—specifically between Computer Aided Systems Engineering (CASE) tools—UML 1.x was again found wanting. UML 1.x's underlying notation rules and its meta-model were (ironically) not formally defined enough to enable machine-to-machine sharing of models.

---

### MDA and Executable UML

Two reasonably new approaches to system development inspired many of the improvements made in UML 2.0. In a nutshell, Model Driven Architectures (MDAs) provide a framework that supports the development of Platform Independent Models (PIMs)—models that capture the system in a generic manner that is divorced from concerns such as implementation language and platform.

PIMs can then be transformed into separate Platform Specific Models (PSMs) that contain concrete specifications for a particular system deployment (containing details such as implementation language and communications protocols, etc.). MDA requires a formally structured and interoperable meta-model to perform its transformations, and this level of meta-model is now provided by UML 2.0.

For many of the same reasons, executable UML provides a means by which a PSM could contain enough complete information so that the model can be effectively run. Some day, you could conceivably drag around a few symbols, and complete, runnable software would pop out! An executable UML engine requires that the UML model be defined well enough for it to be able to generate and execute the modeled system.

Unfortunately, even though UML 2.0 is supposed to provide the mechanisms to make MDA and executable UML a reality, tools support is not yet fully developed.

---

Although UML 1.5 described a system fairly well, the model describing the model—the meta-model—had become patched and overly complex. Like any system that has an overly complex design, and is fragile and difficult to extend, UML had become overly complex, fragile, and difficult to extend; it was time for a re-architecture.

The designers of UML 2.0 were very careful to ensure that UML 2.0 would not be too unfamiliar to people who were already using UML 1.x. Many of the original diagrams and associated notations have been retained and extended in UML 2.0 as shown in Table 1-1. However, new diagram types have been introduced to extend the language just enough so that it can support the latest best practices.

With Version 2.0, UML has evolved to support the new challenges that software and system modelers face today. What began many years ago as a unification of the different methods for software design has now grown into a unified modeling language that is ready and suitable to continue to be the standard language for the myriad of different tasks involved in software and systems design.

---

*Table 1-1. To describe the larger landscape of systems design, UML 2.0 renamed and clarified its diagrams for the new challenges facing system modelers today*

| Diagram type | What can be modeled? | Originally introduced by UML 1.x or UML 2.0 | To learn about this diagram type, go to... |
|---|---|---|---|
| Use Case | Interactions between your system and users or other external systems. Also helpful in mapping requirements to your systems. | UML 1.x | Chapter 2 |
| Activity | Sequential and parallel activities within your system. | UML 1.x | Chapter 3 |
| Class | Classes, types, interfaces, and the relationships between them. | UML 1.x | Chapters 4 and 5 |
| Object | Object instances of the classes defined in class diagrams in configurations that are important to your system. | Informally UML 1.x | Chapter 6 |
| Sequence | Interactions between objects where the order of the interactions is important. | UML 1.x | Chapter 7 |
| Communication | The ways in which objects interact and the connections that are needed to support that interaction. | Renamed from UML 1.x's collaboration diagrams | Chapter 8 |
| Timing | Interactions between objects where timing is an important concern. | UML 2.0 | Chapter 9 |
| Interaction Overview | Used to collect sequence, communication, and timing diagrams together to capture an important interaction that occurs within your system. | UML 2.0 | Chapter 10 |
| Composite Structure | The internals of a class or component, and can describe class relationships within a given context. | UML 2.0 | Chapter 11 |
| Component | Important components within your system and the interfaces they use to interact with each other. | UML 1.x, but takes on a new meaning in UML 2.0 | Chapter 12 |
| Package | The hierarchical organization of groups of classes and components. | UML 2.0 | Chapter 13 |

*Table 1-1. To describe the larger landscape of systems design, UML 2.0 renamed and clarified its diagrams for the new challenges facing system modelers today (continued)*

| Diagram type | What can be modeled? | Originally introduced by UML 1.x or UML 2.0 | To learn about this diagram type, go to… |
|---|---|---|---|
| State Machine | The state of an object throughout its lifetime and the events that can change that state. | UML 1.x | Chapter 14 |
| Deployment | How your system is finally deployed in a given real-world situation. | UML 1.x | Chapter 15 |

# Models and Diagrams

Many newcomers to UML focus on the different types of diagrams used to model their system. It's very easy to assume that the set of diagrams that have been created actually *are* the model. This is an easy mistake to make because when you are using UML, you will normally be interacting with a UML tool and a particular set of diagrams. But UML modeling is not just about diagrams; it's about capturing your system as a model—the diagrams are actually just windows into that model.

A particular diagram will show you some parts of your model but not necessarily everything. This makes sense, since you don't want a diagram showing everything in your model all at once—you want to be able to split contents of your model across several diagrams. However, not everything in your model needs to exist on a diagram for it to be a part of your model.

So, what does this mean? Well, the first thing to understand is that your model sits behind your modeling tool and diagrams as a collection of elements. Each of those elements could be a use case, a class, an activity, or any other construct that UML supports. The collection of all the elements that describe your system, including their connections to each other, make up your model.

However, if all you could do was create a model made up of elements, then you wouldn't have much to look at. This is where diagrams come in. Rather than actually being your model, diagrams are used merely as a canvas on which you can create new elements that are then added to your model and organize related elements into a set of views on your underlying model.

So, when you next use your UML tool to work with a set of diagrams in UML notation, it is worth remembering that what you are manipulating is a view of the contents of your model. You can change elements of your model within the diagram, but the diagram itself is *not* the model—it's just a useful way of presenting some small part of the information your model contains.

# "Degrees" of UML

UML can be used as much or as little as you like. Martin Fowler describes three common ways that people tend to use UML:

*UML as a sketch*
> Use UML to make brief sketches to convey key points. These are throwaway sketches—they could be written on a whiteboard or even a beer coaster in a crunch.

*UML as a blueprint*
> Provide a detailed specification of a system with UML diagrams. These diagrams would not be disposable but would be generated with a UML tool. This approach is generally associated with software systems and usually involves using forward and reverse engineering to keep the model synchronized with the code.

*UML as a programming language*
> This goes directly from a UML model to executable code (not just portions of the code as with forward engineering), meaning that every aspect of the system is modeled. Theoretically, you can keep your model indefinitely and use transformations and code generation to deploy to different environments.

The approach used depends on the type of application you're building, how rigorously the design will be reviewed, whether you are developing a software system, and, if it is software, the software development process you're using.

In certain industries, such as medical and defense, software projects tend to lean toward UML as a blueprint because a high level of quality is demanded. Software design is heavily reviewed since it could be mission-critical: you don't want your heart monitoring machine to suddenly display the "blue screen of death."

Some projects can get away with less modeling. In fact, some commercial industries find that too much modeling is cumbersome and slows down productivity. For such projects, it makes sense to use UML as a sketch and have your model contain some architectural diagrams and a few class and sequence diagrams to illustrate key points.

# UML and the Software Development Process

When you are using UML to model a software system, the "degree of UML" you apply is partially influenced by the software development process you use.

A software development process is a recipe used for constructing software—determining the capabilities it has, how it is constructed, who works on what, and the timeframes for all activities. Processes aim to bring discipline and predictability to software development, increasing the chance of success of a project. Since UML is the language for modeling your software, it's an important part of the software development process.

A few well-known software development processes include:

*Waterfall*
> The waterfall method attempts to pin down the requirements early in the project life cycle. After gathering requirements, software design is performed in full. Once the design is complete, the software is implemented. The problem with this method is that if a change in requirements occurs, the impact can be devastating.

*Iterative*
> Iterative methods attempt to address the shortcomings of the waterfall approach by accepting that change will happen and, in fact, embracing it. The Unified Process is a well-known iterative process. It consists of multiple phases, each phase containing some amount of the following activities: requirements, design, and implementation (coding). Iterative methods encompass a wider range of approaches (e.g., agile iterative processes), and they can range from using UML as sketch to using UML as blueprint.

*Agile methods*
> Agile methods use iterations in extremely short bursts and attempt to minimize risk by always having a working system of expanding capabilities. Methodologies under this category have introduced some of the more interesting development practices, such as pair programming and test-driven development. Agile methods emphasize using UML as a sketch.

# Views of Your Model

There are a number of ways to break up your UML model diagrams into perspectives or views that capture a particular facet of your system. In this book, we use Kruchten's 4+1 view model to help you show you how each diagram type plays a part in the overall model, as shown in Figure 1-7.

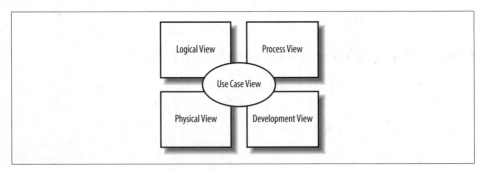

*Figure 1-7. Philippe Kruchten's 4+1 view model*

The 4+1 view model breaks down a model into a set of views, each capturing a specific aspect of your system:

*Logical view*

Describes the abstract descriptions of a system's parts. Used to model what a system is made up of and how the parts interact with each other. The types of UML diagrams that typically make up this view include class, object, state machine, and interaction diagrams.

*Process view*

Describes the processes within your system. It is particularly helpful when visualizing what must happen within your system. This view typically contains activity diagrams.

*Development view*

Describes how your system's parts are organized into modules and components. It is very useful to manage layers within your system's architecture. This view typically contains package and component diagrams.

*Physical view*

Describes how the system's design, as described in the three previous views, is then brought to life as a set of real-world entities. The diagrams in this view show how the abstract parts map into the final deployed system. This view typically contains deployment diagrams.

*Use case view*

Describes the functionality of the system being modeled from the perspective of the outside world. This view is needed to describe what the system is supposed to do. All of the other views rely on the use case view to guide them—that's why the model is called 4+1. This view typically contains use case diagrams, descriptions, and overview diagrams.

Each view offers a different and important perspective on your model. If you find yourself asking, "Why do I care about this?" as you read about a particular notation or diagram, refer to the view that the diagram or notation provides to understand why it is needed.

 To learn more about Kruchten's 4+1 view model, check out "Architectural Blueprints—The '4+1' View Model of Software Architecture" by Philippe Kruchten, at *http://www3.software.ibm.com/ibmdl/pub/software/rational/web/whitepapers/2003/Pbk4p1.pdf*. For an overview, visit *http://www-128.ibm.com/developerworks/wireless/library/wi-arch11/*.

# A First Taste of UML

Before jumping into the different types of diagrams that make up UML, you need to know about two elements of UML notation that are used throughout a model: notes and stereotypes.

## Notes

*Notes* allow you to enter additional comments that aren't captured in your diagrams. You can write anything you want in a note to explain your diagram, similar to a comment in code. Notes are pictured with the folded rectangle notation as shown in Figure 1-8.

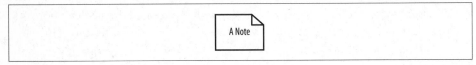

*Figure 1-8. A UML note*

Notes can be placed on a diagram in isolation or attached to a specific part of the diagram as shown in Figure 1-9.

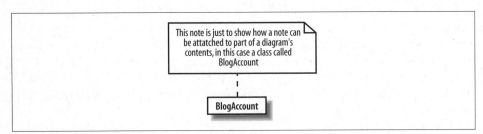

*Figure 1-9. A note is attached to another element on the diagram using a dotted line*

In this book, notes are used to explain something more about a particular diagram. Notes are just aids for the reader of a diagram; they don't change the meaning of the diagram or the underlying model at all.

## Stereotypes

*Stereotypes* signify a special use or intent and can be applied to almost any element of UML notation. Stereotypes modify the meaning of an element and describe the element's role within your model.

A stereotype sometimes has an associated icon, such as in Figure 1-10's stick-figure actor symbol. To learn more about actors, see Chapter 2.

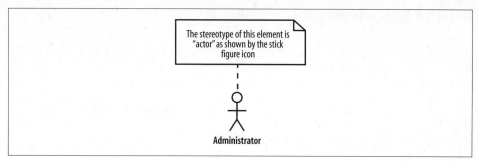

*Figure 1-10. The Administrator is represented in the role of an actor because it is using the stick figure notation associated with that stereotype*

There isn't always a special icon for a stereotype; sometimes they take up too much room and clutter a diagram. In these cases, the stereotype is shown using guillemots at either end of the stereotype name, as in «stereotype_name», shown in Figure 1-11. However, because guillemots require an extended character set, you can substitute them for angle brackets, as in <<stereotype_name>>.

*Figure 1-11. The Administrator element is still an actor, but its stereotype is now specified using a name rather than an icon*

There is no limit to the number of stereotypes with which an element can be associated; sometimes you may end up specifying more than one stereotype, as shown in Figure 1-12.

*Figure 1-12. The Administrator is now stereotyped as an actor and a person*

The UML specification defines a set of "standard" or predefined stereotypes. Some of the more useful standard stereotypes include:

### Stereotype applied to classes (see Chapters 4 and 5)

utility

Represents a class that provides utility services through static methods, just as Java's Math class.

### Stereotypes applied to components (see Chapter 12)

service
> A stateless, functional component that computes a value; could be used to represent a web service.

subsystem
> A large component that is actually a subordinate system of a larger system.

### Stereotypes applied to artifacts (see Chapter 15)

executable
> A physical file that is executable, such as an *.exe* file.

file
> A physical file used by your system; this could be a configuration file such as a *.txt* file.

library
> A static or dynamic library file; you could use this to model *.dll* or *.jar* library files.

source
> A source file containing code, such as a *.java* or *.cpp* file.

### Tagged values

Stereotypes can contain extra information that relates to the element to which they are applied. This extra information is specified using tagged values.

*Tagged values* are associated with a stereotype. Say you had an element in your model that represented a login page on a web site, and it was stereotyped as a form. The form stereotype needs to know whether it should validate the contents of the form or not in this case. This validation decision should be declared as a tagged value of the form stereotype because it is associated with the stereotype that is applied to an element, not with the element itself.

A tagged value is drawn on a diagram using a similar notation to notes, but the folded rectangle contains the name of any stereotypes and settings for any associated tagged values. The tagged value note is then attached to the stereotyped element using a dotted line with a circle at the element end, as shown in Figure 1-13. (This example was adapted from *UML 2.0 in a Nutshell* [O'Reilly].)

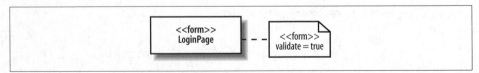

*Figure 1-13. The form stereotype has an associated validate tagged value, which is set to true in this case*

In UML 2.0, stereotypes and their tagged values are defined using profiles. To learn more about stereotypes and how to create roles for the elements of your model, see Appendix B.

## Want More Information?

The next step is to jump into Chapter 2 and start learning UML. If you're a bit of a history buff, then you can also check out a brief history of UML in Appendix C.

UML is a concise language but a big subject. As well as learning about UML, it's worth reading through the tutorials and documentation available at the Object Management Group's web site, *http://www.omg.org*.

# CHAPTER 2

# Modeling Requirements: Use Cases

Imagine that it's Monday morning and your first day on a new project. The requirements folks have just popped in for a coffee—and to leave you the 200-page requirements document they've been working on for the past six months. Your boss's instructions are simple: "Get your team up to speed on these requirements so that you can all start designing the system." Happy Monday, huh?

To make things just a bit more difficult, the requirements are still a little fuzzy, and they are all written in the language of the user—confusing and ambiguous natural language rather than in a language that your system stakeholders can easily understand. See the "Verbosity, Ambiguity, Confusion: Modeling with Informal Languages" section in Chapter 1 for more on the problems of modeling with natural and informal languages.

What is the next step, apart from perhaps a moment or two of sheer panic? How do you take this huge set of loosely defined requirements and distill it into a format for your designers without losing important detail? UML, as you know from Chapter 1, is the answer to both of these questions. Specifically, you need to work with your system's stakeholders to generate a full set of requirements and something new—use cases.

A *use case* is a case (or situation) where your system is used to fulfill one or more of your user's requirements; a use case captures a piece of functionality that the system provides. Use cases are at the heart of your model, shown in Figure 2-1, since they affect and guide all of the other elements within your system's design.

Use cases are an excellent starting point for just about every facet of object-oriented system development, design, testing, and documentation. They describe a system's requirements strictly from the outside looking in; they specify the value that the system delivers to users. Because use cases *are* your system's functional requirements, they should be the first serious output from your model after a project is started. After all, how can you begin to design a system if you don't know what it will be required to do?

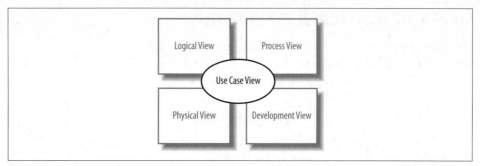

*Figure 2-1. Use cases affect every other facet of your system's design; they capture what is required and the other views on your model, then show how those requirements are met*

 Use cases specify only what your system is supposed to do, i.e., the system's functional requirements. They *do not* specify what the system shall not do, i.e., the system's nonfunctional requirements. Nonfunctional requirements often include performance targets and programming languages, etc.

When you are working on a system's requirements, questions often arise as to whether the system has a particular requirement. Use cases are a means to bring those gaps in the user's requirements to the forefront at the beginning of a project.

This is a real bonus for the system designer since a gap or lack of understanding identified early on in a project's development will cost far less in both time and money than a problem that is not found until the end of a project. Once a gap has been identified, go back to the system's stakeholders—the customers and users—so they can provide the missing information.

 It's even better when a requirement is presented as a use case and the stakeholder sees that the requirement has little or no value to the system. If a stakeholder can discard unnecessary requirements, both money and time are saved.

Once priority and risk are assigned to a use case, it can help manage a project's workload. Your use cases can be assigned to teams or individuals to be implemented and, since a use case represents tangible user value, you can track the progress of the project by use cases delivered. If and when a project gets into schedule trouble, use cases can be jettisoned or delayed to deliver the highest value soonest.

Last but not least, use cases also help construct tests for your system. Use cases provide an excellent starting point for building your test cases and procedures because they precisely capture a user's requirements and success criteria. What better way to test your system than by using the use cases that originally captured what the user wanted in the first place?

# Capturing a System Requirement

Enough theory for now; let's take a look at a simple example. Suppose we're defining requirements for a weblog content management system (CMS).

---

### Requirement A.1

The content management system shall allow an administrator to create a new blog account, provided the personal details of the new blogger are verified using the author credentials database.

---

There's actually no specific "best way" to start analyzing Requirement A.1, but one useful first step is to look at the *things* that interact with your system. In use cases, these external things are called *actors*.

 The terms shall and should have a special and exact meaning when it comes to requirements. A *shall requirement* must be fulfilled; if the feature that implements a shall requirement is not in the final system, then the system does not meet this requirement. A *should requirement* implies that the requirement is not critical to the system working but is still desirable. If a system's development is running into problems that will cause delivery delays, then it's often the should requirements that are sacrificed first.

---

### Blog Features

Weblogs, commonly referred to as blogs, originally started out as privately maintained web pages for authors to write about anything. These days, blogs are usually packaged into an overall CMS. Bloggers submit new entries to the system, administrators allocate blogging accounts, and the systems typically incorporate advanced features, such as RSS feeds. A well-publicized blog can attract thousands of readers (see O'Reilly's blogging site at *http://weblogs.oreillynet.com*).

---

## Outside Your System: Actors

An actor is drawn in UML notation using either a "stick man" or a stereotyped box (see "Stereotypes" in Chapter 1) and is labeled with an appropriate name, as shown in Figure 2-2.

Figure 2-2 captures the Administrator role as it is described in Requirement A.1. The system that is being modeled is the CMS; the requirement's description indicates

---

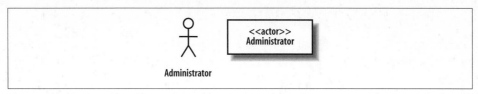

*Figure 2-2. Requirement A.1 contains an Administrator actor that interacts with the system to create a blog account*

that the `Administrator` interacts with the system to create a new blogger's account. The `Administrator` *interacts with* the system and is *not part of* the system; therefore, the `Administrator` is defined as an actor.

---

## What's in a Name?

It's actually worth being very careful when naming your actors. The best approach is to use a name that can be understood by both your customer *and* your system designers. Wherever possible, use the original term for the actor as identified within your customer's requirements; that way, at least your use cases will be familiar to your customers. This approach also lets system designers get comfortable with the system's unique context.

---

Deciding what is and what is not an actor is tricky and is something best learned by experience. Until you've gained some of that experience, Figure 2-3 shows a simple technique for analyzing a "thing" that you've found in your requirements and how to decide whether it is an actor or not.

Actors don't have to be actual people. While an actor might be a person, it could also be a third party's system, such as in a business-to-business (B2B) application. Think of an actor as a black box: you cannot change an actor and you are not interested in how it works, but it must interact with your system.

### Tricky actors

Not all actors are obvious external systems or people that interact with your system. An example of a common tricky actor is the system clock. The name alone implies that the clock is part of the system, but is it really?

The system clock comes into play when it invokes some behavior within your system. It is hard to determine whether the system clock is an actor because the clock is not clearly outside of your system. As it turns out, the system clock *is* often best described as an actor because it is not something that you can influence. Additionally, describing the clock as an actor will help when demonstrating that your system needs to perform a task based on the current time.

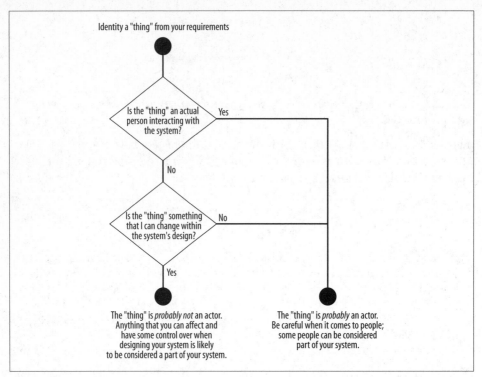

Figure 2-3. *Here are a couple of questions to ask yourself when trying to identify an actor*

It is also tempting to focus on just the users of your systems as the actors in your model, but don't forget about other people, such as auditors, installers, maintainers, upgraders, and so on. If you focus on only the obvious users of your system, then you might forget about some of these other stakeholders, and that can be very dangerous! Those actors may have a veto ("We can't certify this system without proof that the data has not been tampered with") or they may have to enforce important nonfunctional requirements, such as an upgrade in a 10-minute system downtime window and an upgrade without shutting the system down, etc. If these actors are ignored, these important functions of your system won't be documented, and you risk ending up with a worthless system.

### Refining actors

When going through the process of capturing all of the actors that interact with your system, you will find that some actors are related to each other, as shown in Figure 2-4.

The Administrator actor is really a special kind of system user. To show that an administrator can do whatever a regular user can do (with some extra additions), a generalization arrow is used. For more on generalization and the generalization arrow, see Chapter 5.

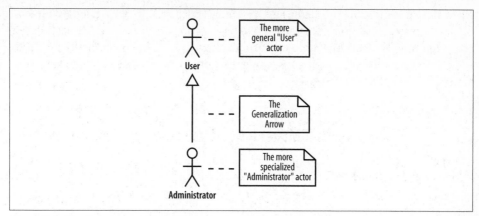

Figure 2-4. Showing that an administrator is a special kind of user

## Use Cases

Once you have captured an initial set of actors that interact with your system, you can assemble the exact model of those interactions. The next step is to find cases where the system is being used to complete a specific job for an actor—use cases, in fact. Use cases can be identified from your user's requirements. This is where those wordy, blurry definitions in the user requirements document should be distilled into a clear set of jobs for your system.

 Remember, if use cases are truly requirements, then they must have very clear pass/fail criteria. The developer, the tester, the technical writer, and the user must explicitly know whether the system fulfils the use case or not.

A use case, or job, might be as simple as allowing the user to log in or as complex as executing a distributed transaction across multiple global databases. The important thing to remember is that a use case—from the user's perspective—is a complete use of the system; there is some interaction with the system, as well as some output from that interaction. For example, Requirement A.1 describes one main use of the CMS: to create a new blog account. Figure 2-5 shows how this interaction is captured as a use case.

Figure 2-5. A use case in UML is drawn as an oval with a name that describes the interaction that it represents

After all that build-up, you might have expected a use case to be a complex piece of notation. Instead, all you get is an oval! The notation for a use case is very simple and often hides its importance in capturing system concerns. Don't be deceived; the use case is probably the single most powerful construct in UML to make sure your system does what it is supposed to.

---

### What Makes a Good Use Case?

Experience will help you determine when you have a good use case, but there is a rule of thumb that can be used to specify a use case:

*A use case is something that provides some measurable result to the user or an external system.*

Any piece of system behavior that meets this simple test is likely to be a good candidate for a use case.

---

## Communication Lines

At this point, we've identified a use case and an actor, but how do we show that the Administrator actor participates in the Create a new Blog Account use case? The answer is by using communication lines.

A *communication line* connects an actor and a use case to show the actor participating in the use case. In this example, the Administrator actor is involved in the Create a new Blog Account use case; this is shown in Figure 2-6 by adding a communication line.

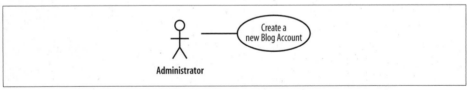

*Figure 2-6. A communication line joins the Administrator actor to the "Create a new Blog Account" use case; the Administrator is involved in the interaction that the use case represents*

This simple example shows a communication line between only one actor and only one use case. There is potential to have any number of actors involved in a use case. There is no theoretical limit to the number of actors that can participate in a use case.

To show a collection of actors participating in a use case, all you have to do is draw a communication line from each of the participating actors to the use case oval, as shown in Figure 2-7.

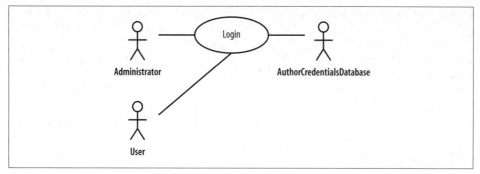

*Figure 2-7. The login use case interacts with three actors during its execution*

Sometimes UML diagrams will have communication lines with navigability; for example, a diagram with an arrow at one end will show the flow of information between the actor and the use case, or show who starts the use case. Although this notation is not really a crime in UML terms, it's not a very good use of communication lines.

The purpose of a communication line is to show that an actor is simply *involved* in a use case, not to imply an information exchange in any particular direction or that the actor starts the use case. That type of information is contained within a use case's detailed description, therefore it doesn't make sense to apply navigation to communication lines. For more on use cases and descriptions, see "Use Case Descriptions," later in this chapter.

## System Boundaries

Although there is an implicit separation between actors (external to your system) and use cases (internal to your system) that marks your system's boundary, UML does provide another small piece of notation if you want to make things crystal clear.

To show your system's boundary on a use case diagram, draw a box around all of the use cases but keep the actors outside of the box. It's also good practice to name your box after the system you are developing, as shown for the CMS in Figure 2-8.

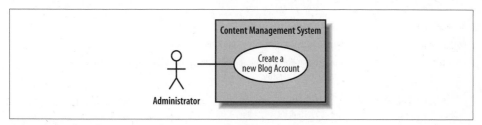

*Figure 2-8. The Administrator actor is located outside of the CMS, explicitly showing that the system boundary box use cases must fall within the system boundary box, since it doesn't make sense to have a use case outside of your system's boundary*

# Use Case Descriptions

A diagram showing your use cases and actors may be a nice starting point, but it does not provide enough detail for your system designers to actually understand exactly how the system's concerns will be met. How can a system designer understand who the most important actor is from the use case notation alone? What steps are involved in the use case? The best way to express this important information is in the form of a text-based description—every use case should be accompanied by one.

There are no hard and fast rules as to what exactly goes into a use case description according to UML, but some example types of information are shown in Table 2-1.

*Table 2-1. Some types of information that you can include in your use case descriptions*

| Use case description detail | What the detail means and why it is useful |
| --- | --- |
| Related Requirements | Some indication as to which requirements this use case partially or completely fulfills. |
| Goal In Context | The use case's place within the system and why this use case is important. |
| Preconditions | What needs to happen before the use case can be executed. |
| Successful End Condition | What the system's condition should be if the use case executes successfully. |
| Failed End Condition | What the system's condition should be if the use case fails to execute successfully. |
| Primary Actors | The main actors that participate in the use case. Often includes the actors that trigger or directly receive information from a use case's execution. |
| Secondary Actors | Actors that participate but are not the main players in a use case's execution. |
| Trigger | The event triggered by an actor that causes the use case to execute. |
| Main Flow | The place to describe each of the important steps in a use case's normal execution. |
| Extensions | A description of any alternative steps from the ones described in the Main Flow. |

Table 2-2 shows an example use case description for the Create a new Blog Account use case and provides a handy template for your own descriptions.

*Table 2-2. A complete use case description for the "Create a new Blog Account" use case*

| Use case name | Create a new Blog Account |
| --- | --- |
| Related Requirements | Requirement A.1. |
| Goal In Context | A new or existing author requests a new blog account from the Administrator. |
| Preconditions | The system is limited to recognized authors and so the author needs to have appropriate proof of identity. |
| Successful End Condition | A new blog account is created for the author. |
| Failed End Condition | The application for a new blog account is rejected. |
| Primary Actors | Administrator. |
| Secondary Actors | Author Credentials Database. |
| Trigger | The Administrator asks the CMS to create a new blog account. |

*Table 2-2. A complete use case description for the "Create a new Blog Account"*
*use case (continued)*

| Use case name | Create a new Blog Account | |
|---|---|---|
| Main Flow | Step | Action |
| | 1 | The Administrator asks the system to create a new blog account. |
| | 2 | The Administrator selects an account type. |
| | 3 | The Administrator enters the author's details. |
| | 4 | The author's details are verified using the Author Credentials Database. |
| | 5 | The new blog account is created. |
| | 6 | A summary of the new blog account's details are emailed to the author. |
| Extensions | Step | Branching Action |
| | 4.1 | The Author Credentials Database does not verify the author's details. |
| | 4.2 | The author's new blog account application is rejected. |

The format and content in Table 2-2 is only an example, but it's worth remembering that use case descriptions and the information that they contain are more than just extra information to accompany the use case diagrams. In fact, a use case's description completes the use case; without a description a use case is, well, not very useful.

The description in Table 2-2 was reasonably straightforward, but something's not quite right when you compare the description to the original use case diagram (shown in Figure 2-9; although the use case description mentions two actors, this use case diagram shows only one).

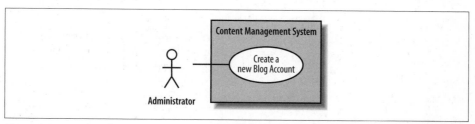

*Figure 2-9. Ensuring that your use case diagrams match the more detailed use case descriptions is critical*

The use case description has identified a new actor, the Author Credentials Database. By creating a complete description of the Create a new Blog Account use case, it becomes clear that this actor is missing.

If you can, it's worth reviewing your use case model with your users as much as possible to ensure that you have captured all of the key uses of your system and that nothing has been missed.

You will often find that items are missing from your diagrams as more detail goes into your use case descriptions. The same goes for any aspect of your model: the more detail you put in, the more you might have to go back and correct what you did before. This is what iterative system development is all about. Don't be too worried though, this refinement of your model is a good thing. With each iteration of development you will (hopefully!) get a better and more accurate model of your system.

Figure 2-10 shows the corrected use case diagram incorporating the new Author Credentials Database actor.

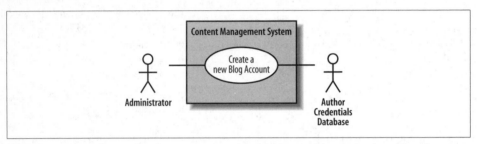

*Figure 2-10. Bring the use case diagram in sync with the use case's description by adding the Author Credentials Database actor*

## How Many Use Cases Should Your Model Have?

There is no set rule for the number of use cases that your use case model should contain for a given system. The number of use cases depends on the of the jobs that your system has to do according to the requirements. This means that for a particular system, you might only need two use cases or you might need hundreds.

It is more important that you have the *right* use cases, rather than worrying about the amount you have. As with most things in system modeling, the best way to get your use cases right is to get used to applying them; experience will teach you what is right for your own systems.

# Use Case Relationships

A use case describes the way your system behaves to meet a requirement. When filling out your use case descriptions, you will notice that there is some similarity between steps in different use cases. You may also find that some use cases work in several different modes or special cases. Finally, you may also find a use case with multiple flows throughout its execution, and it would be good to show those important optional cases on your use case diagrams.

Wouldn't it be great if you could get rid of the repetition between use case descriptions and show important optional flows right on your use case diagrams? OK, so that was a loaded question. You can show reusable, optional, and even specialized use case behavior between use cases.

## The <<include>> Relationship

So far, you have seen that use cases typically work with actors to capture a requirement. Relationships between use cases are more about breaking your system's behavior into manageable chunks than adding anything new to your system. The purpose of use case relationships is to provide your system's designers with some architectural guidance so they can efficiently break down the system's concerns into manageable pieces within the detailed system design.

 In addition to blogs, a CMS can have any number of means for working with its content. One popular mechanism for maintaining documents is by creating a Wiki. Wikis allow online authors to create, edit, and link together web pages to create a web of related content, or a Wiki-web. A great example of a Wiki is available at *http://www.Wikipedia.org*.

Take another look at the `Create a new Blog Account` use case description shown in Table 2-2. The description seems simple enough, but suppose another requirement is added to the `Content Management System`.

---

### Requirement A.2

The content management system shall allow an administrator to create a new personal Wiki, provided the personal details of the applying author are verified using the Author Credentials Database.

---

To capture Requirement A.2 a new use case needs to be added to the `Content Management System`, as shown in Figure 2-11.

Now that we have added the new use case to our model, it's time to fill out a detailed use case description (shown in Table 2-3). See Table 2-1 if you need to refresh your memory about the meaning of each of the details within a use case description.

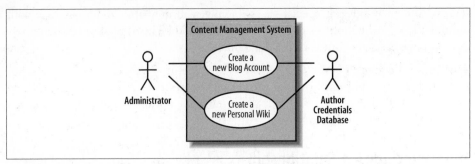

*Figure 2-11. A new requirement can often mean a new use case for the system, although it's not always a one-to-one mapping*

*Table 2-3. The detailed description for the "Create a new Personal Wiki" use case*

| Use case name | Create a new Personal Wiki | |
|---|---|---|
| Related Requirements | Requirement A.2. | |
| Goal In Context | A new or existing author requests a new personal Wiki from the Administrator. | |
| Preconditions | The author has appropriate proof of identity. | |
| Successful End Condition | A new personal Wiki is created for the author. | |
| Failed End Condition | The application for a new personal Wiki is rejected. | |
| Primary Actors | Administrator. | |
| Secondary Actors | Author Credentials Database. | |
| Trigger | The Administrator asks the CMS to create a new personal Wiki. | |
| Main Flow | **Step** | **Action** |
| | 1 | The Administrator asks the system to create a new personal Wiki. |
| | 2 | The Administrator enters the author's details. |
| | 3 | The author's details are verified using the Author Credentials Database. |
| | 4 | The new personal Wiki is created. |
| | 5 | A summary of the new personal Wiki's details are emailed to the author. |
| Extensions | **Step** | **Branching Action** |
| | 3.1 | The Author Credentials Database does not verify the author's details. |
| | 3.2 | The author's new personal Wiki application is rejected. |

The first thing to notice is that we have some redundancy between the two use case descriptions (Tables 2-2 and 2-3). Both Create a new Blog Account and Create a new Personal Wiki need to check the applicant's credentials. Currently, this behavior is simply repeated between the two use case descriptions.

This repetitive behavior shared between two use cases is best separated and captured within a totally new use case. This new use case can then be reused by the `Create a new Blog Account` and `Create a new Personal Wiki` use cases using the `<<include>>` relationship (as shown in Figure 2-12).

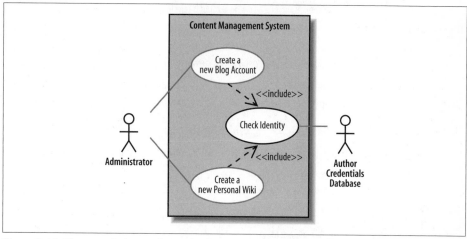

Figure 2-12. The <<include>> relationship supports reuse between use cases

The `<<include>>` relationship declares that the use case at the tail of the dotted arrow *completely* reuses all of the steps from the use case being included. In Figure 2-12, the `Create a new Blog Account` and `Create a new Personal Wiki` completely reuse all of the steps declared in the `Check Identity` use case.

You can also see in Figure 2-12 that the `Check Identity` use case is not directly connected to the `Administrator` actor; it picks this connection up from the use cases that include it. However, the connection to the `Author Credentials Database` is now solely owned by the `Check Identity` use case. A benefit of this change is that it emphasizes that the `Check Identity` use case is the only one that relies directly on a connection to the `Author Credentials Details Database` actor.

To show the `<<include>>` relationship in your use case descriptions, you need to remove the redundant steps from the `Create a new Blog Account` and `Create new Personal Wiki` use case descriptions and instead use the `Included Cases` field and `include::<use case name>` syntax to indicate the use case where the reused steps reside, as shown in Tables 2-4 and 2-5.

Table 2-4. Showing <<include>> in a use case description using Included Cases and include::<use case name>

| Use case name | Create a new Blog Account |
|---|---|
| Related Requirements | Requirement A.1. |
| Goal In Context | A new or existing author requests a new blog account from the Administrator. |
| Preconditions | The author has appropriate proof of identity. |

*Table 2-4. Showing <<include>> in a use case description using Included Cases and include::<use case name> (continued)*

| Use case name | Create a new Blog Account | |
|---|---|---|
| Successful End Condition | A new blog account is created for the author. | |
| Failed End Condition | The application for a new blog account is rejected. | |
| Primary Actors | Administrator | |
| Secondary Actors | **None** | |
| Trigger | The Administrator asks the CMS to create a new blog account. | |
| Included Cases | **Check Identity** | |
| Main Flow | **Step** | **Action** |
| | 1 | The Administrator asks the system to create a new blog account. |
| | 2 | The Administrator selects an account type. |
| | 3 | The Administrator enters the author's details. |
| | 4 | The author's details are checked. |
| | **include::Check Identity** | |
| | 5 | The new account is created. |
| | 6 | A summary of the new blog account's details are emailed to the author. |

*Table 2-5. The Create a new Personal Wiki use case description also gets a makeover*

| Use case name | Create a new Personal Wiki | |
|---|---|---|
| Related Requirements | Requirement A.2 | |
| Goal In Context | A new or existing author requests a new personal Wiki from the Administrator. | |
| Preconditions | The author has appropriate proof of identity. | |
| Successful End Condition | A new personal Wiki is created for the author. | |
| Failed End Condition | The application for a new personal Wiki is rejected. | |
| Primary Actors | Administrator | |
| Secondary Actors | **None** | |
| Trigger | The Administrator asks the CMS to create a new personal Wiki. | |
| Included Cases | **Check Identity** | |
| Main Flow | **Step** | **Action** |
| | 1 | The Administrator asks the system to create a new personal Wiki. |
| | 2 | The Administrator enters the author's details. |
| | 3 | The author's details are checked. |
| | **include::Check Identity** | |

*Table 2-5. The Create a new Personal Wiki use case description also gets a makeover (continued)*

| Use case name | Create a new Personal Wiki | |
|---|---|---|
| | 5 | The new personal Wiki is created. |
| | 6 | A summary of the new personal Wiki's details are emailed to the author. |

Now you can create a use case description for the reusable steps within the Check Identity use case, as shown in Table 2-6.

*Table 2-6. The Check Identity use case description contains the reusable steps*

| Use case name | Check Identity | |
|---|---|---|
| Related Requirements | Requirement A.1, Requirement A.2. | |
| Goal In Context | An author's details need to be checked and verified as accurate. | |
| Preconditions | The author being checked has appropriate proof of identity. | |
| Successful End Condition | The details are verified. | |
| Failed End Condition | The details are not verified. | |
| Primary Actors | Author Credentials Database. | |
| Secondary Actors | None. | |
| Trigger | An author's credentials are provided to the system for verification. | |
| Main Flow | **Step** | **Action** |
| | 1 | The details are provided to the system. |
| | 2 | The Author Credentials Database verifies the details. |
| | 3 | The details are returned as verified by the Author Credentials Database. |
| Extensions | **Step** | **Branching Action** |
| | 2.1 | The Author Credentials Database does not verify the details. |
| | 2.2 | The details are returned as unverified. |

Why bother with all this hassle with reuse between use cases? Why not just have two use cases and maintain the similar steps separately? All this reuse has two important benefits:

- Reuse using <<include>> removes the need for tedious cut-and-paste operations between use case descriptions, since updates are made in only one place instead of every use case.
- The <<include>> relationship gives you a good indication at system design time that the implementation of Check Identity will need to be a reusable part of your system.

## Special Cases

Sometimes you'll come across a use case whose behavior, when you start to analyze it more carefully, can be applied to several different cases, but with small changes. Unlike the <<include>> relationship, which allows you to reuse a small subset of behavior, this is applying a use case with small changes for a collection of specific situations. In object-oriented terms, you potentially have a number of specialized cases of a generalized use case.

Let's take a look at an example. Currently, the Content Management System contains a single Create a new Blog Account use case that describes the steps required to create an account. But what if the CMS supports several different types of blog accounts, and the steps required to create each of these accounts differs ever so slightly from the original use case? You want to describe the *general* behavior for creating a blog account—captured in the Create a new Blog Account use case—and then define specialized use cases in which the account being created is a specific type, such as a regular account with one blog or an editorial account that can make changes to entries in a set of blogs.

This is where *use case generalization* comes in. A more common way of referring to generalization is using the term inheritance. *Use case inheritance* is useful when you want to show that one use case is a special type of another use case. To show use case inheritance, use the generalization arrow to connect the more general, or *parent*, use case to the more specific use case. Figure 2-13 shows how you could extend the CMS's use cases to show that two different types of blog accounts can be created.

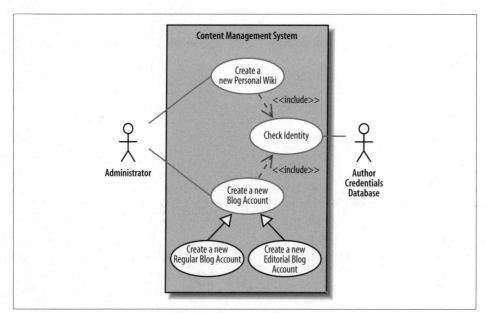

*Figure 2-13. Two types of blog account, regular and editorial, can be created by the Management System*

Taking a closer look at the Create a new Editorial Blog Account specialized use case description, you can see how most of the behavior from the more general Create a new Blog Account use case is reused. Only the details that are specific to creating a new editorial account need to be added (see Table 2-7).

*Table 2-7. You can show that a use case is a special case of a more general use case within the detailed description using the Base Use Cases field*

| Use case name | Create a new Editorial Blog Account | |
|---|---|---|
| Related Requirements | Requirement A.1. | |
| Goal In Context | A new or existing author requests a new **editorial** blog account from the Administrator . | |
| Preconditions | The author has appropriate proof of identity. | |
| Successful End Condition | A new **editorial** blog account is created for the author. | |
| Failed End Condition | The application for a new **editorial** blog account is rejected. | |
| Primary Actors | Administrator. | |
| Secondary Actors | **None**. | |
| Trigger | The Administrator asks the CMS to create a new **editorial** account that will allow an author to edit entries in a set of blogs. | |
| Base Use Cases | **Create a new Blog Account** | |
| Main Flow | **Step** | **Action** |
| | 1 | The Administrator asks the system to create a new blog account. |
| | 2 | **The Administrator selects the editorial account type.** |
| | 3 | The Administrator enters the author's details. |
| | 4 | **The Administrator selects the blogs that the account is to have editorial rights over.** |
| | 5<br>include::Check Identity | The author's details are checked. |
| | 6 | The new editorial account is created. |
| | 7 | A summary of the new editorial account's details are emailed to the author. |
| Extensions | **Step** | **Branching Action** |
| | 5.1 | **The author is not allowed to edit the indicated blogs.** |
| | 5.2 | **The editorial blog account application is rejected.** |
| | 5.3 | **The application rejection is recorded as part of the author's history.** |

Use case inheritance is a powerful way of reusing a use case so that you only have to specify the extra steps that are needed in the more specific use cases. See Chapter 5 for more information on inheritance between classes.

But be careful—by using inheritance, you are effectively saying that *every* step in the general use case *must* occur in the specialized use cases. Also, every relationship that the general use case has with external actors or use cases, as shown with the <<include>> relationship between Create a new Blog Account and Check Identity, must also make sense in the more specialized cases, such as Create a new Editorial Blog Account.

If you really don't want your more specific use case to do everything that the general use case describes, then *don't use generalization.* Instead, you might want to consider using either the <<include>> relationship shown in the previous section or the <<extend>> relationship coming up in the next section.

## The <<extend>> Relationship

Any explanation of the <<extend>> stereotype should be preceded by a warning that it is the most heavily debated type of use case relationship. Almost nothing is less understood or harder to accurately communicate within the UML modeling community than the <<extend>> use case relationship, and this presents a bit of a problem when you are trying to learn about it. Figure 2-14 shows you how <<extend>> works; take a look, and then let's dive into some UML concept and theory.

*Figure 2-14. The <<extend>> use case relationship looks a bit like the <<include>> relationship, but that's where the similarities end*

At first glance—particularly if you are a Java programmer—<<extend>> seems very similar to inheritance between classes. In Java, a class can extend from a base class. Similarly, in C++ and C#, you can declare inheritance between classes, and you would often say that a class extends another class. In both these cases, the extend relationship between classes *means inheritance.* So, for a programmer, it follows that <<extend>> should mean something like inheritance, right?

Alarm bells should definitely be going off now. You already saw in the previous section how use cases declare inheritance using a generalization arrow, so why would you need yet another type of arrow with an <<extend>> stereotype? Does the generalization arrow mean the same thing as the <<extend>> stereotype? Unfortunately, the <<extend>> stereotype has *very little in common with inheritance*, and so the two definitely do not mean the same thing.

The designers of UML 2.0 took a very different view as to the meaning of <<extend>> between use cases. They wanted a means for you to show that a use case *might* completely reuse another use case's behavior, similar to the <<include>> relationship, but that this reuse was *optional* and dependent either on a runtime or system implementation decision.

From the CMS example, the Create a new Blog Account use case might want to record that a new author applied for an account and was rejected, adding this information to the author's application history. Extra steps can be added to the Create a new Blog Account use case's description to show this optional behavior, as shown in Step 4.3 in Table 2-8.

*Table 2-8. Behavior that is a candidate for <<extend>> relationship reuse can usually be found in the Extensions section of a use case description*

| Use case name | Create a new Blog Account | |
|---|---|---|
| Related Requirements | Requirement A.1. | |
| Goal In Context | A new or existing author requests a new blog account from the Administrator. | |
| Preconditions | The author has appropriate proof of identity. | |
| Successful End Condition | A new blog account is created for the author. | |
| Failed End Condition | The application for a new blog account is rejected. | |
| Primary Actors | Administrator. | |
| Secondary Actors | None . | |
| Trigger | The Administrator asks the CMS to create a new blog account. | |
| Included Cases | Check Identity | |
| Main Flow | **Step** | **Action** |
| | 1 | The Administrator asks the system to create a new blog account. |
| | 2 | The Administrator selects an account type. |
| | 3 | The Administrator enters the author's details. |
| | 4 | The author's details are checked. |
| | include::Check Identity | |
| | 5 | The new account is created. |
| | 6 | A summary of the new blog account's details are emailed to the author. |
| Extensions | **Step** | **Branching Action** |
| | 4.1 | The author is not allowed to create a new blog. |
| | 4.2 | The blog account application is rejected. |
| | 4.3 | **The application rejection is recorded as part of the author's history.** |

The same behavior captured in Step 4.3 would also be useful if the customer was refused an account for some reason during the `Create a new Personal Wiki` use case's execution. According to the requirements, this reusable behavior is *optional* in both cases; you don't want to record a rejection if the application for a blog account or a personal Wiki was accepted. The <<extend>> relationship is ideal in this sort of reuse situation, as shown in Figure 2-15.

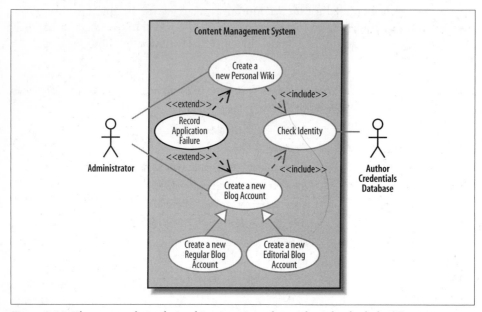

*Figure 2-15. The <<extend>> relationship comes into play to show that both the "Create a new Personal Wiki" and "Create a new Blog Account" use cases might occasionally share the application rejection recording behavior*

The new `Record Application Failure` use case, as the name implies, captures all of the behavior associated with recording an author's application failure whether it be for a personal Wiki or for a specific type of blog account. Using the <<extend>> relationship, the `Record Application Failure` use case's behavior is *optionally* reused by the `Create a new Blog Account` and `Create a new Personal Wiki` use cases if an application is rejected.

## Use Case Overview Diagrams

When you are trying to understand a system, it is sometimes useful to get a glimpse of the context within which it sits. For this purpose, UML provides the *Use Case Overview* diagram. Use Case Overview diagrams give you an opportunity to paint a broad picture of your system's context or domain (see Figure 2-16 for an example).

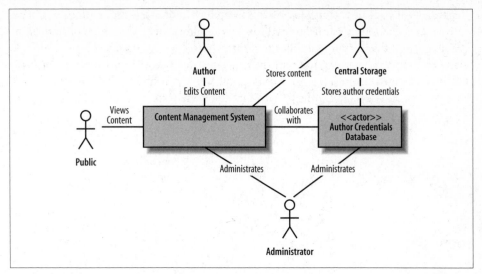

*Figure 2-16. The CMS's context as shown on a Use Case Overview diagram*

Unfortunately, Use Case Overviews are badly named as they don't usually contain any use cases. The use cases are not shown because the overview is designed to provide a context to your system; the system's internals—captured by use cases—are not normally visible.

Use Case Overviews are a useful place to show any extra snippets of information when understanding your system's place within the world. Those snippets often include relationships and communication lines between actors. These contextual pieces of information do not usually contain a great deal of detail, they are more a placeholder and starting point for the rest of your model's detail.

# What's Next?

Although this book, like UML, does not push any particular system development process, there are some common steps that are taken after the first cut of use cases are captured.

With your use case model in hand, it is often a good time to start delving into the high-level activities that your system will have to execute to fulfill its use cases. See Chapter 3 for information on activity diagrams.

Once you have a good grip on the high-level activities, look at the classes and components that will actually make up the parts of your system. You already might have some idea of what those classes contain, and so the next stop naturally would be to create a few rudimentary class diagrams. See Chapter 4 for information on class diagrams.

Regardless of your next step, just because you have a use case model does not necessarily mean that you are finished with use cases altogether. The only constant in life is change, and this certainly applies to your system's requirements. As a requirement changes—either because some new system constraint has been found or because a user has changed his mind—you need to go back and refine your use cases to make sure you are still developing the system that the users want.

# CHAPTER 3

# Modeling System Workflows: Activity Diagrams

Use cases show *what* your system should do. Activity diagrams allow you to specify *how* your system will accomplish its goals. Activity diagrams show high-level actions chained together to represent a process occurring in your system. For example, you can use an activity diagram to model the steps involved with creating a blog account.

Activity diagrams are particularly good at modeling *business processes*. A business process is a set of coordinated tasks that achieve a business goal, such as shipping customers' orders. Some business process management (BPM) tools allow you to define business processes using activity diagrams, or a similar graphical notation, and then execute them. This allows you to define and execute, for example, a payment approval process where one of the steps invokes a credit card approval web service—using an easy graphical notation such as activity diagrams.

Activity diagrams are the only UML diagram in the process view of your system's model, as shown in Figure 3-1.

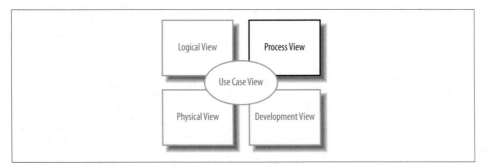

*Figure 3-1. The Process View shows the high-level processes in your system—this is exactly what activity diagrams are good at doing*

Activity diagrams are one of the most accessible UML diagrams since they use symbols similar to the widely-known flowchart notation; therefore, they are useful for describing processes to a broad audience. In fact, activity diagrams have their roots in flowcharts, as well as UML state diagrams, data flow diagrams, and Petri Nets.

# Activity Diagram Essentials

Let's look at the basic elements of activity diagrams by modeling a process encoun-tered earlier in the book—the steps in the blog account creation use case. Table 3-1 contains the Create a new Blog Account use case description (originally Table 2-1). The Main Flow and Extension sections describe steps in the blog account creation process.

*Table 3-1. Create a new Blog Account use case description*

| Use case name | Create a new Blog Account | |
|---|---|---|
| Related Requirements | Requirement A.1. | |
| Goal In Context | A new or existing author requests a new blog account from the Administrator. | |
| Preconditions | The system is limited to recognized authors, and so the author needs to have appropriate proof of identity. | |
| Successful End Condition | A new blog account is created for the author. | |
| Failed End Condition | The application for a new blog account is rejected. | |
| Primary Actors | Administrator. | |
| Secondary Actors | Author Credentials Database. | |
| Trigger | The Administrator asks the Content Management System to create a new blog account. | |
| **Main Flow** | **Step** | **Action** |
| | 1 | The Administrator asks the system to create a new blog account. |
| | 2 | The Administrator selects an account type. |
| | 3 | The Administrator enters the author's details. |
| | 4 | The author's details are verified using the Author Credentials Database. |
| | 5 | The new blog account is created. |
| | 6 | A summary of the new blog account's details are emailed to the author. |
| **Extensions** | **Step** | **Branching Action** |
| | 4.1 | The Author Credentials Database does not verify the author's details. |
| | 4.2 | The author's new blog account applica-tion is rejected. |

Figure 3-2 shows this blog account creation process in activity diagram notation. An activity diagram is useful here because it helps you to better visualize a use case's steps (compared to the table notation in the use case description), especially the branching steps that depend on whether the author is verified.

In Figure 3-2, the activity is launched by the *initial node*, which is drawn as a filled circle. The initial node simply marks the start of the activity. At the other end of the

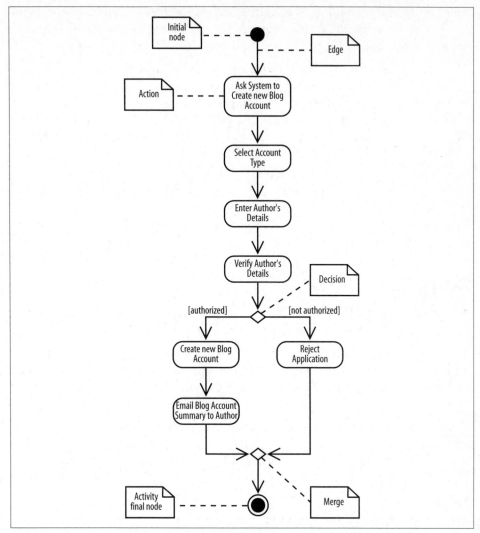

*Figure 3-2. Activity diagrams model dynamic behavior with a focus on processes; the basic elements of activity diagrams are shown in this blog account creation process*

diagram, the *activity final node*, drawn as two concentric circles with a filled inner circle, marks the end of the activity.

In between the initial node and the activity final node are *actions*, which are drawn as rounded rectangles. Actions are the important steps that take place in the overall activity, e.g., Select Account Type, Enter Author's Details, and so on. An action could be a behavior performed, a computation, or any key step in the process.

The flow of the activity is shown using arrowed lines called *edges* or *paths*. The arrowhead on an activity edge shows the direction of flow from one action to the next. A line going into a node is called an *incoming edge*, and a line exiting a node is called an *outgoing edge*. Edges string the actions together to determine the overall activity flow: first the initial node becomes active, then Ask System to create new Blog Account, and so on.

The first diamond-shaped node is called a *decision*, analogous to an if-else statement in code. Notice that there are two outgoing edges from the decision in Figure 3-2, each labeled with Boolean conditions. Only one edge is followed out of the decision node depending on whether the author is authorized. The second diamond-shaped node is called a *merge*. A merge node combines the edges starting from a decision node, marking the end of the conditional behavior.

The word "flow" was mentioned several times previously and you may ask—what's flowing? The answer depends on the context. Typically, it's the flow of control from one action to the next: one action executes to completion, then gives up its control to the next action. In later sections you'll see that, along with control, objects can flow through an activity.

## Activities and Actions

Actions are active steps in the completion of a process. An action can be a calculation, such as Calculate Tax, or a task, such as Verify Author's Details.

The word "activity" is often mistakenly used instead of "action" to describe a step in an activity diagram, but they are not the same. An *activity* is the process being modeled, such as washing a car. An *action* is a step in the overall activity, such as Lather, Rinse, and Dry.

The actions in this simple car-washing activity are shown in Figure 3-3.

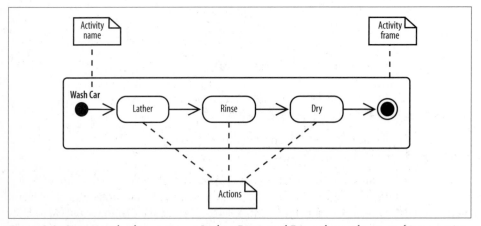

*Figure 3-3. Capturing the three actions—Lather, Rinse, and Dry—that make up washing a car in an activity diagram*

In Figure 3-3, the entire activity is enclosed within the rounded rectangle called an *activity frame*. The activity frame is used to contain an activity's actions and is useful when you want to show more than one activity on the same diagram. Write the name of the activity in the upper left corner.

The activity frame is optional and is often left out of an activity diagram, as shown in the alternative Wash Car activity in Figure 3-4.

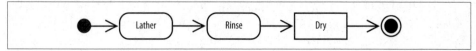

*Figure 3-4. The activity frame can be omitted*

Although you lose the name of the activity being displayed on the diagram itself, it is often more convenient to leave out the activity frame when constructing a simple activity diagram.

## Decisions and Merges

*Decisions* are used when you want to execute a different sequence of actions depending on a condition. Decisions are drawn as diamond-shaped nodes with one incoming edge and multiple outgoing edges, as shown in Figure 3-5.

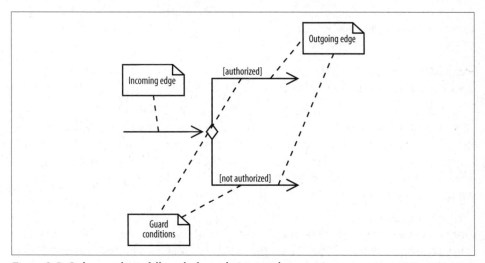

*Figure 3-5. Only one edge is followed after a decision node*

Each branched edge contains a *guard condition* written in brackets. Guard conditions determine which edge is taken after a decision node.

They are statements that evaluate to true or false, for example:

[authorized]
> If the authorized variable evaluates to true, then follow this outgoing edge.

[wordCount >= 1000]
> If the wordCount variable is greater than or equal to 1,000, then follow this outgoing edge.

The branched flows join together at a *merge* node, which marks the end of the conditional behavior started at the decision node. Merges are also shown with diamond-shaped nodes, but they have multiple incoming edges and one outgoing edge, as shown in Figure 3-6.

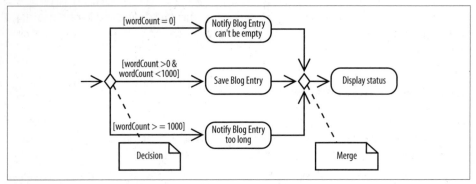

*Figure 3-6. If the input value of age is 1200, then the Notify Blog Entry too long action is performed*

Activity diagrams are clearest if the guards at decision nodes are complete and mutually exclusive. Figure 3-7 shows a situation in which the paths are not mutually exclusive.

If an item is in stock and the order is a rush order, then two guards evaluate to true. So which edge is followed? According to the UML specifications, if multiple guards evaluate to true, then only one edge is followed and that choice is out of your control unless you specify an order. You can avoid this complicated situation by making guards mutually exclusive.

The other situation to avoid is incomplete guards. For example, if Figure 3-7 had no guard covering out of stock items, then an out of stock item can't follow any edge out of the decision node. This means the activity is frozen at the decision node. Modelers sometimes leave off guards if they expect a situation not to occur (or if they want to defer thinking about it until later), but to minimize confusion, you should always include a guard to cover every possible situation. If it's possible in your activity, it's helpful to label one path with else, as shown in Figure 3-7, to make sure all situations are covered.

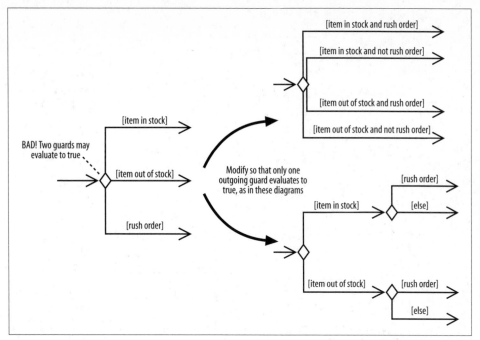

*Figure 3-7. Beware of diagrams where multiple guards evaluate to true*

If you're coming from a UML 1.x background, it may not seem necessary to show merge nodes. In UML 1.x, it was common to see multiple edges starting at a decision node flow directly into an action, as shown in the top part of Figure 3-8. This meant the flows were merged implicitly.

As of UML 2.0, when multiple edges lead directly into an action, all incoming flows are waited on before proceeding. But this doesn't make sense because only one edge is followed out of a decision node. You can avoid confusing your reader by explicitly showing merge nodes.

# Doing Multiple Tasks at the Same Time

Consider a computer assembly workflow that involves the following steps:

1. Prepare the case.
2. Prepare the motherboard.
3. Install the motherboard.
4. Install the drives.
5. Install the video card, sound card, and modem.

So far we've covered enough activity diagram notation to model this workflow sequentially. But suppose the entire workflow can be sped up by preparing the case

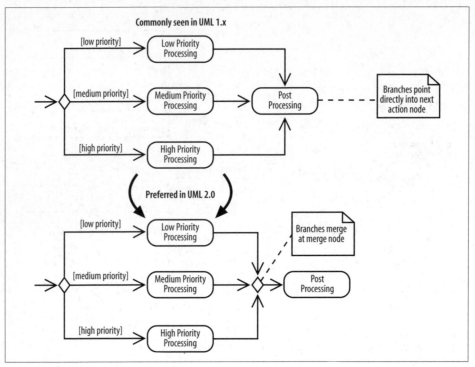

Figure 3-8. In UML 2.0, it's better to be as clear as possible and to show merge nodes

and the motherboard at the same time since these actions don't depend on each other. Steps that occur at the same time are said to occur *concurrently* or *in parallel*.

You represent parallel actions in activity diagrams by using *forks* and *joins*, as shown in the activity diagram fragment in Figure 3-9.

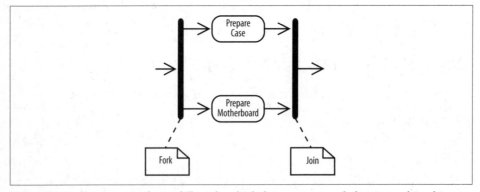

Figure 3-9. Both outgoing paths are followed at the fork, in contrast with decision nodes, where only one outgoing path is taken

After a fork in Figure 3-9, the flow is broken up into two or more simultaneous flows, and the actions along all forked flows execute. In Figure 3-9, Prepare Case and Prepare Motherboard begin executing at the same time.

The join means that all incoming actions must finish before the flow can proceed past the join. Forks and joins *look* identical—they are both drawn with thick bars— but you can tell the difference because forks have multiple outgoing flows, whereas joins have multiple incoming flows.

 In a detailed design model, you can use forks to represent multiple processes or multiple threads in a program.

Figure 3-10 completes the activity diagram for the computer assembly workflow.

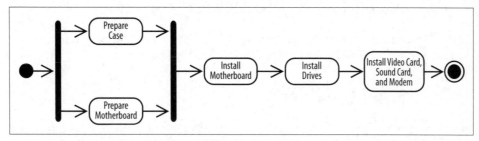

*Figure 3-10. The computer assembly workflow demonstrates how forks and joins work in a complete activity diagram*

When actions occur in parallel, it doesn't necessarily mean they will finish at the same time. In fact, one task will most likely finish before the other. However, the join prevents the flow from continuing past the join until all incoming flows are complete. For example, in Figure 3-10 the action immediately after the join—Install Motherboard—executes only after both the Prepare Case and Prepare Motherboard actions finish.

## Time Events

Sometimes *time* is a factor in your activity. You may want to model a wait period, such as waiting three days after shipping an order to send a bill. You may also need to model processes that kick off at a regular time interval, such as a system backup that happens every week.

*Time events* are drawn with an hourglass symbol. Figure 3-11 shows how to use a time event to model a wait period. The text next to the hourglass—Wait 3 Days— shows the amount of time to wait. The incoming edge to the time event means that the time event is activated once. In Figure 3-11, the bill is sent only once—not every three days.

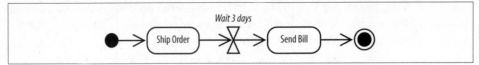

*Figure 3-11. A time event with an incoming edge represents a timeout*

A time event with no incoming flows is a *recurring* time event, meaning it's activated with the frequency in the text next to the hourglass. In Figure 3-12, the progress bar is updated every second.

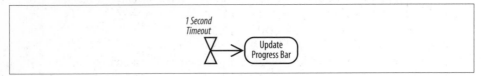

*Figure 3-12. A time event with no incoming flows models a repeating time event*

Notice that there is no initial node in Figure 3-12; a time event is an alternate way to start an activity. Use this notation to model an activity that is launched periodically.

## Calling Other Activities

As detail is added to your activity diagram, the diagram may become too big, or the same sequence of actions may occur more than once. When this happens, you can improve readability by providing details of an action in a separate diagram, allowing the higher level diagram to remain less cluttered.

Figure 3-13 shows the computer assembly workflow from Figure 3-10, but the Prepare Motherboard action now has an upside-down pitchfork symbol indicating that it is a *call activity* node. A call activity node calls the activity corresponding to its node name. This is similar to calling a software procedure.

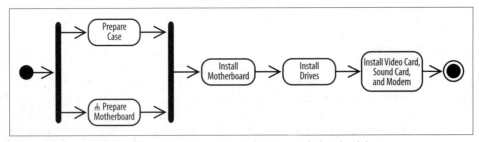

*Figure 3-13. Rather than cluttering up the top-level diagram with details of the Prepare Motherboard action, details are provided in another activity diagram*

The Prepare Motherboard node in Figure 3-13 invokes the Prepare Motherboard activity in Figure 3-14. You associate a call activity node with the activity it invokes by giving them the same name. Call activities essentially break an action down into more details without having to show everything in one diagram.

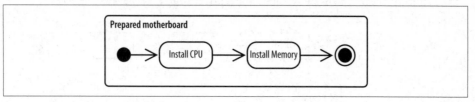

*Figure 3-14. The Prepare Motherboard activity elaborates on the motherboard preparation process*

The `Prepare Motherboard` activity diagram has its own initial and activity final nodes. The activity final node marks the end of `Prepare Motherboard`, but it doesn't mean the calling activity is complete. When `Prepare Motherboard` terminates, control is returned to the calling activity, which proceeds as normal. This is another reason call activities resemble invoked software procedures.

 Although it's acceptable to omit the activity frame for top-level activities, you should always show it for invoked activities. The name of the activity in the activity frame will help you associate invoked activities with the invoker.

# Objects

Sometimes data objects are an important aspect of the process you're modeling. Suppose your company decides to sell the CMS as a commercial product, and you want to define a process for approving incoming orders. Each step in the order approval process will need information about the order, such as the payment information and transaction cost. This can be modeled in your activity diagram with an `Order` object, which contains the order information needed by the steps. Activity diagrams offer a variety of ways to model objects in your processes.

 Objects don't have to be software objects. For example, in a non-automated computer assembly activity, an object node may be used to represent a physical work order that starts the process.

## Showing Objects Passed Between Actions

In activity diagrams, you can use *object nodes* to show data flowing through an activity. An object node represents an object that is available at a particular point in the activity, and can be used to show that the object is used, created, or modified by any of its surrounding actions.

An object node is drawn with a rectangle, as shown in the order approval process in Figure 3-15. The Order object node draws attention to the fact that the Order object flows from the Receive Order Request action to the Approve Payment action.

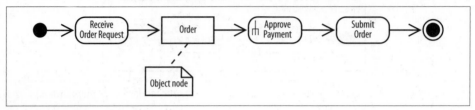

*Figure 3-15. The Order object node emphasizes that it is important data in this activity and shows which actions interact with it*

See "Sending and Receiving Signals" for a more precise way of modeling the Receive Order Request action—as a receive signal node.

## Showing Action Inputs and Outputs

Figure 3-16 shows a different perspective on the previous activity using *pins*. Pins show that an object is input to or output from an action.

An *input pin* means that the specified object is input to an action. An *output pin* means that the specified object is output from an action. In Figure 3-16, an Order object is input to the Approve Payment action and an Order object is output from the Receive Order Request action.

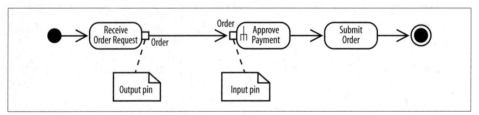

*Figure 3-16. Pins in this change request approval process allow finer-grained specification of input and output parameters*

Figures 3-15 and 3-16 show similar situations, but pins are good at emphasizing that an object is required input and output, whereas an object node simply means that the object is available at that particular point in the activity. However, object nodes have their own strength; they are good at emphasizing the flow of data through an activity.

If the Approve Payment action needs only parts of the Order object—not the whole object—you can use a *transformation* to show which parts are needed. Transformations allow you to show how the output from one action provides the input to another action.

Figure 3-17 specifies that the Approve Payment action requires the Cost object as input and shows how this data is obtained from the Order object using the transformation specified in a note.

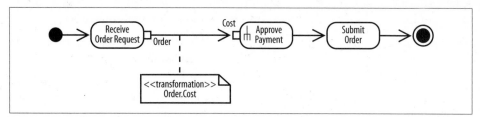

*Figure 3-17. Transformations show where input parameters come from*

## Showing How Objects Change State During an Activity

You can also show an object changing state as it flows through an activity. Figure 3-18 shows that the Order object's state is pending before Approve Payment and changes to approved afterward. The state is shown in brackets.

*Figure 3-18. The focus of this diagram is the change of state of the Order object throughout the order approval process*

## Showing Input to and Output from an Activity

In addition to acting as inputs to and outputs from actions, object nodes can be inputs to and outputs from an activity. Activity inputs and outputs are drawn as object nodes straddling the boundary of the activity frame, as shown in Figure 3-19. This notation is useful for emphasizing that the entire activity requires input and provides output.

Figure 3-19 shows the Order object as input and output for the Approve Payment activity. When input and output parameters are shown, the initial node and activity final node are omitted from the activity.

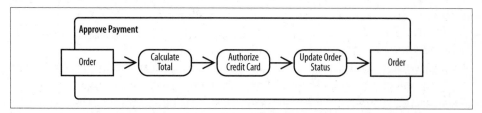

*Figure 3-19. Object nodes can be used to emphasize input to and output from an activity*

# Sending and Receiving Signals

Activities may involve interactions with external people, systems, or processes. For example, when authorizing a credit card payment, you need to verify the card by interacting with an approval service provided by the credit card company.

In activity diagrams, *signals* represent interactions with external participants. Signals are messages that can be sent or received, as in the following examples:

- Your software sends a request to the credit card company to approve a credit card transaction, and your software receives a response from the credit card company (sent and received, from the perspective of your credit card approval activity).
- The receipt of an order prompts an order handling process to begin (received, from the perspective of the order handling activity).
- The click of a button causes code associated with the button to execute (received, from the perspective of the button event handling activity).
- The system notifies a customer that his shipment has been delayed (sent, from the perspective of the order shipping activity).

A *receive signal* has the effect of waking up an action in your activity diagram. The recipient of the signal knows how to react to the signal and expects that a signal will arrive at some time but doesn't know exactly when. *Send signals* are signals sent to an external participant. When that external person or system receives the message, it probably does something in response, but that isn't modeled in your activity diagram.

Figure 3-20 refines the steps in Figure 3-19 to show that the credit card approval action requires interaction with external software. The send signal node shows that a signal is sent to an outside participant. In this example, the signal is a credit card approval request. Signals are sent asynchronously, meaning the activity does not wait for the response but moves immediately to the next action after the signal is sent.

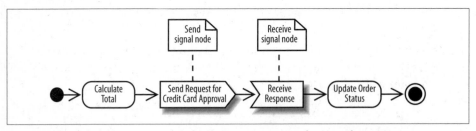

*Figure 3-20. Send and receive signal nodes show interactions with external participants*

The receive signal node shows that a signal is received from an external process. In this case, the system waits for a response from the credit card company. At a receive signal node, the action waits until a signal is received and proceeds only when a signal is received.

Notice that combining send and receive signals results in behavior similar to a synchronous call, or a call that waits for a response. It's common to combine send and receive signals in activity diagrams because you often need a response to the signal you sent.

When you see a receive signal node with no incoming flows, it means that the node is *always* waiting for a signal when its containing activity is active. In the case of Figure 3-21, the activity is launched every time an account request signal is received.

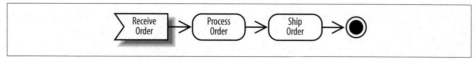

*Figure 3-21. Starting an activity with a receive signal node: the receive signal node replaces the usual initial node*

This differs from a receive signal node with an incoming edge, such as the Receive Response node in Figure 3-20; a receive signal node with an incoming edge only starts waiting when the previous action is complete.

## Starting an Activity

The simplest and most common way to start an activity is with a single initial node; most of the diagrams you've seen so far in this chapter use this notation. There are other ways to represent the start of an activity that have special meanings:

- The activity starts by receiving input data, shown previously in "Showing Input to and Output from an Activity."
- The activity starts in response to a time event, shown previously in "Time Events."
- The activity starts as a result of being woken up by a signal.

To specify that an activity starts as a result of being woken up by a signal, use a *receive signal node* instead of an initial node. Inside the receive signal, node you specify what type of event starts the activity. Figure 3-21 shows an activity starts upon receipt of an order.

## Ending Activities and Flows

The end nodes in this chapter haven't been very interesting so far; in fact, they haven't acted as much more than end markers. In the real world, you can encounter more complex endings to processes, including flows that can be interrupted and flows that end without terminating the overall activity.

## Interrupting an Activity

Figure 3-21 above shows a typical activity diagram with a simple ending. Notice there's only one path leading into the activity final node; every action in this diagram gets a chance to finish.

Sometimes you need to model that a process can be terminated by an event. This could happen if you have a long running process that can be interrupted by the user. Or, in the CMS order handling activity, you may need to account for an order being canceled. You can show interruptions with *interruption regions*.

Draw an interruption region with a dashed, rounded rectangle surrounding the actions that can be interrupted along with the event that can cause the interruption. The interrupting event is followed by a line that looks like a lightning bolt. Figure 3-22 extends Figure 3-21 to account for the possibility that an order might be canceled.

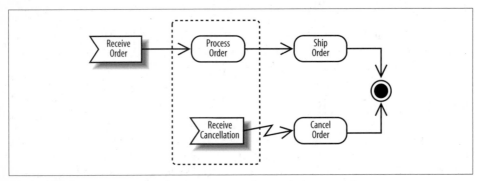

*Figure 3-22. Interruption region showing a process that can be interrupted*

In Figure 3-22, if a cancellation is received while `Process Order` is active, `Process Order` will be interrupted and `Cancel Order` will become active. Cancellation regions are relevant only to the contained actions. If a cancellation is received while `Ship Order` is active, `Ship Order` won't be interrupted since it's not in the cancellation region.

 Sometimes you'll see activity diagrams with multiple activity final nodes instead of multiple flows into a single activity final node. This is legal and can help detangle lines in a diagram that has many branches. But activity diagrams are usually easier to understand if they contain a single activity final node.

## Ending a Flow

A new feature of UML 2.0 is the ability to show that a flow dies without ending the whole activity. A *flow final* node terminates its own path—not the whole activity. It is shown as a circle with an X through it, as in Figure 3-23.

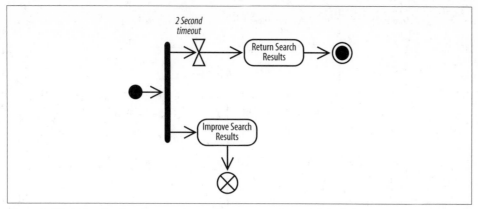

*Figure 3-23. A flow final node terminates only its own path—not the whole activity*

Figure 3-23 shows a search engine for the CMS with a two-second window to generate the best possible search results. When the two-second timeout occurs, the search results are returned, and the entire activity ends, including the `Improve Search Results` action. However, if `Improve Search Results` finishes before the two-second timeout, it will not stop the overall activity since its flow ends with a flow final node.

> Be careful when using a flow final node after a fork. As soon as the activity final node is reached, all other actions in the activity (including the ones before the final node) terminate. If you want all forked actions to run to completion, make sure to add a join.

# Partitions (or Swimlanes)

Activities may involve different participants, such as different groups or roles in an organization or system. The following scenarios require multiple participants to complete the activity (participant names are italicized):

*An order processing activity*
> Requires the *shipping department* to ship the products and the *accounts department* to bill the customer.

*A technical support process*
> Requires different levels of support, including *1st level Support*, *Advanced Support*, and *Product Engineering*.

You use *partitions* to show which participant is responsible for which actions. Partitions divide the diagram into columns or rows (depending on the orientation of your activity diagram) and contain actions that are carried out by a responsible group. The columns or rows are sometimes referred to as *swimlanes*.

Figure 3-24 shows a technical support process involving three types of participants: 1st level Support, Advanced Support, and Product Engineering.

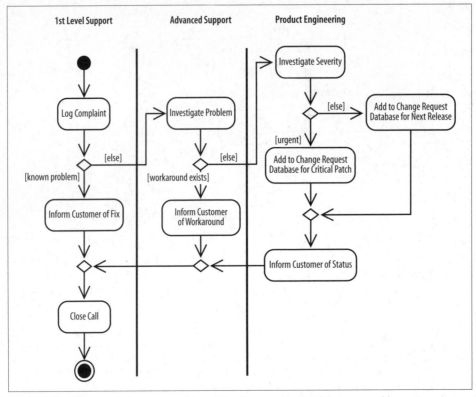

*Figure 3-24. Partitions help organize this activity diagram by clarifying responsible parties*

You can also show responsibility by using *annotations*. Notice that there are no swimlanes; instead, the name of the responsible party is put in parentheses in the node, shown in Figure 3-25. This notation typically makes your diagram more compact, but it shows the participants less clearly than swimlanes.

# Managing Complex Activity Diagrams

Activity diagrams have many additional symbols to model a wide range of processes. The following sections feature some convenient shortcuts for simplifying your activity diagrams. See *UML 2.0 in a Nutshell* (O'Reilly) for a more complete list.

## Connectors

If your activity diagram has a lot of actions, you can end up with long, crossing lines, which make the diagram hard to read. This is where connectors can help you out.

*Connectors* help untangle your diagrams, connecting edges with symbols instead of explicit lines. A connector is drawn as a circle with its name written inside. Connectors are typically given single character names. In Figure 3-26, the connector name is n.

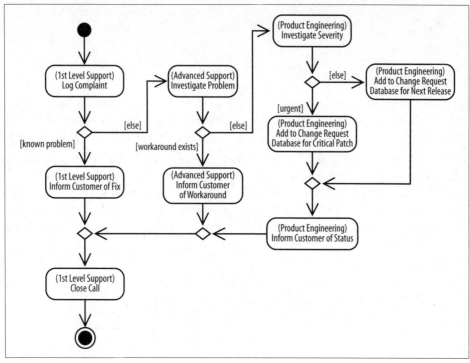

*Figure 3-25. Annotations can be used instead of swimlanes as a way of showing responsibility directly in the action*

Connectors come in pairs: one has an incoming edge and the other has an outgoing edge. The second connector picks up where the first connector left off. So the flow in Figure 3-26 is the same as if Step 3 had an edge leading directly into Step 4.

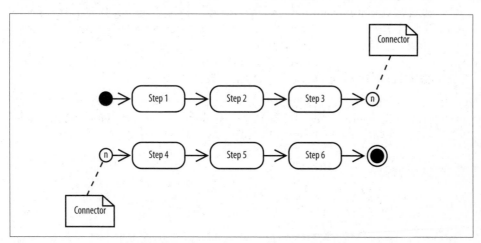

*Figure 3-26. Connectors can improve the readability of a large activity diagram*

Be careful with connectors: if you use too many different connectors in one diagram, the reader may have a hard time pairing them.

## Expansion Regions

*Expansion regions* show that actions in a region are performed for each item in an input collection. For example, an expansion region could be used to model a software function that takes a list of files as input and searches each file for a search term.

Draw an expansion region as a large rounded rectangle with dashed lines and four aligned boxes on either side. The four boxes represent input and output collections (but they don't imply that the collection size is four). Figure 3-27 shows that the bug report is discussed for each bug report in an input collection. If it's a real bug, then the activity proceeds; otherwise the bug is discarded and the flow for that input ends.

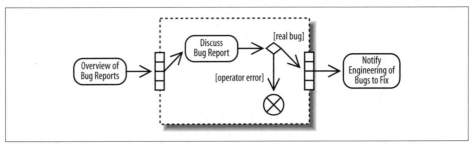

*Figure 3-27. The actions in an expansion region are performed for each item in a collection*

# What's Next?

Sequence and communication diagrams are other UML diagrams that can model the dynamic behavior of your system. These diagrams focus on showing detailed interactions, such as which objects are involved in an interaction, which methods are invoked, and the sequence of events. Sequence diagrams can be found in Chapter 7. Communication diagrams are covered in Chapter 8.

If you haven't already, it's also worth reading Chapter 2 on use cases because activity diagrams offer a great way of showing a visual representation of a use case's flow.

# CHAPTER 4

# Modeling a System's Logical Structure: Introducing Classes and Class Diagrams

Classes are at the heart of any object-oriented system; therefore, it follows that the most popular UML diagram is the class diagram. A system's structure is made up of a collection of pieces often referred to as *objects*. Classes describe the different types of objects that your system can have, and class diagrams show these classes and their relationships. Class relationships are covered in Chapter 5.

Use cases describe the behavior of your system as a set of concerns. Classes describe the different types of objects that are needed within your system to meet those concerns. Classes form part of your model's logical view, as shown in Figure 4-1.

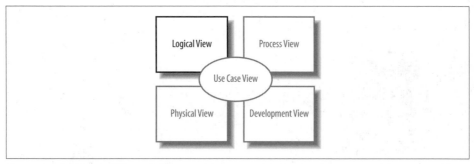

Figure 4-1. *The Logical View on your model contains the abstract descriptions of your system's parts, including classes*

## What Is a Class?

Like any new concept, when first coming to grips with what classes are, it's usually helpful to start with an analogy. The analogy we'll use here is that of guitars, and my favorite guitar is the Burns Brian May Signature (BMS) guitar, shown in Figure 4-2.

The guitar in Figure 4-2 is an example of an object. It has an identity: it's the one I own. However, I'm not going to pretend that Burns made only one of this type of

*Figure 4-2. One of my guitars: a good example of an object*

guitar and that it was just for me—I'm not that good a guitarist! Burns as a company will make hundreds of this *type* of guitar or, to put it another way, this *class* of guitar.

A class is a type of something. You can think of a class as being the blueprint out of which objects can be constructed, as shown in Figure 4-3.

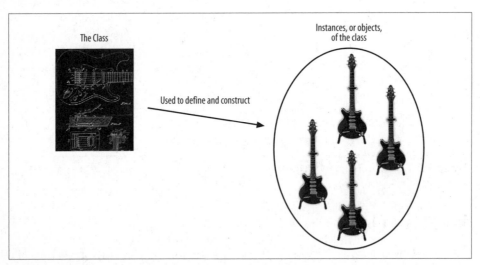

*Figure 4-3. The class defines the main characteristics of the guitar; using the class, any number of guitar objects can be constructed*

In this analogy, the BMS guitar that Burns manufactures is an example of a class of guitar. Burns know how to build this type of guitar from scratch based on its blueprints. Each guitar constructed from the class can be referred to as an *instance* or *object* of the class, and so my guitar in Figure 4-2 is an instance of the Burns BMS Guitar class.

At its simplest, a class's description will include two pieces of information: the state information that objects of the class will contain and the behavior that they will support. This is what differentiates OO from other forms of system development. In OO, closely related state and behavior are combined into class definitions, which are then used as the blueprints from which objects can be created.

In the case of the Burns BMS Guitar class, the class's state could include information about how many strings the guitar has and what condition the guitar is in. Those pieces of information are the class's attributes.

To complete the description, we need to know what the guitar can do. This includes behavior such as tuning and playing the guitar. A class's behavior is described as the different operations that it supports.

Attributes and operations are the mainstays of a class's description (see "Class State: Attributes"). Together, they enable a class to describe a group of parts within your system that share common characteristics such as state—represented by the class's attributes—and behavior—represented by the class's operations (see "Class Behavior: Operations" later in this chapter).

## Abstraction

A class's definition contains the details about that class that are important to you and the system you are modeling. For example, my BMS guitar might have a scratch on the back—or several—but if I am creating a class that will represent BMS guitars, do I need to add attributes that contain details about scratches? I might if the class were to be used in a repair shop; however, if the class were to be used only in the factory system, then scratches are one detail that I can hopefully ignore. Discarding irrelevant details within a given context is called *abstraction*.

Let's have a look at an example of how a class's abstraction changes depending on its context. If Burns were creating a model of its guitar production system, then it would probably be interested in creating a Burns BMS Guitar class that models how one is constructed, what materials are to be used, and how the guitar is to be tested. In contrast, if a Guitar World store were creating a model of its sales system, then the Burns BMS Guitar class might contain only relevant information, such as a serial number, price, and possibly any special handling instructions.

Getting the right level of abstraction for your model, or even just for a class, is often a real challenge. Focus on the information that your system needs to know rather than becoming bogged down with details that may be irrelevant to your system. You will then have a good starting point when designing your system's classes.

Abstraction is key not only to class diagrams but to modeling in general. A model, by definition, is an abstraction of the system that it represents. The actual system *is* the real thing; the model contains only enough information to be an *accurate representation* of the actual system. In most cases, the model abstracts away details that are not important to the accuracy of the representation.

## Encapsulation

Before we take a more detailed look at attributes, operations, and how classes can work together, it's worth focusing on what is the most important characteristic of classes and object orientation: *encapsulation*.

According to the object-oriented approach to system development, for an object to be an object, it needs to contain both data—attributes—and the instructions that affect the data—operations. This is *the* big difference between object orientation and other approaches to system development: in OO, there is the concept of an object that contains, or encapsulates, both the data *and* the operations that work on that data.

Referring back to the guitar analogy, the Burns BMS Guitar class could encapsulate its strings, its body, its neck, and probably some neat electrics that no one should mess around with. These parts of the guitar are effectively its attributes, and some of the attributes, such as the strings, are accessible to the outside world and others, such as electrics, are hidden away. In addition to these attributes, the Burns BMS Guitar class will contain some operations that will allow the outside world to work with the guitar's attributes. At a minimum, the guitar class should at least have an operation called play so that the guitar objects can be played, but other operations such as clean and possibly even serviceElectrics may also be encapsulated and offered by the class.

Encapsulation of operations and data within an object is probably the single most powerful and useful part of the object-oriented approach to system design. Encapsulation enables a class to hide the inner details of how it works from the outside world—like the electrics from the example guitar class—and only expose the operations and data that it chooses to make accessible.

Encapsulation is very important because with it, a class can change the way it works internally and as long as those internals are not visible to the rest of the system, those changes will have no effect on how the class is interacted with. This is a useful feature of the object-oriented approach because with the right classes, small changes to how those classes work internally shouldn't cause your system to break.

# Getting Started with Classes in UML

So far we've been looking at what a class is and how it enables the key benefits of the object-oriented approach of system development: abstraction and encapsulation. Now it's time to take a look at how classes are represented in UML.

At its simplest, a class in UML is drawn as a rectangle split into up to three sections. The top section contains the name of the class, the middle section contains the attributes or information that the class contains, and the final section contains the operations that represent the behavior that the class exhibits. The attributes and operations sections are optional, as shown in Figure 4-4. If the attributes and operations sections are not shown, it does not necessarily imply that they are empty, just that the diagram is perhaps easier to understand with that information hidden.

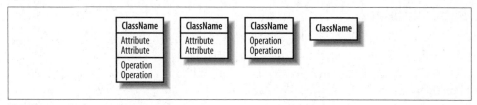

*Figure 4-4. Four different ways of showing a class using UML notation*

A class's name establishes a type for the objects that will be instantiated based on it. Figure 4-5 shows a couple of classes from the CMS in Chapter 2: the `BlogAccount` class defines the information that the system will hold relating to each of the user's accounts, and the `BlogEntry` class defines the information contained within an entry made by a user into her blog.

*Figure 4-5. Two classes of objects have been identified in the CMS*

The interaction diagrams covered in Chapters 7 through 10 are used to show how class instances, or objects, work together when a system is running.

# Visibility

How does a class selectively reveal its operations and data to other classes? By using *visibility*. Once visibility characteristics are applied, you can control access to attributes, operations, and even entire classes to effectively enforce encapsulation. See "Encapsulation" earlier in this chapter for more information on why encapsulation is such a useful aspect of object-oriented system design.

There are four different types of visibility that can be applied to the elements of a UML model, as shown in Figure 4-6. Typically these visibility characteristics will be used to control access to both attributes, operations, and sometimes even classes (see the "Packages" section in Chapter 13 for more information on class visibility).

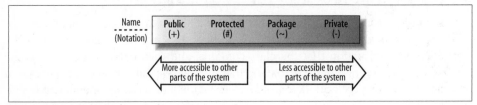

Figure 4-6. UML's four different visibility classifications

## Public Visibility

Starting with the most accessible of visibility characteristics, *public visibility* is specified using the plus (+) symbol before the associated attribute or operation (see Figure 4-7). Declare an attribute or operation public if you want it to be accessible directly by any other class.

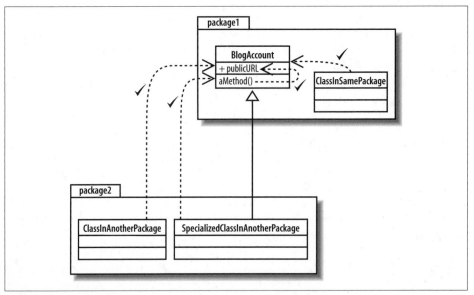

Figure 4-7. Using public visibility, any class within the model can access the publicURL attribute

The collection of attributes and operations that are declared public on a class create that class's public interface. The *public interface* of a class consists of the attributes and operations that can be accessed and used by other classes. This means the public interface is the part of your class that other classes will depend on the most. It is important that the public interface to your classes changes as little as possible to prevent unnecessary changes wherever your class is used.

## Protected Visibility

*Protected* attributes and operations are specified using the hash (#) symbol and are more visible to the rest of your system than private attributes and operations, but are less visible than public. Declared protected elements on classes can be accessed by methods that are part of your class and also by methods that are declared on any class that inherits from your class. Protected elements cannot be accessed by a class that does not inherit from your class whether it's in the same package or not, as shown in Figure 4-8. See Chapter 5 for more information on inheritance relationships between classes.

Protected visibility is crucial if you want to allow specialized classes to access an attribute or operation in the base class without opening that attribute or operation to the entire system. Using protected visibility is like saying, "This attribute or operation is useful inside my class and classes extending my class, but no one else should be using it."

Java confuses the matter a little further by allowing access to protected parts of a class to any other class in the same package. This is like combining the accessibility of protected and package visibility, which is covered in the next section.

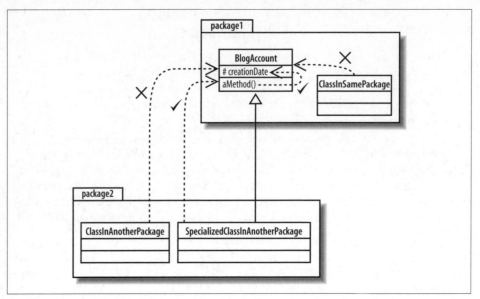

*Figure 4-8. Any methods in the BlogAccount class or classes that inherit from the BlogAccount class can access the protected creationDate attribute*

## Package Visibility

Package visibility, specified with a tilde (~), when applied to attributes and operations, sits in between protected and private. As you'd expect, packages are the key factor in determining which classes can see an attribute or operation that is declared with package visibility.

The rule is fairly simple: if you add an attribute or operation that is declared with package visibility to your class, then any class in the same package can directly access that attribute or operation, as shown in Figure 4-9. Classes outside the package cannot access protected attributes or operations even if it's an inheriting class.In practice, package visibility is most useful when you want to declare a collection of methods and attributes across your classes that can only be used within your package.

For example, if you were designing a package of utility classes and wanted to reuse behavior between those classes, but not expose the rest of the system to that behavior, then you would declare package visibility to those particular operations internally to the package. Any functionality of utility classes that you wanted to expose to the rest of the application could then be declared with public visibility.

See "Package Diagrams" in Chapter 13 for more on how packages control visibility of elements such as classes.

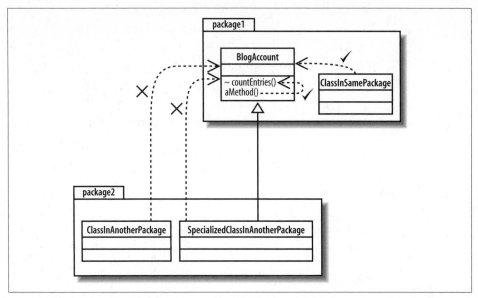

Figure 4-9. *The countEntries operation can be called by any class in the same package as the BlogAccount class or by methods within the BlogAccount class itself*

## Private Visibility

Last in line in the UML visibility scale is private visibility. *Private visibility* is the most tightly constrained type of visibility classification, and it is shown by adding a minus (-) symbol before the attribute or operation. Only the class that contains the private element can see or work with the data stored in a private attribute or make a call to a private operation, as shown in Figure 4-10.

Private visibility is most useful if you have an attribute or operation that you want no other part of the system to depend on. This might be the case if you intend to change an attribute or operation at a later time but don't want other classes with access to that element to be changed.

It's a commonly accepted rule of thumb that attributes should always be private and only in extreme cases opened to direct access by using something more visible. The exception to this rule is when you need to share your class's attribute with classes that inherit from your class. In this case, it is common to use protected. In well-designed OO systems, attributes are usually private or protected, but very rarely public.

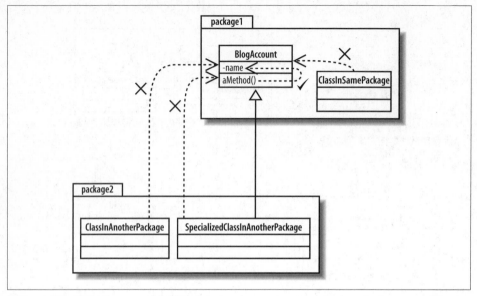

*Figure 4-10. aMethod is part of the BlogAccount class, so it can access the private name attribute; no other class's methods can see the name attribute*

# Class State: Attributes

A class's *attributes* are the pieces of information that represent the state of an object. These attributes can be represented on a class diagram either by placing them inside their section of the class box—known as inline attributes—or by association with another class, as shown in Figure 4-11. Associations are covered in more detail in Chapter 5.

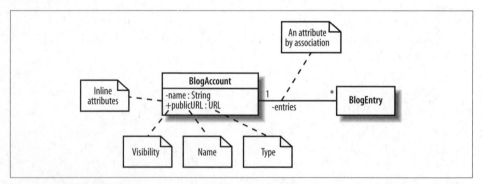

*Figure 4-11. The BlogAccount class contains two inlined attributes, name and publicURL, as well as an attribute that is introduced by the association between the BlogAccount and BlogEntry classes*

It doesn't matter if you are declaring an inline or associated attribute. At a minimum, your attribute will usually have a signature that contains a visibility property, a name, and a type, although the attribute's name is the only part of its signature that absolutely must be present for the class to be valid.

## Name and Type

An attribute's name can be any set of characters, but no two attributes in the same class can have the same name. The type of attribute can vary depending on how the class will be implemented in your system but it is usually either a class, such as String, or a primitive type, such as an int in Java.

---

### Choosing Attribute Names

Remember, one of the primary aims of modeling your system is to communicate your design to others. When picking names of attributes, operations, classes, and packages, make sure that the name accurately describes what is being named. When naming attributes, it's worth trying to come up with a name that describes the information that the attribute represents.

Also, if your class is to be implemented in a specific software language, check to make sure that the name meets the conventions of that language. In Java, it is common to use an uppercase character for each word in your class's names, e.g., BlogAccount, while Java packages are usually named all in lowercase (see Chapter 13).

---

In Figure 4-11, the name attribute is declared as private (indicated by the minus (-) sign at the beginning of the signature) and after the colon, the type is specified as being of the class String. The associated entries attribute is also private, and because of that association, it represents a number of instances of the BlogEntry class.

If the BlogAccount class in Figure 4-11 was going to be implemented as a Java class in software, then the source code would look something like that shown in Example 4-1.

*Example 4-1. Java inline and by-association attributes*

```java
public class BlogAccount
{
    // The two inline attributes from Figure 4-11.
    private String name;
    private URL publicURL;

    // The single attribute by association, given the name 'entries'
    BlogEntries[] entries;

    // ...

}
```

It's pretty clear how the two inline attributes are implemented in the BlogAccount Java class; the name attribute is just a Java String and the publicURL attribute is a Java URL object. The entries attribute is a bit more interesting since it is introduced by association. Associations and relationships between classes are covered in Chapter 5.

## Multiplicity

Sometimes an attribute will represent more than one object. In fact, an attribute could represent any number of objects of its type; in software, this is like declaring that an attribute is an array. Multiplicity allows you to specify that an attribute actually represents a collection of objects, and it can be applied to both inline and attributes by association, as shown in Figure 4-12.

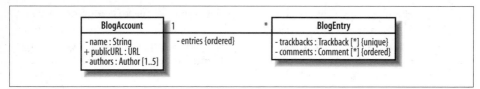

*Figure 4-12. Applying several flavors of attribute multiplicity to the attributes of the BlogAccount and BlogEntry classes*

In Figure 4-12, the trackbacks, comments, and authors attributes all represent collections of objects. The * at the end of the trackbacks and comments attributes specifies that they could contain any number of objects of the Trackback and Comment class, respectively. The authors attribute is a little more constrained since it specifies that it contains between one and five authors.

The entries attribute that is introduced using an association between the BlogAccount class and the BlogEntry class has two multiplicity properties specified at either end of the association. A * at the BlogEntry class end of the association indicates that any number of BlogEntry objects will be stored in the entries attribute within the BlogAccount class. The 1 specified at the other end of the association indicates that each BlogEntry object in the entries attribute is associated with one and only one BlogAccount object.

Those with a keen eye will have also noticed that the trackbacks, comments, and entries attributes also have extra properties to describe in even more detail what the multiplicity on the attributes means. The trackbacks attribute represents any number of objects of the Trackback class, but it also has the unique multiplicity property applied to it. The unique property dictates that no two Trackback objects within the array should be the same. This is a reasonable constraint since we don't want an entry in another blog cross-referencing one of our entries more than once; otherwise the list of trackbacks will get messy.

By default, all attributes with multiplicity are unique. This means that, as well as the trackbacks attribute in the BlogEntry class, no two objects in the authors attributes collection in the BlogAccount class should be the same because they are also declared unique. This makes sense since it specifies that a BlogAccount can have up to five *different* authors; however, it wouldn't make sense to specify that the same author represents two of the possible five authors that work on a blog! If you want to specify that duplicates are allowed, then you need to use the not unique property, as used on the comments attribute in the BlogEntry class.

The final property that an attribute can have that is related to multiplicity is the ordered property. As well as not having to be unique, the objects represented by the comments attribute on the BlogEntry class need to be ordered. The ordered property is used in this case to indicate that each of the Comment objects is stored in a set order, most likely in order of addition to the BlogEntry. If you don't care about the order in which objects are stored within an attribute that has multiplicity, then simply leave out the ordered property.

## Attribute Properties

As well as visibility, a unique name, and a type, there is also a set of properties that can be applied to attributes to completely describe an attribute's characteristics.

Although a complete description of the different types attribute properties is probably a bit beyond this book—also, some of the properties are rarely used in practice—it is worth looking at what is probably the most popular attribute property: the readOnly property.

 Other properties supported by attributes in UML include union, subsets, redefines, and composite. For a neat description of all of the different properties that can be applied to attributes, check out *UML 2.0 in a Nutshell* (O'Reilly).

If an attribute has the readOnly property applied, as shown in Figure 4-13, then the value of the attribute cannot be changed once its initial value has been set.

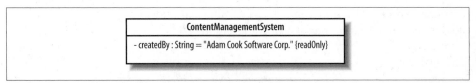

*Figure 4-13. The createBy attribute in the ContentManagementSystem class is given a default initial value and a property of readOnly so that the attribute cannot be changed throughout the lifetime of the system*

If the ContentManagementSystem class were to be implemented in Java source code, then the createdBy attribute would be translated into a final attribute, as shown in Example 4-2.

*Example 4-2. Final attributes in Java are often referred to as constants since they keep the same constant value that they are initially set up with for their entire lifetime*

```java
public class ContentManagementSystem
{
    private final String createdBy = "Adam Cook Software Corp.";
}
```

## Inline Attributes Versus Attributes by Association

So, why confuse things with two ways of showing a class's attributes? Consider the classes and associations shown in Figure 4-14.

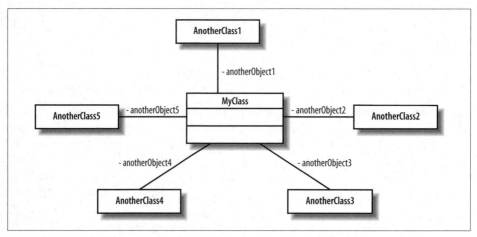

*Figure 4-14. The MyClass class has five attributes, and they are all shown using associations*

When attributes are shown as associations, as is the case in Figure 4-14, the diagram quickly becomes busy—and that's just to show the associations, nevermind all of the other relationships that classes can have (see Chapter 5). The diagram is neater and easier to manage with more room for other information when the attributes are specified inline with the class box, as shown in Figure 4-15.

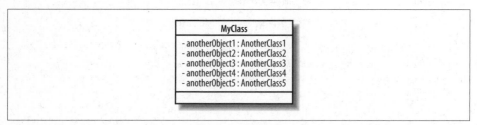

*Figure 4-15. The MyClass class's five attributes shown inline within the class box*

Choosing whether an attribute should be shown inline or as an association is really a question of what the focus of the diagram should be. Using inline attributes takes the spotlight away from the associations between MyClass and the other classes, but is a much more efficient use of space. Associations show relationships between classes very clearly on a diagram but they can get in the way of other relationships, such as inheritance, that are more important for the purpose of a specific diagram.

 One useful rule of thumb: "simple" classes, such as the String class in Java, or even standard library classes, such as the File class in Java's io package, are generally best shown as inline attributes.

# Class Behavior: Operations

A class's operations describe *what* a class can do but not necessarily *how* it is going to do it. An operation is more like a promise or a minimal contract that declares that a class will contain some behavior that does what the operation says it will do. The collection of all the operations that a class contains should totally encompass all of the behavior that the class contains, including all the work that maintains the class's attributes and possibly some additional behavior that is closely associated with the class.

Operations in UML are specified on a class diagram with a signature that is at minimum made up of a visibility property, a name, a pair of parentheses in which any parameters that are needed for the operation to do its job can be supplied, and a return type, as shown in Figure 4-16.

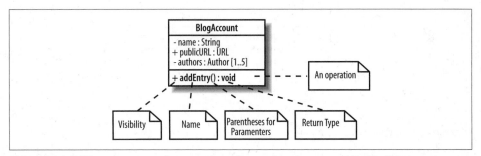

*Figure 4-16. Adding a new operation to a class allows other classes to add a BlogEntry to a BlogAccount*

In Figure 4-16, the addEntry operation is declared as public; it does not require any parameters to be passed to it (yet), and it does not return any values. Although this is a perfectly valid operation in UML, it is not even close to being finished yet. The operation is supposed to add a new BlogEntry to a BlogAccount, but at the moment, there is no way of knowing what entry to actually add.

## Parameters

Parameters are used to specify the information provided to an operation to allow it to complete its job. For example, the addEntry(..) operation needs to be supplied with the BlogEntry that is to be added to the account, as shown in Figure 4-17.

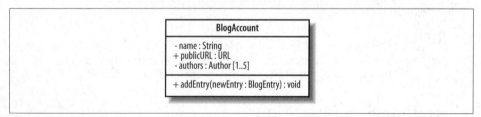

*Figure 4-17. Adding a new parameter to the addEntry operation saves a bit of embarrassment when it comes to implementing this class; at least the addEntry operation will now know which entry to add to the blog!*

The newEntry parameter that is passed to the addEntry operation in Figure 4-17 shows a simple example of a parameter being passed to an operation. At a minimum, a parameter needs to have its type specified—in this case, BlogEntry class. More than one parameter can be passed to an operation by splitting the parameters with a comma, as shown in Figure 4-18. For more information on all the nuances of parameter notation, see *UML 2.0 in a Nutshell* (O'Reilly).

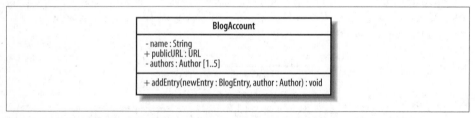

*Figure 4-18. As well as passing the new blog entry that is to be added, by adding another parameter, we can also indicate which author wrote the entry*

## Return Types

As well as a name and parameters, an operation's signature also contains a return type. A return type is specified after a colon at the end of an operation's signature and specifies the type of object that will be returned by the operation, as shown in Figure 4-19.

There is one exception where you don't need to specify a return type: when you are declaring a class's constructor. A constructor creates and returns a new instance of the class that it is specified in, therefore, it does not need to explicitly declare any return type, as shown in Figure 4-20.

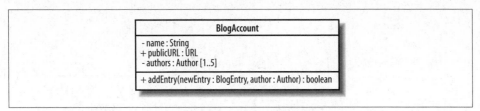

*Figure 4-19. The addEntry(..) operation now returns a Boolean indicating whether the entry was successfully added*

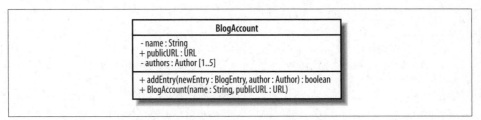

*Figure 4-20. The BlogAccount(..) constructor must always return an instance of BlogAccount, so there is no need to explicitly show a return type*

# Static Parts of Your Classes

To finish off this introduction to the fundamentals of class diagrams, let's take a look at one of the most confusing characteristics of classes: when a class operation or attribute is static.

In UML, operations, attributes, and even classes themselves can be declared static. To help us understand what static means, we need to look at the lifetime of regular non-static class members. First, lets take another look at the BlogAccount class from earlier on in this chapter, shown in Figure 4-21.

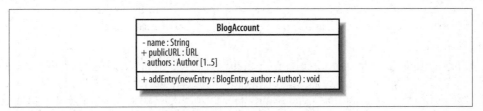

*Figure 4-21. The BlogAccount class is made up of three regular attributes and one regular operation*

Because each of the attributes and operations on the BlogAccount class are non-static, they are associated with instances, or objects, of the class. This means that each object of the BlogAccount class will get their own copy of the attributes and operations, as shown in Figure 4-22.

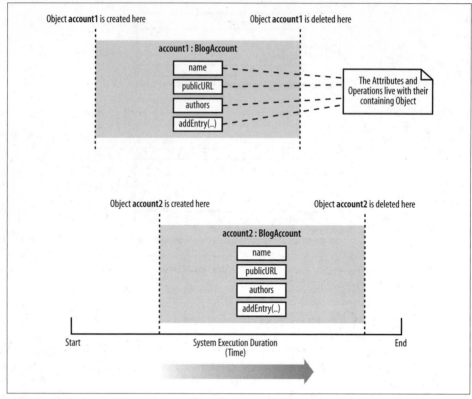

*Figure 4-22. Both account1 and account2 contain and exhibit their own copy of all the regular non-static attributes and operations declared on the BlogAccount class*

Sometimes you want all of the objects in a particular class to share the same copy of an attribute or operation. When this happens, a class's attributes and operations are associated with the class itself and have a lifetime beyond that of the any objects that are instantiated from the class. This is where static attributes and operations become useful.

For example (and let's ignore the possibility of multiple classloaders for now), if we wanted to keep a count of all the BlogAccount objects currently alive in the system, then this counter would be a good candidate for being a static class attribute. Rather than the counter attribute being associated with any one object, it is associated with the BlogAccount class and is therefore a static attribute, as shown in Figure 4-23.

The accountCounter attribute needs to be incremented every time a new BlogAccount is created. The accountCounter attribute is declared static because the same copy needs to be shared between all of the instances of the BlogAccount class. The instances can increment it when they are created and decrement it when they are destroyed, as shown in Figure 4-24.

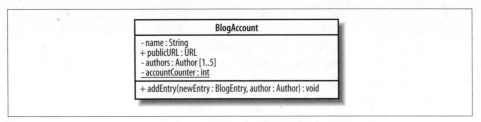

*Figure 4-23. An attribute or operation is made static in UML by underlining it; the accountCounter attribute will be used to keep a running count of the number of objects created from the BlogAccount class*

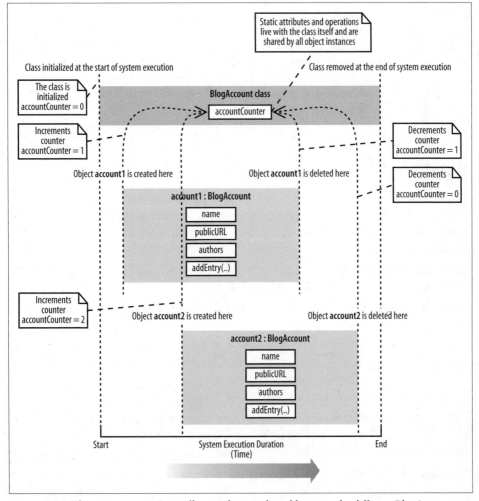

*Figure 4-24. The static accountController attribute is shared between the different BlogAccount objects to keep a count of the currently active BlogAccount objects within the system*

If the `accountCounter` attribute were not static, then every `BlogAccount` instance would get its own copy of the `accountCounter` attribute. This would not be very useful at all since each `BlogAccount` object would update only its own copy of accountCounter rather than contributing to a master object instance counter—in fact, if accountCounter were not static, then every object would simply increment its own copy to 1 and then decrement it to 0 when it is destroyed, which is not very useful at all!

---

### The Singleton Design Pattern

Another great example of when static attributes and operations are used is when you want to apply the Singleton design pattern. In a nutshell, the Singleton design pattern ensures that one and only one object of a particular class is ever constructed during the lifetime of your system. To ensure that only one object is ever constructed, typical implementations of the Singleton pattern keep an internal static reference to the single allowed object instance, and access to that instance is controlled using a static operation. To learn more about the Singleton pattern, check out *Head First Design Patterns* (O'Reilly).

---

## What's Next

This chapter has given you only a first glimpse of all that is possible with class diagrams. Classes can be related to one another, and there are even advanced forms of classes, such as templates, that can make your system's design even more effective. Class relationships, abstract classes, and class templates are all covered in Chapter 5.

Class diagrams show the types of objects in your system; a useful next step is to look at object diagrams because they show how classes come alive at runtime as object instances, which is useful if you want to show runtime configurations. Object diagrams are covered in Chapter 6.

Composite structures are a diagram type that loosely shows context-sensitive class diagrams and patterns in your software. Composite structures are described in Chapter 11.

After you've decided the responsibilities of the classes in your system, it's common to then create sequence and communication diagrams to show interactions between the parts. Sequence diagrams can be found in Chapter 7. Communication diagrams are covered in Chapter 8.

It's also common to step back and organize your classes into packages. Package diagrams allow you to view dependencies at a higher level, helping you understand the stability of your software. Package diagrams are described in Chapter 13.

# CHAPTER 5

# Modeling a System's Logical Structure: Advanced Class Diagrams

If all you could do with class diagrams was declare classes with simple attributes and operations, then UML would be a pretty poor modeling language. Luckily, object orientation and UML allows much more to be done with classes than just simple declarations. For starters, classes can have relationships to one another. A class can be a type of another class—generalization—or it can contain objects of another class in various ways depending on how strong the relationship is between the two classes.

Abstract classes help you to partly declare a class's behavior, allowing other classes to complete the missing—abstract—bits of behavior as they see fit. Interfaces take abstract classes one stage further by specifying only the needed operations of a class but without any operation implementations. You can even apply constraints to your class diagrams that describe how a class's objects can be used with the Object Constraint Language (OCL).

Templates complete the picture by allowing you to declare classes that contain completely generic and reusable behavior. With templates, you can specify what a class will do and then wait—as late as runtime if you choose—to decide which classes it will work with.

Together, these techniques complete your class diagram toolbox. They represent some of the most powerful concepts in object-oriented design and, when applied correctly, can make the difference between an OK design and a *great* piece of reusable design.

## Class Relationships

Classes do not live in a vacuum—they work together using different types of relationships. Relationships between classes come in different strengths, as shown in Figure 5-1.

The strength of a class relationship is based on how dependent the classes involved in the relationship are on each other. Two classes that are strongly dependent on one another are said to be *tightly coupled*; changes to one class will most likely affect the

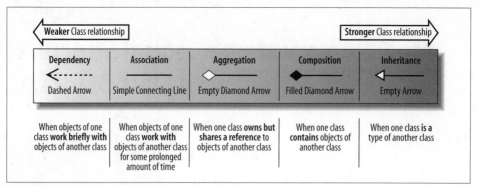

| Weaker Class relationship | | | | Stronger Class relationship |
|---|---|---|---|---|
| Dependency | Association | Aggregation | Composition | Inheritance |
| Dashed Arrow | Simple Connecting Line | Empty Diamond Arrow | Filled Diamond Arrow | Empty Arrow |
| When objects of one class **work briefly with** objects of another class | When objects of one class **work with** objects of another class for some prolonged amount of time | When one class **owns but shares a reference** to objects of another class | When one class **contains** objects of another class | When one class **is a** type of another class |

*Figure 5-1. UML offers five different types of class relationship*

other class. Tight coupling is usually, but not always, a bad thing; therefore, the stronger the relationship, the more careful you need to be.

## Dependency

A *dependency* between two classes declares that a class needs to know about another class to use objects of that class. If the UserInterface class of the CMS needed to work with a BlogEntry class's object, then this dependency would be drawn using the dependency arrow, as shown in Figure 5-2.

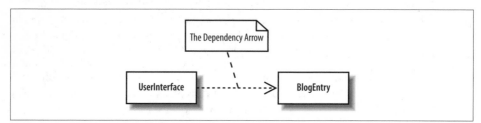

*Figure 5-2. The UserInterface is dependent on the BlogEntry class because it will need to read the contents of a blog's entries to display them to the user*

The UserInterface and BlogEntry classes simply work together at the times when the user interface wants to display the contents of a blog entry. In class diagram terms, the two classes of object are dependent on each other to ensure they work together at runtime.

A dependency implies only that objects of a class *can* work together; therefore, it is considered to be the weakest direct relationship that can exist between two classes.

The dependency relationship is often used when you have a class that is providing a set of general-purpose utility functions, such as in Java's regular expression (java.util.regex) and mathematics (java.math) packages. Classes depend on the java.util.regex and java.math classes to use the utilities that those classes offer.

# Association

Although dependency simply allows one class to use objects of another class, *association* means that a class will actually contain a reference to an object, or objects, of the other class in the form of an attribute. If you find yourself saying that a class *works with* an object of another class, then the relationship between those classes is a great candidate for association rather than just a dependency. Association is shown using a simple line connecting two classes, as shown in Figure 5-3.

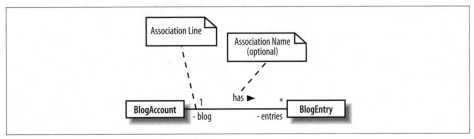

*Figure 5-3. The BlogAccount class is optionally associated with zero or more objects of the BlogEntry class; the BlogEntry is also associated with one and only one BlogAccount*

*Navigability* is often applied to an association relationship to describe which class contains the attribute that supports the relationship. If you take Figure 5-3 as it currently stands and implement the association between the two classes in Java, then you would get something like that shown in Example 5-1.

*Example 5-1. The BlogAccount and BlogEntry classes without navigability applied to their association relationship*

```
public class BlogAccount {

    // Attribute introduced thanks to the association with the BlogEntry class
    private BlogEntry[] entries;

    // ... Other Attributes and Methods declared here ...
}

public class BlogEntry {

    // Attribute introduced thanks to the association with the Blog class
    private BlogAccount blog;

    // ... Other Attributes and Methods declared here ...
}
```

Without more information about the association between the `BlogAccount` and `BlogEntry` classes, it is impossible to decide which class should contain the association introduced attribute; in this case, both classes have an attribute added. If this was intentional, then there might not be a problem; however, it is more common to have only one class referencing the other in an association.

In our system, it makes more sense to be able to ask a blog account what entries it contains, rather than asking the entry what blog account it belongs to. In this case, we use navigability to ensure that the BlogAccount class gets the association introduced attribute, as shown in Figure 5-4.

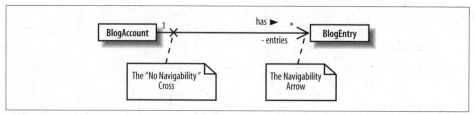

*Figure 5-4. If we change Figure 5-3 to incorporate the navigability arrow, then we can declare that you should be able to navigate from the blog to its entries*

Updating the association between the BlogAccount class and the BlogEntry class as shown in Figure 5-4 would result in the code shown in Example 5-2.

*Example 5-2. With navigability applied, only the BlogAccount class contains an association introduced attribute*

```
public class BlogAccount {

    // Attribute introduced thanks to the association with the BlogEntry class
    private BlogEntry[] entries ;

    // ... Other Attributes and Methods declared here ...
}

public class BlogEntry
{
    // The blog attribute has been removed as it is not necessary for the
    // BlogEntry to know about the BlogAccount that it belongs to.

    // ... Other Attributes and Methods declared here ...
}
```

## Association classes

Sometimes an association itself introduces new classes. Association classes are particularly useful in complex cases when you want to show that a class is related to two classes *because* those two classes have a relationship with each other, as shown in Figure 5-5.

In Figure 5-5, the BlogEntry class is associated with a BlogAccount. However, depending on the categories that the account contains, the blog entry is also associated with any number of categories. In short, the association relationship between a blog account and a blog entry results in an association relationship with a set of categories (whew!).

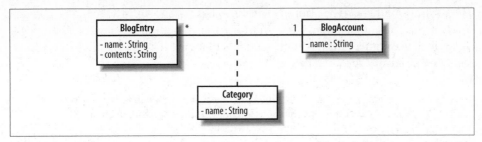

Figure 5-5. A BlogEntry is associated with a Category by virtue of the fact that it is associated with a particular BlogAccount

There are no hard and fast rules for exactly how an association class is implemented in code, but, for example, the relationships shown in Figure 5-5 could be implemented in Java, as shown in Example 5-3.

Example 5-3. One method of implementing the BlogEntry to BlogAccount relationship and the associated Category class in Java

```java
public class BlogAccount {
    private String name;
    private Category[] categories;
    private BlogEntry[] entries;
}

public class Category {
    private String name;
}

public class BlogEntry {
    private String name;
    private Category[] categories
}
```

## Aggregation

Moving one step on from association, we encounter the aggregation relationship. Aggregation is really just a stronger version of association and is used to indicate that a class actually *owns but may share* objects of another class.

Aggregation is shown by using an empty diamond arrowhead next to the owning class, as shown in Figure 5-6.

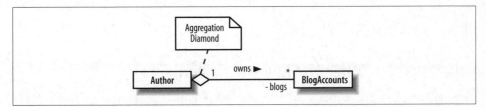

Figure 5-6. An aggregation relationship can show that an Author owns a collection of blogs

The relationship between an author and his blogs, as shown in Figure 5-6, is much stronger than just association. An author owns his blogs, and even though he *might* share them with other authors, in the end, his blogs are his own, and if he decides to remove one of his blogs, then he can!

 Where's the code? Actually, the Java code implementation for an aggregation relationship is exactly the same as the implementation for an association relationship; it results in the introduction of an attribute.

## Composition

Moving one step further down the class relationship line, composition is an even stronger relationship than aggregation, although they work in very similar ways. Composition is shown using a closed, or filled, diamond arrowhead, as shown in Figure 5-7.

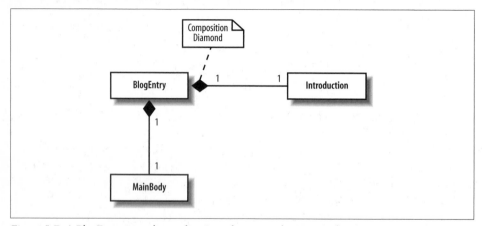

*Figure 5-7. A BlogEntry is made up of an Introduction and a MainBody*

A blog entry's introduction and main body sections are actually *parts of* the blog entry itself and won't usually be shared with other parts of the system. If the blog entry is deleted, then its corresponding parts are also deleted. This is exactly what composition is all about: you are modeling the internal parts that make up a class.

 Similar to aggregation, the Java code implementation for a composition relationship results only in the introduction of an attribute.

## Generalization (Otherwise Known as Inheritance)

Generalization and inheritance are used to describe a class that *is a type of* another class. The terms *has a* and *is a type of* have become an accepted way of deciding whether a relationship between two classes is aggregation or generalization for many years now. If you find yourself stating that a class has a part that is an object of another class, then the relationship is likely to be one of association, aggregation, or composition. If you find yourself saying that the class is a type of another class, then you might want to consider using generalization instead.

In UML, the generalization arrow is used to show that a class is a type of another class, as shown in Figure 5-8.

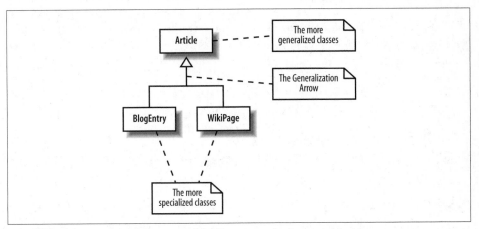

*Figure 5-8. Showing that a BlogEntry and WikiPage are both types of Article*

The more generalized class that is inherited from—at the arrow end of the generalization relationship, `Article` in this case—is often referred to as the parent, base, or superclass. The more specialized classes that do the inheriting—`BlogEntry` and `WikiPage` in this case—are often referred to as the children or derived classes. The specialized class inherits all of the attributes and methods that are declared in the generalized class and may add operations and attributes that are only applicable in specialized cases.

The key to why inheritance is called generalization in UML is in the difference between what a parent class and a child class each represents. Parent classes describe a more *general* type, which is then made more specialized in child classes.

 If you need to check that you've got a generalization relationship correct, this rule of thumb can help: generalization relationships make sense only in one direction. Although it's true to say that a guitarist is a musician, it is not true to say that all musicians are guitarists.

### Generalization and implementation reuse

A child class inherits and reuses all of the attributes and methods that the parent contains and that have public, protected, or default visibility. So, generalization offers a great way of expressing that one class is a type of another class, and it offers a way of reusing attributes and behavior between the two classes. That makes generalization look like the answer to your reuse prayers, doesn't it?

Just hold on a second! If you are thinking of using generalization just so you can reuse some behavior in a particular class, then you probably need to think again. Since a child class can see most of the internals of its parent, it becomes tightly coupled to its parent's implementation.

One of the principles of good object-oriented design is to avoid tightly coupling classes so that when one class changes, you don't end up having to change a bunch of other classes as well. Generalization is the strongest form of class relationship because it creates a tight coupling between classes. Therefore, it's a good rule of thumb to use generalization only when a class really is a more specialized type of another class and not just as a convenience to support reuse.

 If you still want to reuse a class's behavior in another class, think about using delegation. For more information on how delegation works and why it is preferred over inheritance, check out the excellent book, *Design Patterns: Elements of Reusable Object-Oriented Software* (Addison Wesley).

## Multiple inheritance

Multiple inheritance—or multiple generalization in the official UML terminology—occurs when a class inherits from two or more parent classes, as shown in Figure 5-9.

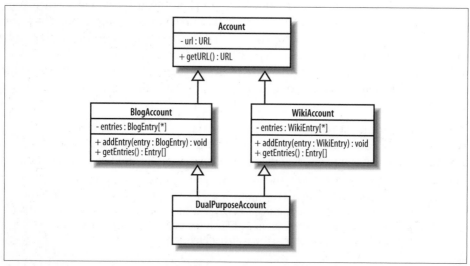

*Figure 5-9. The DualPurposeAccount is a BlogAccount and a WikiAccount all combined into one*

Although multiple inheritance is supported in UML, it is still not considered to be the best practice in most cases. This is mainly due to the fact that multiple inheritance presents a complicated problem when the two parent classes have overlapping attributes or behavior.

So, why the complication? In Figure 5-9, the DualPurposeAccount class inherits all of the behavior and attributes from the BlogAccount and WikiAccount classes, but there is quite a bit of duplication between the two parent classes. For example, both BlogAccount and WikiAccount contain a copy of the name attribute that they in turn inherited from the Account class. Which copy of this attribute does the DualPurposeAccount class get, or does it get two copies of the same attribute? The situation becomes even more complicated when the two parent classes contain the same operation. The BlogAccount class has an operation called getEntries( ) and so does the WikiAccount.

Although the BlogAccount and WikiAccount classes are kept separate, the fact that they both have a getEntries( ) operation is not a problem. However, when both of these classes become the parent to another class through inheritance, a conflict is created. When DualPurposeAccount inherits from both of these classes, which version of the getEntries( ) method does it get? If the DualPurposeAccount's getEntries( ) operation is invoked, which method should be executed to get the Wiki entries or the blog entries?

The answers to these question are unfortunately often hidden in implementation details. For example, if you were using the C++ programming language, which supports multiple inheritance, you would use the C++ language's own set of rules about how to resolve these conflicts. Another implementation language may use a different set of rules completely. Because of these complications, multiple inheritance has become something of a taboo subject in object-oriented software development—to the point where the current popular development languages, such as Java and C#, do not even support it. However, the fact remains that there are situations where multiple inheritance can make sense and be implemented—in languages such as C++, for example—so UML still needs to support it.

# Constraints

Sometimes you will want to restrict the ways in which a class can operate. For example, you might want to specify a *class invariant*—a rule that specifies that a particular condition should never happen within a class—or that one attribute's value is based on another, or that an operation should never leave the class in an irregular state. These types of constraints go beyond what can be done with simple UML notation and calls for a language in its own right: the OCL.

There are three types of constraint that can be applied to class members using OCL:

*Invariants*
>    An *invariant* is a constraint that must always be true; otherwise the system is in an invalid state. Invariants are defined on class attributes.

*Preconditions*

> A *precondition* is a constraint that is defined on a method and is checked before the method executes. Preconditions are frequently used to validate input parameters to a method.

*Postconditions*

> A *postcondition* is also defined on a method and is checked after the method executes. Postconditions are frequently used to describe how values were changed by a method.

Constraints are specified using either the OCL statement in curly brackets next to the class member or in a separate note, as shown in Figure 5-10.

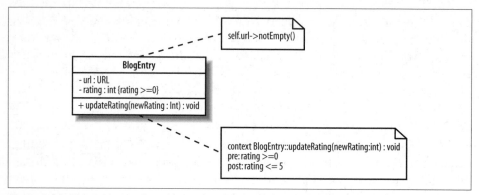

*Figure 5-10. Three constraints are set on the BlogEntry class: self.url>notEmpty() and rating>=0 are both invariants, and there is a postcondition constraint on the updateRating(..) operation*

In Figure 5-10, the url attribute is constrained to never being null and the rating attribute is constrained so that it must never be less than 0. To ensure that the updateRating(..) operation checks that the rating attribute is not less than 0, a precondition constraint is set. Finally, the rating attribute should never be more than 5 after it has been updated, so this is specified as a postcondition constraint on the updateRating(..) operation.

> OCL allows you to specify all sorts of constraints that limit how your classes can operate. For more information on OCL, see Appendix A.

# Abstract Classes

Sometimes when you are using generalization to declare a nice, reusable, generic class, you will not be able to implement all of the behavior that is needed by the general class. If you are implementing a Store class to store and retrieve the CMS's articles, as shown in Figure 5-11, you might want to indicate that exactly how a Store stores and retrieves the articles is not known at this point and should be left to subclasses to decide.

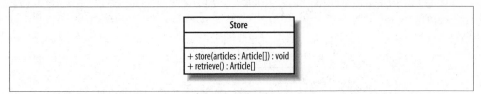

*Figure 5-11. Using regular operations, the Store class needs to know how to store and retrieve a collection of articles*

To indicate that the implementation of the store(..) and retrieve(..) operations is to be left to subclasses by declaring those operations as abstract, write their signatures in italics, as shown in Figure 5-12.

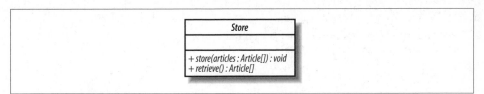

*Figure 5-12. The store(..) and retrieve(..) operations do not now need to be implemented by the Store class*

An abstract operation does not contain a method implementation and is really a placeholder that states, "I am leaving the implementation of this behavior to my subclasses." If any part of a class is declared abstract, then the class itself also needs to be declared as abstract by writing its name in italics, as shown in Figure 5-13.

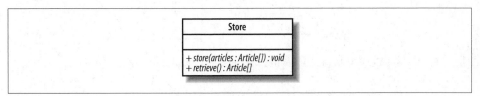

*Figure 5-13. The complete abstract Store class*

Now that the store(..) and retrieve(..) operations on the Store class are declared as abstract, they do not have to have any methods implemented, as shown in Example 5-4.

*Example 5-4. The problem of what code to put in the implementation of the play()operation is solved by declaring the operation and the surrounding class as abstract*

```
public abstract class Store {
    public abstract void store(Article[] articles);
    public abstract Article[] retrieve();
}
```

An abstract class cannot be instantiated into an object because it has pieces missing. The Store class might implement the store(..) and retrieve(..) operations but because it is abstract, children who inherit from the Store class will have to implement or declare abstract the Store class's abstract operations, as shown in Figure 5-14.

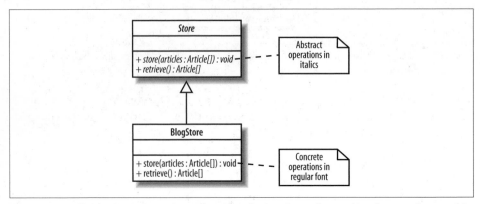

Figure 5-14. The BlogStore class inherits from the abstract Store class and implements the store(..) and retrieve(..) operations; classes that completely implement all of the abstract operations inherited from their parents are sometimes referred to as "concrete"

By becoming abstract, the Store class has delayed the implementation of the store(..) and retrieve(..) operations until a subclass has enough information to implement them. The BlogStore class can implement the Store class's abstract operations because it knows how to store away a blog, as shown in Example 5-5.

Example 5-5. The BlogStore class completes the abstract parts of the Store class

```
public abstract class Store {

    public abstract void store(Article[] articles);
    public abstract Article[] retrieve();
}

public class BlogStore {

    public void store(Article[] articles) {
        // Store away the blog entries here ...
    }

    public Article[] retrieve() {
        // Retrieve and return the stored blog entries here...
    }
}
```

An abstract class cannot be instantiated as an object because there are parts of the class definition missing: the abstract parts. Child classes of the abstract class can be instantiated as objects if they complete all of the abstract parts missing from the parent, thus becoming a concrete class, as shown in Example 5-6.

*Example 5-6. You can create objects of non-abstract classes, and any class not declared as abstract needs to implement any abstract behavior it may have inherited*

```
public abstract class Store {

    public abstract void store(Article[] articles);
    public abstract Article[] retrieve();
}

public class BlogStore {

    public void store(Article[] articles) {
        // Store away the blog entries here ...
    }

    public Article[] retrieve() {
        // Retrieve and return the stored blog entries here...
    }
}
public class MainApplication {

    public static void main(String[] args) {

        // Creating an object instance of the BlogStore class.
        // This is totally fine since the BlogStore class is not abstract.
        BlogStore store = new BlogStore();
        blogStore.store(new Article[]{new BlogEntry()});
        Article[] articlesInBlog = blogStore.retrieve();

        // Problem! It doesn't make sense to create an object of
        // an abstract class because the implementations of the
        // abstract pieces are missing!
        Store store = new Store(); // Compilation error here!
    }
}
```

Abstract classes are a very powerful mechanism that enable you to define common behavior and attributes, but they leave some aspects of how a class will work to more concrete subclasses. A great example of where abstract classes and interfaces are used is when defining the generic roles and behavior that make up design patterns. However, to implement an abstract class, you have to use inheritance; therefore, you need to be aware of all the baggage that comes with the strong and tightly coupling generalization relationship.

See the "Generalization (Otherwise Known as Inheritance)" section earlier in this chapter for more information on the trials and tribulations of using generalization. For more on design patterns and how they make good use of abstract classes, check out the definitive book on the subject *Design Patterns: Elements of Reusable Object-Oriented Software* (Addison-Wesley).

# Interfaces

If you want to declare the methods that concrete classes should implement, but not use abstraction since you have only one inheritance relationship (if you're coding in Java), then interfaces could be the answer.

An *interface* is a collection of operations that have no corresponding method implementations—very similar to an abstract class that contains only abstract methods. In some software implementation languages, such as C++, interfaces are implemented as abstract classes that contain no operation implementations. In newer languages, such as Java and C#, an interface has its own special construct.

> Interfaces tend to be much safer to use than abstract classes because they avoid many of the problems associated with multiple inheritance (see the "Multiple inheritance" section earlier in this chapter). This is why programming languages such as Java allow a class to implement any number of interfaces, but a class can inherit from only one regular or abstract class.

Think of an interface as a very simple contract that declares, "These are the operations that must be implemented by classes that intend to meet this contract." Sometimes an interface will contain attributes as well, but in those cases, the attributes are usually static and are often constants. See Chapter 4 for more on the use of static attributes.

In UML, an interface can be shown as a stereotyped class notation or by using its own ball notation, as shown in Figure 5-15.

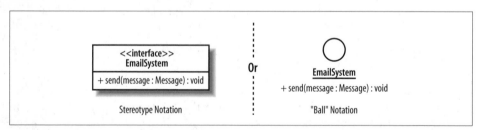

*Figure 5-15. Capturing an interface to an EmailSystem using the stereotype and "ball" UML notation; unlike abstract classes, an interface does not have to show that its operations are not implemented, so it doesn't have to use italics*

If you were implementing the EmailSystem interface from Figure 5-15 in Java, then your code would look like Example 5-7.

*Example 5-7. The EmailSystem interface is implemented in Java by using the interface keyword and contains the single send(..) operation signature with no operation implementation*

```
public interface EmailSystem {
   public void send(Message message);
}
```

You can't instantiate an interface itself, much like you can't instantiate an abstract class. This is because all of the implementations for an interface's operations are missing until it is realized by a class. If you are using the "ball" interface notation, then you realize an interface by associating it with a class, as shown in Figure 5-16.

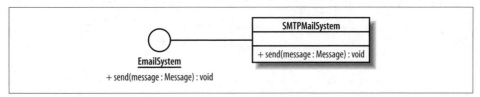

Figure 5-16. *The SMTPMailSystem class implements, or realizes, all of the operations specified on the EmailSystem interface*

If you have used the stereotype notation for your interface, then a new arrow is needed to show that this is a realization relationship, as shown in Figure 5-17.

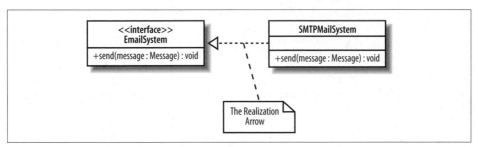

Figure 5-17. *The realization arrow specifies that the SMTPMailSystem realizes the EmailSystem interface*

Both Figures 5-16 and 5-17 and would have resulted in the same Java code being generated, as shown in Example 5-8.

Example 5-8. *Java classes realize interfaces using the implements keyword*

```java
public interface EmailSystem
{
    public void send(Message message));
}

public class SMTPMailSystem implements EmailSystem
{
    public void send(Message message)
    {
        // Implement the interactions with an SMTP server to send the message
    }

    // ... Implementations of the other operations on the Guitarist class ...
}
```

If a class realizes an interface but does not implement all of the operations that the interface specifies, then that class needs to be declared abstract, as shown in Figure 5-18.

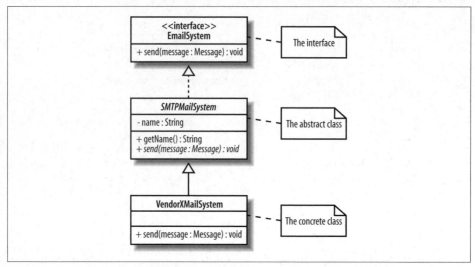

*Figure 5-18. Because the SMTPMailSystem class does not implement the send(..) operation as specified by the EmailSystem interface, it needs to be declared abstract; the VendorXMailSystem class completes the picture by implementing all of its operations*

Interfaces are great at completely separating the behavior that is required of a class from exactly how it is implemented. When a class implements an interface, objects of that class can be referred to using the interface's name rather than the class name itself. This means that other classes can be dependent on interfaces rather than classes. This is generally a good thing since it ensures that your classes are as loosely coupled as possible. If your classes are loosely coupled, then when a class implementation changes other classes should not break (because they are dependent on the interface, not on the class itself).

## Using Interfaces

It is good practice to de-couple dependencies between your classes using interfaces; some programming environments, such as the Spring Framework, enforce this interface-class relationship. The use of interfaces, as opposed to abstract classes, is also useful when you are implementing design patterns. In languages such as Java, you don't really want to use up the single inheritance relationship just to use a design pattern. A Java class can implement any number of interfaces, so they offer a way of enforcing a design pattern without imposing the burden of having to expend that one inheritance relationship to do it.

# Templates

Templates are an advanced but useful feature of object orientation. A *template*—or parameterized class, as they are sometimes referred to—is helpful when you want to postpone the decision as to which classes a class will work with. When you declare a template, as shown in Figure 5-19, it is similar to declaring, "I know this class will have to work with other classes, but I don't know or necessarily care what those classes actually end up being."

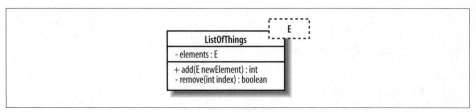

*Figure 5-19. A template in UML is shown by providing an extra box with a dashed border to the top right of the regular class box*

The ListOfThings class in Figure 5-19 is parameterized with the type referred to as E. There is no class in our model called E; E is nothing more than a placeholder that can be used at a later point to tell the ListOfThings class the type of object that it will need to store.

---

## Lists

Lists tend to be the most common examples of how to use templates, and with very good reason. Lists and their cousins, such as maps and sets, all store objects in different ways, but they don't actually care what classes those objects are constructed from. For this reason, one of the best real-world uses of templates is in the Java collection classes. Prior to Java 5, the Java programming language did not have a means of specifying templates. With the release of Java 5 and its generics feature, you can now not only create your own templates, but the original collection classes are all available to use as templates as well. To find out more about Java 5 generics, check out the latest edition of *Java in a Nutshell* (O'Reilly).

---

To use a class that is a template, you first need to bind its parameters. The ListOfSomething class template doesn't yet know what it's supposed to be storing; you need to tell the template what actual classes it will be working with; you need to bind the parameter referred to so far as just E to an actual class.

You can bind a template's parameters to a specific set of classes in one of two ways. First, you can subclass the template, binding the parameters as you go, as shown in Figure 5-20.

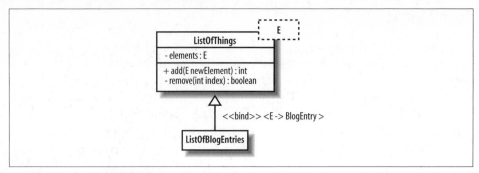

*Figure 5-20. The ListOfThings class is subclassed into a ListOfBlogEntries, binding the single parameter E to the concrete BlogEntry class*

Binding by subclass in Figure 5-20 allows you to reuse all of the generic behavior in the ListOfThings class and restrict that behavior in the ListOfBlogEntries class to only adding and removing BlogEntry objects.

The real power of templates is much more obvious when you use the second approach to template parameter binding—binding at runtime. You bind at runtime when a template is told the type of parameters it will have *as it is constructed into an object*.

Runtime template binding is about objects rather than classes; therefore, a new type of diagram is needed: the object diagram. Object diagrams use classes to show some of the important ways they are used as your system runs. As luck would have it, object diagrams are the subject of the very next chapter.

# What's Next

Class diagrams show the types of objects in your system. A useful next step is to look at object diagrams since they show how classes come alive at runtime as object instances, which is useful if you want to show runtime configurations. Object diagrams are covered in Chapter 6.

Composite structures are a diagram type that loosely shows context sensitive class diagrams and patterns in your software. Composite structures are described in Chapter 11.

After you've decided the responsibilities of the classes in your system, it's common to then create sequence and communication diagrams to show interactions between the parts. Sequence diagrams can be found in Chapter 7; communication diagrams are covered in Chapter 8.

It's also common to step back and organize your classes into packages. Package diagrams allow you to view dependencies at a higher level, helping you understand the stability of your software. Package diagrams are described in Chapter 13.

# CHAPTER 6

# Bringing Your Classes to Life: Object Diagrams

Objects are at the heart of any object-oriented system at runtime. When the system you designed is actually in use, *objects* make up its parts and bring all of your carefully designed classes to life.

Compared to class diagrams, object diagram notation is very simple. Despite having a fairly limited vocabulary, object diagrams are particularly useful when you want to describe how the objects within the system would work together in a particular scenario. Class diagrams describe how all of the different types of objects within your system interact with each other. They also draw attention to the many ways that the objects will exist and interact within your system at runtime. In addition to class diagrams, object diagrams help you capture the logical view of your model, shown in Figure 6-1.

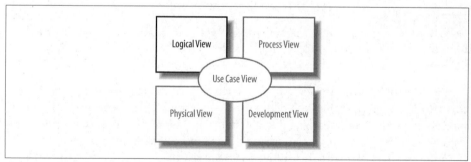

*Figure 6-1. The Logical View of your model contains the abstract descriptions of your system's parts, including which objects exist within your system at runtime*

## Object Instances

To draw an object diagram, the first thing you need to add are the actual objects themselves. Object notation is actually very simple if you're already familiar with class notation; an object is shown with a rectangle, just like a class, but to show that this is an instance of a class rather than the class itself, the title is underlined, as shown in Figure 6-2.

Figure 6-2. You show an instantiated object by using a rectangle but with the name of the object—its identifier—underlined

The entry object in Figure 6-2 has only an identity with which the object can be referred to—the entry name. However, if you happen to also know the class that this object instantiates, then you can also add the class name to the object name, as shown in Figure 6-3.

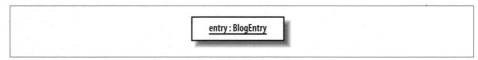

Figure 6-3. The entry object is an instance of the BlogEntry class from Chapter 4

There is one final type of object that you might want to use on your object diagrams—the anonymous object, shown in Figure 6-4.

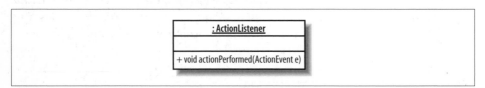

Figure 6-4. The class of this object is ActionListener, but the name or identity is not specified; this object also shows the single actionPerformed(…) method that is required by the ActionListener interface

Anonymous objects are typically useful when the name of the object is not important within the context that it is being used. For example, it is a common programming idiom when you create an event handler in Java using an anonymous object because you don't care what the name of the object is, just that it is registered with the appropriate event source, as shown in Example 6-1.

Example 6-1. Using an anonymous object in Java code to register an ActionListener with a JButton

```
public void initialiseUI( ) {
    //... Other method implementation code ...

    JButton button = new Jbutton("Submit");
    button.addActionListener(new ActionListener{
        public void actionPerformed(ActionEvent e)
        {
```

*Example 6-1. Using an anonymous object in Java code to register an ActionListener with a JButton (continued)*

```
        System.out.println("The button was pressed so it's time to do something ...");
    }
});

//... Other method implementation code ...
}
```

You might also notice in Example 6-1 that the anonymous object is implementing an interface as it is declared. As the anonymous object is instantiated, it implements the `actionPerformed(...)` method that is required by the `ActionListener` interface.

# Links

Objects on their own are not very interesting or helpful. To really show how your objects will work together in a particular runtime configuration, you need to tie those objects together using links, as shown in Figure 6-5.

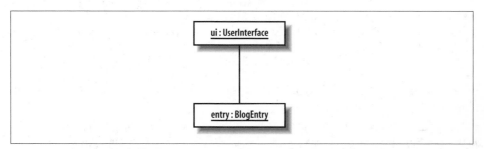

*Figure 6-5. Links are shown using a line between the two objects that are being linked*

Links between objects on an object diagram show that the two objects can communicate with each other. However, you can't just link any two objects together. If you create a link between two objects, there must be a corresponding association between the classes.

The links on an object diagram work in a similar fashion to links on a communication diagram (see Chapter 8). However, unlike communication diagrams, the only additional piece of information that you can optionally add to a link is a label that indicates the purpose of the link, as shown in Figure 6-6.

## Links and Constraints

Links between objects correspond to associations between the object's classes. This means that where constraint rules have been applied to an association, the link must keep to those rules.

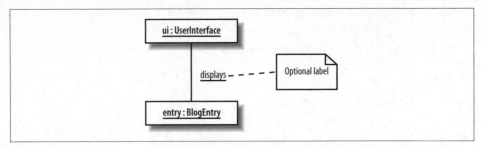

Figure 6-6. To play some tunes, a BlogEntry object is connected to a UserInterface object

In Chapter 5, the relationship between BlogEntry, BlogAccount, and Category was modeled using an association class, as shown in Figure 6-7.

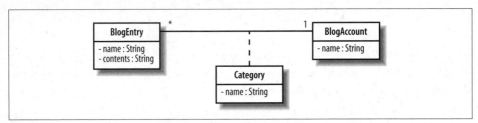

Figure 6-7. When a BlogEntry is added to a BlogAccount, it will be grouped under one or more categories; the Category class is associated with the relationship between a BlogEntry and a BlogAccount

If the diagram in Figure 6-7 were left as it is, then the two object diagrams shown in Figure 6-8 would be perfectly valid.

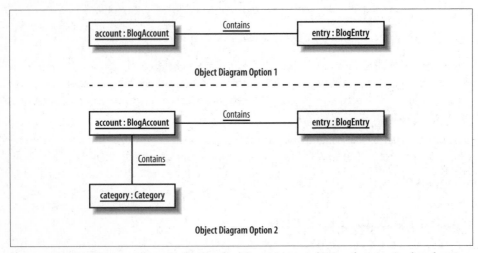

Figure 6-8. A BlogEntry can be associated with a BlogAccount and a set of categories, but there is no rule that states that a BlogEntry must be associated with a category

If you wanted to show that an entry must be associated with a category when it is contained within a blog account, you need to add some OCL to the original class diagram, as shown in Figure 6-9. OCL was briefly covered in Chapter 5 and is covered in more depth in Appendix A.

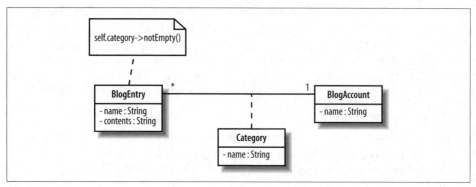

*Figure 6-9. The constraint states that within the context of the BlogEntry, a BlogEntry object should be associated with a category and that the association should not be null; in other words, for a BlogEntry to be added to a BlogAccount, it must have a category assigned*

Objects and their links must abide by the rules set by the OCL statements—this is one of the reasons why OCL is called the object constraint language, and not the class constraint language. With the constraints applied to the class diagram in Figure 6-9, the possible options for an object diagram based on these classes is reduced to something that makes much more sense, as shown in Figure 6-10.

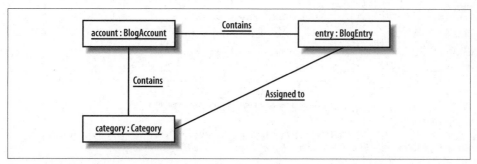

*Figure 6-10. The self.category->notEmpty( ) constraint affects the options available when you create an object diagram, ensuring that an entry is associated with a category for it to be added to a BlogAccount*

# Binding Class Templates

In Chapter 5, we saw how the parameters declared on class templates could be realized using subclassing on a class diagram. Although this approach works fine, the real power of templates comes when you bind template parameters at runtime. To do this, you take a template and tell it the types that its parameters are going to be *as it is constructed into an object.*

Object diagrams are ideal for modeling how runtime binding takes place. When you use runtime template parameter binding, you are really talking about objects rather than classes, so you can't really model this information on a regular class diagram.

Although this book talks about UML in terms of diagram types, the UML specification is not actually constrained to a particular set of diagrams. In fact, you could show object diagram notation on a class diagram if you wanted to group your classes and their runtime bindings on the same diagram.

Figure 6-11 shows a simple class template for a list collection taken from Chapter 4. Collections are great candidates for templates because they need to manage a collection of objects, but they don't usually care what classes those objects are.

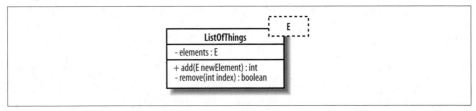

*Figure 6-11. The ListOfThings collection can store and remove any class of object to which the E parameter is bound*

To model that the ListOfThings template's E parameter is to be bound at runtime to a particular class, all you need to do is add the parameter binding details to the end of the object's class description, as shown in Figure 6-12.

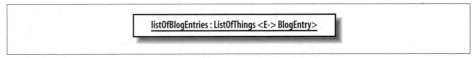

*Figure 6-12. The listOfBlogEntries reuses the generic ListOfThings template, binding the E parameter to the BlogEntry class to store only objects of the BlogEntry class*

Up until recently, showing runtime binding of templates in Java would have been impossible; the language did not support templates at all. However, with the release of Java 5 and the new generics language features, the runtime binding of the BlogEntry class to the E parameter on the ListOfThings template can now be implemented, as shown in Example 6-2.

*Example 6-2. Using Java 5 generics to implement the ListOfThings template and a runtime binding to the ListOfBlogEntries*

```java
public class ListOfThings<E> {

    // We're cheating a bit here; Java actually already has a List template
    // and so we're using that for our ListOfThings templates operations.
    private List[E] elements;

    public ListOfThings {
        elements = new ArrayList<E>();
    }

    public int add(E object) {
        return elements.add(object);
    }

    public E remove(int index) {
        return elements.remove(index);
    }
}

public class Application {

    public static void main(String[] args) {
        // Binding the E parameter on the ListOfThings template to a Musician class
        // to create a ListOfThings that will only store Musician objects.
        ListOfThings <BlogEntry>listOfBlogEntries= new ListOfThings<BlogEntry>();
    }
}
```

There is a lot more to generics in Java than the simple template implementation provided here. For more examples, see *Java 5 Tiger: A Developer's Notebook* (O'Reilly).

# What's Next?

Now that you're considering runtime characteristics of your system, it's natural to continue on this path by studying sequence diagrams and communication diagrams. These show messages passing between parts on your system, demonstrating how your objects get used.

You can find sequence diagrams in Chapter 7; communication diagrams are covered in Chapter 8.

# CHAPTER 7

# Modeling Ordered Interactions: Sequence Diagrams

Use cases allow your model to describe what your system must be able to do; classes allow your model to describe the different types of parts that make up your system's structure. There's one large piece that's missing from this jigsaw; with use cases and classes alone, you can't yet model *how* your system is actually going to its job. This is where interaction diagrams, and specifically sequence diagrams, come into play.

Sequence diagrams are an important member of the group known as interaction diagrams. *Interaction diagrams* model important runtime interactions between the parts that make up your system and form part of the logical view of your model, shown in Figure 7-1.

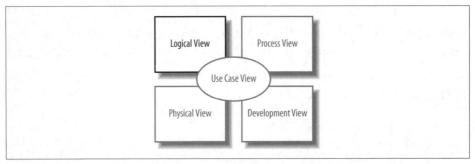

*Figure 7-1. The Logical View of your model contains the abstract descriptions of your system's parts, including the interactions between those parts*

Sequence diagrams are not alone in this group; they work alongside communication diagrams (see Chapter 8) and timing diagrams (see Chapter 9) to help you accurately model how the parts that make up your system interact.

 Sequence diagrams are the most popular of the three interaction diagram types. This could be because they show the right sorts of information or simply because they tend to make sense to people new to UML.

*Sequence diagrams* are all about capturing the *order* of interactions between parts of your system. Using a sequence diagram, you can describe which interactions will be triggered when a particular use case is executed and in what order those interactions will occur. Sequence diagrams show plenty of other information about an interaction, but their forté is the simple and effective way in which they communicate the order of events within an interaction.

# Participants in a Sequence Diagram

A sequence diagram is made up of a collection of *participants*—the parts of your system that interact with each other during the sequence. Where a participant is placed on a sequence diagram is important. Regardless of where a participant is placed vertically, participants are always arranged horizontally with no two participants overlapping each other, as shown in Figure 7-2.

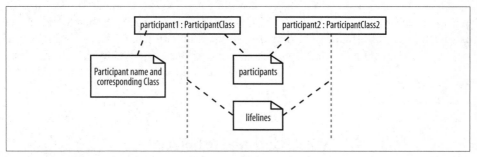

*Figure 7-2. At its simplest, a sequence diagram is made up of one or more participants—only one participant would be a very strange sequence diagram, but it would be perfectly legal UML*

Each participant has a corresponding lifeline running down the page. A participant's *lifeline* simply states that the part exists at that point in the sequence and is only really interesting when a part is created and/or deleted during a sequence (see "Participant Creation and Destruction Messages" later in this chapter).

## Participant Names

Participants on a sequence diagram can be named in number of different ways, picking elements from the standard format:

    name [selector] : class_name ref decomposition

The elements of the format that you pick to use for a particular participant will depend on the information known about a participant at a given time, as explained in Table 7-1.

*Table 7-1. How to understand the components of a participant's name*

| Example participant name | Description |
| --- | --- |
| admin | A part is named `admin`, but at this point in time the part has not been assigned a class. |
| : ContentManagementSystem | The class of the participant is `ContentManagementSystem`, but the part currently does not have its own name. |
| admin : Administrator | There is a part that has a name of `admin` and is of the class `Administrator`. |
| eventHandlers [2] : EventHandler | There is a part that is accessed within an array at element 2, and it is of the class `EventHandler`. |
| : ContentManagementSystem ref cmsInteraction | The participant is of the class `ContentManagementSystem`, and there is another interaction diagram called `cmsInteraction` that shows how the participant works internally (see "A Brief Overview of UML 2.0's Fragment Types," later in this chapter). |

The format used when creating names for your participants is totally up to you—or maybe your company's style guide. In this book, we lowercase the first word in the participant name to make sure that there is as little confusion as possible with the name of a class. However, this is just our convention—similar to the conventions used when naming objects and classes in Java—and is not something specified by UML.

---

## What Happened to Objects?

In UML 1.x, participants on an interaction diagram were usually software objects in the traditional object-oriented programming sense. Each object was an instance of a class, and the object name was underlined to indicate this. Because UML 2.0 is more of a general system modeling language, it makes much more sense to think of it in terms of system *parts* interacting with each other rather than software *objects*. This is why we've used the term "participant" to describe a part that is involved in the interactions on a sequence diagram. A participant could still be a software object, a la UML 1.x, but it could equally be any other part of the system in keeping with the spirit of UML 2.0.

---

# Time

A sequence diagram describes the order in which the interactions take place, so time is an important factor. How time relates to a sequence diagram is shown in Figure 7-3.

Time on a sequence diagram starts at the top of the page, just beneath the topmost participant heading, and then progresses down the page. The order that interactions

---

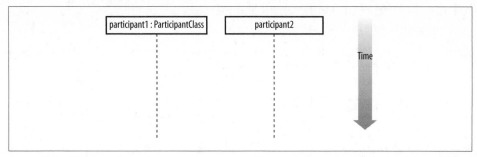

*Figure 7-3. Time runs down the page on a sequence diagram in keeping with the participant lifeline*

are placed down the page on a sequence diagram indicates the order in which those interactions will take place in time.

Time on a sequence diagram is all about ordering, not duration. Although the time at which an interaction occurs is indicated on a sequence diagram by where it is placed vertically on the diagram, how much of the vertical space the interaction takes up has nothing to do with the duration of time that the interaction will take. Sequence diagrams are first about the ordering of the interactions between participants; more detailed timing information is better shown on timing diagrams (see Chapter 9).

## Events, Signals, and Messages

The smallest part of an interaction is an event. An *event* is any point in an interaction where something occurs, as shown on Figure 7-4.

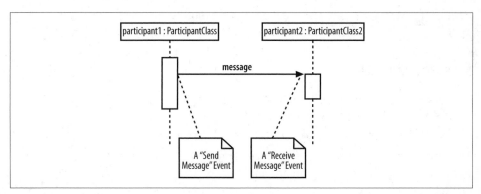

*Figure 7-4. Probably the most common examples of events are when a message or signal is sent or received*

Events are the building blocks for signals and messages. Signals and messages are really different names for the same concept: a signal is the terminology often used by system designers, while software designers often prefer messages.

In terms of sequence diagrams, signals and messages act and look the same, so we'll stick to using the term "messages" in this book.

An interaction in a sequence diagram occurs when one participant decides to send a message to another participant, as shown in Figure 7-5.

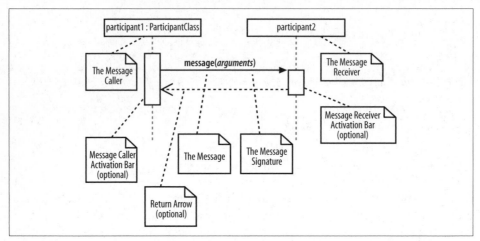

*Figure 7-5. Interactions on a sequence diagram are shown as messages between participants*

*Messages* on a sequence diagram are specified using an arrow from the participant that wants to pass the message, the Message Caller, to the participant that is to receive the message, the Message Receiver. Messages can flow in whatever direction makes sense for the required interaction—from left to right, right to left, or even back to the Message Caller itself. Think of a message as an event that is passed from a Message Caller to get the Message Receiver to do something.

## Message Signatures

A message arrow comes with a description, or signature. The format for a message signature is:

    attribute = signal_or_message_name (arguments) : return_type

You can specify any number of different arguments on a message, each separated using a comma. The format of an argument is:

    <name>:<class>

The elements of the format that you use for a particular message will depend on the information known about a particular message at any given time, as explained in Table 7-2.

*Table 7-2. How to understand the components of a message's signature*

| Example message signature | Description |
| --- | --- |
| doSomething( ) | The message's name is doSomething, but no further information is known about it. |
| doSomething(number1 : Number, number2 : Number) | The message's name is doSomething, and it takes two arguments, number1 and number2, which are both of class Number. |
| doSomething( ) : ReturnClass | The message's name is doSomething; it takes no arguments and returns an object of class ReturnClass. |
| myVar = doSomething( ) : ReturnClass | The message's name is doSomething; it takes no arguments, and it returns an object of class ReturnClass that is assigned to the myVar attribute of the message caller. |

## Activation Bars

When a message is passed to a participant it triggers, or invokes, the receiving participant into doing something; at this point, the receiving participant is said to be *active*. To show that a participant is active, i.e., doing something, you can use an activation bar, as shown in Figure 7-6.

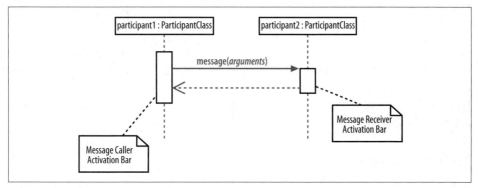

*Figure 7-6. Activation bars show that a participant is busy doing something for a period of time*

An activation bar can be shown on the sending and receiving ends of a message. It indicates that the sending participant is busy while it sends the message and the receiving participant is busy after the message has been received

 Activation bars are optional—they can clutter up a diagram.

# Nested Messages

When a message from one participant results in one or more messages being sent by the receiving participant, those resulting messages are said to be nested within the triggering message, as shown in Figure 7-7.

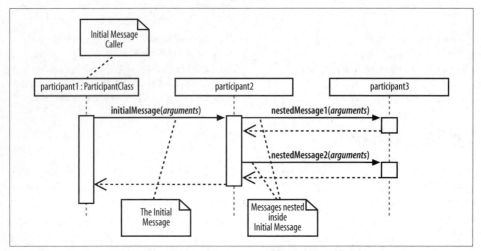

*Figure 7-7. Two nested messages are invoked when an initial message is received*

In Figure 7-7, participant1 sends initialMessage(..) to participant2. When participant2 receives initialMessage(..), participant2 becomes active and sends two nested messages to participant3. You can have any number of nested messages inside a triggering message and any number of levels of nested messages on a sequence diagram.

# Message Arrows

The type of arrowhead that is on a message is also important when understanding what type of message is being passed. For example, the Message Caller may want to wait for a message to return before carrying on with its work—a synchronous message. Or it may wish to just send the message to the Message Receiver without waiting for any return as a form of "fire and forget" message—an asynchronous message.

Sequence diagrams need to show these different types of message using various message arrows, as shown in Figure 7-8.

To explain how the different types of messages work, let's look at some simple examples where the participants are actually software objects implemented in Java.

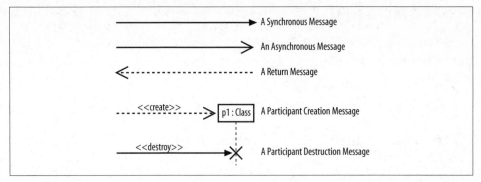

*Figure 7-8. There are five main types of message arrow for use on sequence diagram, and each has its own meaning*

## Synchronous Messages

As mentioned before, a synchronous message is invoked when the Message Caller waits for the Message Receiver to return from the message invocation, as shown in Figure 7-9.

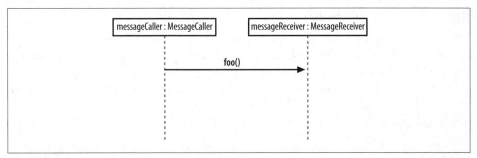

*Figure 7-9. The messageCaller participant makes a single synchronous message invocation on the messageReceiver participant*

The interaction shown in Figure 7-9 is implemented in Java using nothing more than a simple method invocation, as shown in Example 7-1.

*Example 7-1. The messageCaller object makes a regular Java method call to the foo( ) method on the messageReceiver object and then waits for the messageReceiver.foo( ) method to return before carrying on with any further steps in the interaction*

```
public class MessageReceiver
{
   public void foo( )
   {
      // Do something inside foo.
   }
}
```

*Example 7-1. The messageCaller object makes a regular Java method call to the foo( ) method on the messageReceiver object and then waits for the messageReceiver.foo( ) method to return before carrying on with any further steps in the interaction (continued)*

```
public class MessageCaller
{
    private MessageReceiver messageReceiver;

    // Other Methods and Attributes of the class are declared here

    // The messageRecevier attribute is initialized elsewhere in
    // the class.

    public doSomething(String[] args)
    {
        // The MessageCaller invokes the foo( ) method

        this.messageReceiver.foo( ); // then waits for the method to return

        // before carrying on here with the rest of its work
    }
}
```

## Asynchronous Messages

It would be great if all the interactions in your system happened one after the other in a nice simple order. Each participant would pass a message to another participant and then calmly wait for the message to return before carrying on. Unfortunately, that's not how most systems work. Interactions can happen at the same point in time, and sometimes you will want to initiate a collection of interactions all at the same time and not wait for them to return at all.

For example, say you are designing a piece of software with a user interface that supports the editing and printing of a set of documents. Your application offers a button for the user to print a document. Printing could take some time, so you want to show that after the print button is pressed and the document is printing, the user can go ahead and work with other things in the application. The regular synchronous message arrow is not sufficient to show these types of interactions. You need a new type of message arrow: the asynchronous message arrow.

An asynchronous message is invoked by a Message Caller on a Message Receiver, but the Message Caller does not wait for the message invocation to return before carrying on with the rest of the interaction's steps. This means that the Message Caller will invoke a message on the Message Receiver and the Message Caller will be busy invoking further messages before the original message returns, as shown in Figure 7-10.

A common way of implementing asynchronous messaging in Java is to use threads, as shown in Example 7-2.

---

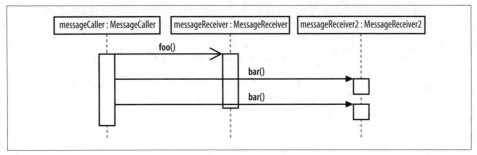

*Figure 7-10. While the foo() message is being worked on by the messageReceiver object, the messageCaller object has carried on with the interaction by executing further synchronous messages on another object*

If you're not too familiar with how threads work in Java, check out *Java in a Nutshell*, Fifth Edition (O'Reilly) or *Java Threads* (O'Reilly). See "Applying Asynchronous Messages" later in this chapter for a practical example of asynchronous messages.

*Example 7-2. The operation1() asynchronous message invokes an internal thread on the message receiver that in turn spurs the message, immediately returning the flow of execution to the messageCaller*

```
public class MessageReceiver implements Runable {

    public void operation1( ) {
        // Receive the message and trigger off the thread

        Thread fooWorker = new Thread(this);
        fooWorker.start(); // This call starts a new thread, calling the run( )
                           // method below

        // As soon as the thread has been started, the call to foo( ) returns.

    }

    public void run( ) {
        // This is where the work for the foo( ) message invocation will
        // be executed.
    }
}

public class MessageCaller
{
    private MessageReceiver messageReceiver;

    // Other Methods and Attributes of the class are declared here

    // The messageRecevier attribute is initialized elsewhere in
    // the class.

    public void doSomething(String[] args) {
```

*Example 7-2. The operation1() asynchronous message invokes an internal thread on the message receiver that in turn spurs the message, immediately returning the flow of execution to the messageCaller (continued)*

```
        // The MessageCaller invokes the operation1() operation

        this.messageReceiver.operation1();

        // then immediately carries on with the rest of its work
    }
}
```

## The Return Message

The *return message* is an optional piece of notation that you can use at the end of an activation bar to show that the control flow of the activation returns to the participant that passed the original message. In code, a return arrow is similar to reaching the end of a method or explicitly calling a return statement.

You *don't* have to use return messages—sometimes they can really make your sequence diagram too busy and confusing. You don't have to clutter up your sequence diagrams with a return arrow for every activation bar since there is an implied return arrow on any activation bars that are invoked using a synchronous message.

 Although a message will often be passed between two different participants, it is totally normal for a participant to pass a message to itself. Messages from an object to itself are a good way of splitting up a large activation into smaller and more manageable pieces and, in terms of software, can be thought of as being very similar to making a method call to the this reference in Java and C#.

## Participant Creation and Destruction Messages

Participants do not necessarily live for the entire duration of a sequence diagram's interaction. Participants can be created and destroyed according to the messages that are being passed, as shown in Figure 7-11.

To show that a participant is created, you can either simply pass a create(..) message to the participant's lifeline or use the dropped participant box notation where it is absolutely clear that the participant does not exist before the create call is invoked. Participant deletion is shown by the ending of the participant's lifeline with the deletion cross.

Software participant creation in Java and C# is implemented using the new keyword, as shown in Example 7-3.

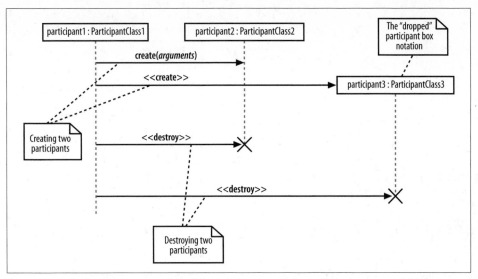

*Figure 7-11. Both participant2 and participant3 are created throughout the course of this sequence diagram*

*Example 7-3. The MessageCaller creates a new MessageReceiver object simply by using the new keyword*

```
public class MessageReceiver {
   // Attributes and Methods of the MessageReceiver class
}

public class MessageCaller {

   // Other Methods and Attributes of the class are declared here

   public void doSomething( ) {
      // The MessageReceiver object is created
      MessageReceiver messageReceiver = new MessageReceiver( );
   }
}
```

With some implementation languages, such as Java, you will not have an explicit destroy method, so it doesn't make sense to show one on your sequence diagrams. Example 7-3 is one such case where the messageReceiver object will be flagged for destruction when the doSomething( ) method completes its execution. However, no additional messages have to be passed to the messageReceiver to make it destroy itself since this is all handled implicitly by the Java garbage collector.

In these cases, where another factor such as the garbage collector is involved, you can either leave the object as alive but unused or imply that it is no longer needed by using the destruction cross without an associated destroy method, as shown in Figure 7-12.

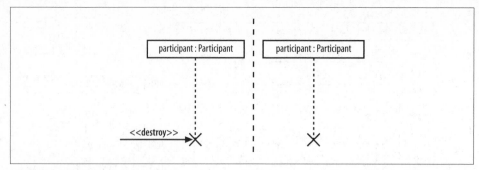

Figure 7-12. Using an explicit destroy message or implying that a participant has been discarded using just a destruction cross

# Bringing a Use Case to Life with a Sequence Diagram

It's time to take a closer look at a sequence. Specifically, let's look at a sequence diagram that is going to model the interactions that need to occur to make the Create a new Regular Blog Account use case happen.

Figure 7-13 should look familiar; it is just a quick reminder of what the Create a new Regular Blog Account use case looks like (see Chapter 2).

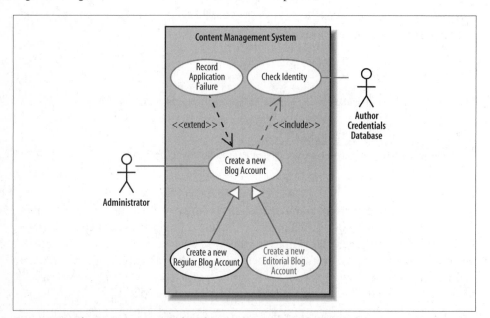

Figure 7-13. The Create a new Regular Blog Account use case diagram

Briefly, the Create a new Regular Blog Account use case is a special case of the Create a new Blog Account use case. It also includes all of the steps provided by the Check Identity use case and may optionally execute the steps provided by the Record Application Failure use case, if the application for a new account is denied.

Figure 7-13 is a pretty busy use case diagram, so feel free to jump back to Chapter 2 to remind yourself of what is going on.

---

## Supporting the Dropped Title Box Technique

It is a sad fact that many standard UML tools do not support the dropped title box technique for showing participant creation or the cross notation for participant destruction. For example, you will often find that your tool does not allow you to place the participant's title box anywhere else but at the top of the diagram. In these cases, the best approach is to show that the creation or deletion message invokes the object being created and to rely on the reader of the diagram to realize that you mean that the participant is being created (a note to this effect is often helpful too). Unfortunately, this approach is not the best use of UML, but sometimes it is all you can get the tool to do.

---

## A Top-Level Sequence Diagram

Before you can specify what types of interaction are going to occur when a use case executes, you need a more detailed description of what the use case does. If you've already completed a use case description, you already have a good reference for this detailed information.

Table 7-3 shows the steps that occur in the `Create a new Regular Blog Account` use case according to its detailed description.

*Table 7-3. Most of the detailed information that you will need to start constructing a sequence diagram for a use case should already be available as the Main Flow within the use case's description*

| Main Flow | Step | Action |
|-----------|------|--------|
| | 1 | The Administrator asks the system to create a new blog account. |
| | 2 | The Administrator selects the regular blog account type. |
| | 3 | The Administrator enters the author's details. |
| | 4 | The author's details are checked using the Author Credentials Database. |
| | 5 | The new regular blog account is created. |
| | 6 | A summary of the new blog account's details are emailed to the author. |

Table 7-3 actually shows all of the steps involved in the `Create a new Regular Blog Account` use case, including any steps that it has inherited from `Create a new Blog Account` or reused from `Check Identity`. This has been done just so you can easily see all of the Main Flow steps in one place.

In practice, you would probably just look up all three use case descriptions separately without actually going to the bother of actually merging them.

Table 7-3 only shows the Main Flow—that is the steps that would occur without worrying about any extensions—but this is a good enough starting point for creating a top-level sequence diagram, as shown in Figure 7-14.

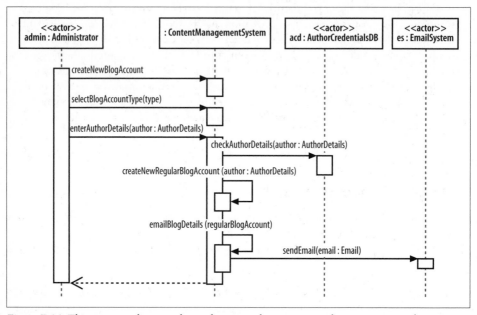

Figure 7-14. This sequence diagram shows the actors that interact with your system and your system is shown simply as a single part in the sequence

 Figure 7-14 focuses on the participants and messages that are involved in the use case. The same use case was modeled in Chapter 3 as an activity diagram, which focused on the processes involved rather than the particpants.

## Breaking an Interaction into Separate Participants

At this point, Figure 7-14 shows only the interactions that must happen between the external actors and your system because that is the level at which the use case description's steps were written. On the sequence diagram, your system is represented as a single participant, the ContentManagementSystem; however, unless you intend on implementing your content management system as a single monolithic piece of code (generally not a good idea!), it's time to break apart ContentManagementSystem to expose the pieces that go inside, as shown in Figure 7-15.

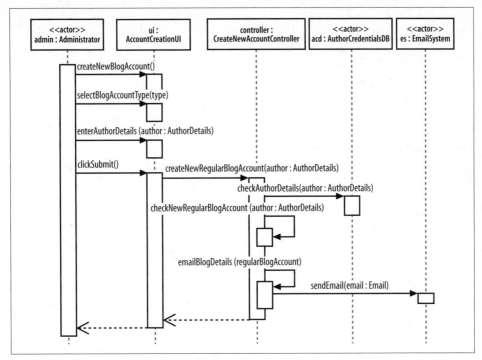

*Figure 7-15. Adding more detail about the internals of your system*

Sequence diagrams can get much more complicated by simply adding a couple of extra participants and some more detailed interactions. In Figure 7-15, the original sequence diagram has been refined so that the single ContentManagementSystem participant has been removed and in its place, more detail has been added showing the actual participants that will be involved.

Work on sequence diagrams invariably goes on throughout the life of your system's model, and even getting the right participants and interactions in a detailed sequence diagram at the beginning can be hard work. Keeping your sequence diagrams up to date is also a challenge (see "Managing Complex Interactions with Sequence Fragments" later in this chapter); therefore, expect to spend some time working with your sequence diagrams until you get things right.

## Applying Participant Creation

Something critical is missing from the sequence diagram shown in Figure 7-15. The title of the use case in which the sequence diagram is operating is Create a new Regular Blog Account, but where is the actual *creation* of the blog account? Figure 7-16 adds the missing pieces to the model to show the actual creation of a regular blog account.

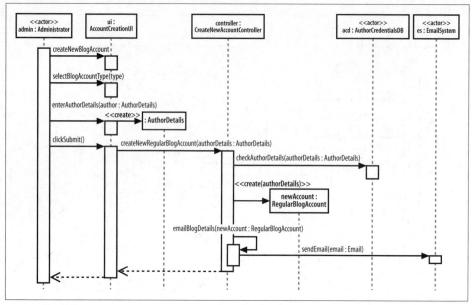

*Figure 7-16. Showing the lifelines of your sequence diagram's participants*

Participant lifelines are particularly useful when showing that a participant has been created. In Figure 7-16, the AuthorDetails and RegularBlogAccount participants are not in existence when the sequence diagram begins but they are created during its execution.

The AuthorDetails and newAccount:RegularBlogAccount participants are created by corresponding create messages. Each create message connects directly into the title box for the participant being created, passing any information needed when creating the new participant. By dropping the participant's title box to the point where the create message is actually invoked, the diagram can clearly show the point where the participant's lifeline begins.

## Applying Participant Deletion

Let's say that the authorDetails:AuthorDetails participant is no longer required once the newAccount:RegularBlogAccount has been created. To show that the authorDetails:AuthorDetails participant is discarded at this point, you can use an explicit destroy message connected to the destruction cross, as shown in Figure 7-17.

## Applying Asynchronous Messages

So far, all of the messages on our example sequence diagram have been synchronous; they are executed one after the other in order, and nothing happens concurrently. However, there is at least one message in the example sequence that is a great candidate for being an asynchronous message, as shown in Figure 7-18.

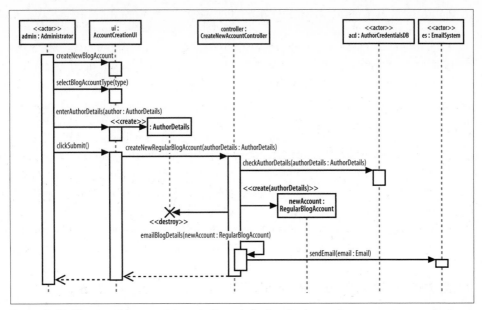

*Figure 7-17. Showing that a participant is discarded using the destruction cross*

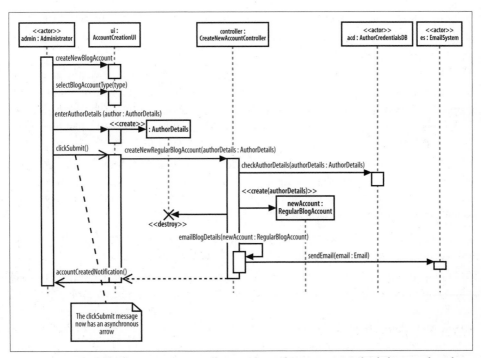

*Figure 7-18. The clickSubmit() message will currently produce some irregular behavior when the admin creates a new account*

In Figure 7-18, when the `Administrator` clicks on the submit button the system freezes, until the new blog account has been created. It would be useful to show that the user interface allows the `Administrator` to carry on with other tasks while the content management system creates the new account. What we need is for the `clickSubmit( )` message to be asynchronous.

Converting the `clickSubmit( )` from a synchronous to an asynchronous message means that the sequence diagram now shows that when the new regular blog account information is submitted, the user interface will not lock and wait for the new account to be created. Instead, the user interface allows the `Administrator` actor to continue working with the system.

For the `Administrator` to receive feedback as to whether the new blog account has been created, the simple return arrow has to be replaced with a new `accountCreationNotification( )` asynchronous message since asynchronous messages do not have return values.

# Managing Complex Interactions with Sequence Fragments

Most of what you've seen in this chapter will have been pretty familiar to anyone who has used sequence diagrams in UML 1.x. But now it's time for something completely different.

In the bad old days of pre-UML 2.0, sequence diagrams quickly became huge and messy, and contained far too much detail to be easily understood or maintained. There were no built-in, standard ways to show loops and alternative flows, so you had to "grow your own" solutions. This tended to contribute to the size and complexity of the sequence diagrams rather than helping to manage it.

Something new was needed to help the modeler work with the detail that a sequence diagram needed to capture, allowing her to create organized and structured sequence diagrams that showed complex interactions such as loops and alternate flows. The answer from the UML 2.0 designers was the *sequence fragment*.

A sequence fragment is represented as a box that encloses a portion of the interactions within a sequence diagram, as shown in Figure 7-19.

A sequence fragment's box overlaps the region of the sequence diagram where the fragment's interactions take place. A fragment box can contain any number of interactions and, for large complex interactions, further nested fragments as well. The top left corner of the fragment box contains an operator. The *fragment operator* indicates which type of fragment this is.

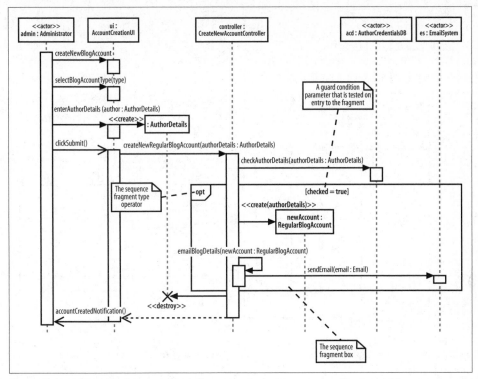

*Figure 7-19. A sequence fragment located as part of a larger sequence diagram, with notes to indicate the fragment box, any parameters, and its operator*

In Figure 7-19, the operator is opt, which means that this is an optional fragment. All the interactions contained within the fragment box will be executed according to the result of the fragments guard condition parameter.

Some fragment types do not need additional parameters as part of their specification, such as the ref fragment type discussed in the next section, but the guard condition parameter is needed by the opt fragment type to make a decision as to whether it should execute its interactions or not. In the case of the opt fragment type, the interactions that the fragment contains will be executed only if the associated guard condition logic evaluates to true.

## Using a Sequence Fragment: The ref Fragment

The ref type of sequence fragment finally alleviates some of the maintenance nightmare presented by the huge sequence diagrams that are often created for complex systems. In Figure 7-20, the ref fragment represents a piece of a larger sequence diagram.

The interactions by which the Administrator actor selects a blog account type for creation are now contained within the referenced sequence fragment. Figure 7-21 shows how the referenced fragment can be expressed on a separate sequence diagram.

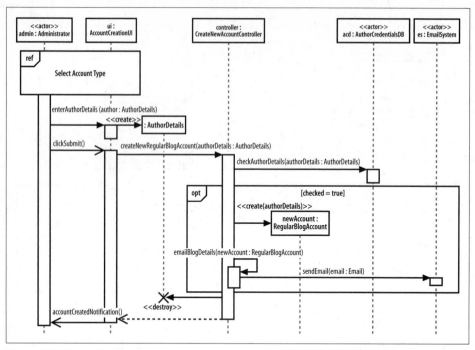

*Figure 7-20. Capturing the interactions used to select an account type within a ref sequence fragment*

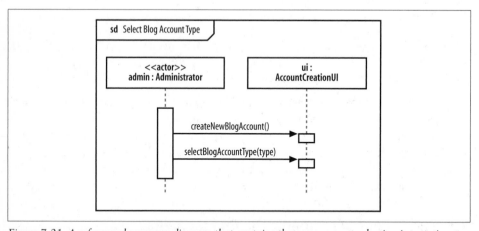

*Figure 7-21. A referenced sequence diagram that contains the new account selection interactions*

Along with managing the sheer size of large sequence diagrams, the ref fragment also presents an opportunity to reuse a set of common interactions. Several ref fragment boxes can reference the same set of interactions, thereby reusing the interactions in multiple places.

The ref fragment type works in a very similar manner to the <<include>> use case relationship. See Chapter 2 for more about the <<include>> use case relationship.

# A Brief Overview of UML 2.0's Fragment Types

UML 2.0 contains a broad set of different fragment types that you can apply to your sequence diagrams to make them more expressive, as shown in Table 7-4.

*Table 7-4. The fragment family and explanations why each type might be useful when creating sequence diagrams*

| Type | Parameters | Why is it useful? |
|---|---|---|
| ref | None | Represents an interaction that is defined elsewhere in the model. Helps you manage a large diagram by splitting, and potentially reusing, a collection of interactions. Similar to the reuse modeled when the <<include>> use case relationship is applied. |
| assert | None | Specifies that the interactions contained within the fragment box must occur exactly as they are indicated; otherwise the fragment is declared invalid and an exception should be raised. Works in a similar fashion to the assert statement in Java. Useful when specifying that every step in an interaction must occur successfully, i.e., when modeling a transaction. |
| loop | min times, max times, [guard_condition] | Loops through the interactions contained within the fragment a specified number of times until the guard condition is evaluated to false. Very similar to the Java and C# for(..) loop. Useful when you are trying execute a set of interactions a specific number of times. |
| break | None | If the interactions contained within the break fragment occur, then any enclosing interaction, most commonly a loop fragment, should be exited. Similar to the break statement in Java and C#. |
| alt | [guard_condition1] ... [guard_condition2] ... [else] | Depending on which guard condition evaluates to true first, the corresponding sub-collection of interactions will be executed. Helps you specify that a set of interactions will be executed only under certain conditions. Similar to an if(..) else statement in code. |
| opt | [guard_condition] | The interactions contained within this fragment will execute only if the guard condition evaluates to true. Similar to a simple if(..) statement in code with no corresponding else. Especially useful when showing steps that have been reused from another use case's sequence diagrams, where <<extend>> is the use case relationship. |
| neg | None | Declares that the interactions inside this fragment are not to be executed, ever. Helpful if you are just trying to mark a collection of interactions as not executed until you're sure that those interactions can be removed. Most useful if you happen to be lucky enough to be using an Executable UML tool where your sequence diagrams are actually being run. Also can be helpful to show that something cannot be done, e.g., when you want to show that a participant cannot call read( ) on a socket after close( ). Works in a similar fashion to commenting out some method calls in code. |

*Table 7-4. The fragment family and explanations why each type might be useful when creating sequence diagrams (continued)*

| Type | Parameters | Why is it useful? |
|---|---|---|
| par | None | Specifies that interactions within this fragment can happily execute in parallel. This is similar to saying that there is no need for any thread-safe locking required within a set of interactions. |
| region | None | Interactions within this type of fragment are said to be part of a critical region. A critical region is typically an area where a shared participant is updated. Combined with parallel interactions, specified using the par fragment type, you can model where interactions are not required to be thread- or process-safe (par fragment) and where locks are required to prevent parallel interactions interleaving (region fragment). Has similarities synchronized blocks and object locks in Java. |

Sequence fragments make it easier to create and maintain accurate sequence diagrams. However, it's worth remembering that no fragment is an island; you can mix and match any number of fragments to accurately model the interactions on a sequence diagram. Be wary if your diagrams become huge and unwieldy even when you are using fragments, since you might simply be trying to model too much in one sequence.

We've given you a brief overview of sequence diagram fragments here. All the different sequence diagram fragment types are a big subject in their own right and are a little beyond the scope of this book. For a more in-depth look at the different types of sequence diagram fragments, see *UML 2.0 in a Nutshell* (O'Reilly).

# What's Next?

Sequence diagrams are closely related to communication diagrams. So closely, in fact, that many modelers often don't know when to use sequence versus communication diagrams. Chapter 8 describes communication diagrams and concludes with a comparison between the two, providing some tips about when to use which diagram type.

Sequence and communication diagrams are both interaction diagrams; timing diagrams are yet another type of interaction diagram. Timing diagrams specialize at showing time constraints involved with interactions, which is especially useful for real-time systems. Timing diagrams are covered in Chapter 9.

If your sequence diagram is getting cluttered with too many messages, step back and look at interaction diagrams on a higher level with interaction overview diagrams. Interaction overview diagrams model the big picture perspective on interactions that occur within your system. Interaction overview diagrams are described in Chapter 10.

# CHAPTER 8

# Focusing on Interaction Links: Communication Diagrams

The main purpose of sequence diagrams is to show the order of events between the parts of your system that are involved in a particular interaction. Communication diagrams add another perspective to an interaction by focusing on the links *between* the participants.

*Communication diagrams* are especially good at showing which links are needed between participants to pass an interaction's messages. With a quick glance at a communication diagram, you can tell which participants need to be connected for an interaction to take place.

On a sequence diagram, the links between participants are *implied* by the fact that a message is passed between them. Communication diagrams provide an intuitive way to show the links between participants that are required for the events that make up an interaction. On a communication diagram, the order of the events involved in an interaction is almost a secondary piece of information.

Sequence and communication diagrams are so similar that most UML tools can automatically convert from one diagram type to the other. The difference between the two approaches is largely personal preference. If you're happier looking at interactions from a link perspective, then communication diagrams are likely to be for you; however, if you prefer to see the order of the interactions as clearly as possible, then you're likely to be in the sequence diagram camp.

## Participants, Links, and Messages

A communication diagram is made up of three things: participants, the communication links between those participants, and the messages that can be passed along those communication links, as shown in Figure 8-1.

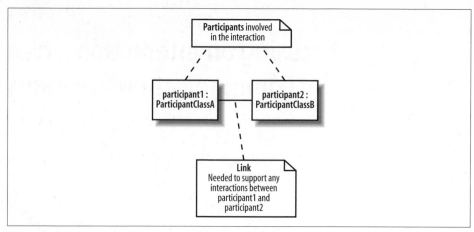

*Figure 8-1. Much simpler than sequence diagrams, communication diagrams are made up of participants and links*

*Participants* on a communication diagram are represented by a rectangle. The participant's name and class are then placed in the middle of the rectangle. A participant's name is formatted as *<name>* : *<class>*, similar to participants on a sequence diagram.

You need to specify either the participant's name or class (or both). If, for some reason, you do not have both the name and class information—sometimes a participant is anonymous and does not have a name—then either the class or the name can be left out.

A *communication link* is shown with a single line that connects two participants. A link's purpose is to allow messages to be passed between the different participants; without a link, the two participants cannot interact with each other. A communication link is shown in Figure 8-2.

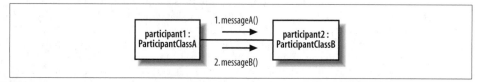

*Figure 8-2. Two messages are passed along the link between participant1 and participant2*

A message on a communication diagram is shown using a filled arrow from the message sender to the message receiver. Similar to messages on a sequence diagram, a message's signature is made up of the message name and a list of parameters. However, unlike sequence diagrams, the message signature alone is not enough for a communication diagram—you also need to show the order in which the messages are invoked during the interaction.

Communication diagrams do not necessarily flow down the page like sequence diagrams; therefore, message order on a communication diagram is shown using a number before each message. Each message number indicates the order in which that message is invoked, starting at 1 and increasing until all of the messages on the diagram are accounted for. Following this rule, in Figure 8-2, `1. messageA( )` is invoked first and then `2. messageB( )`.

Things get more complicated when a message sent to a participant directly causes that participant to invoke another message. When a message causes another message to be invoked, the second message is said to be *nested* inside the original message, as shown on Figure 8-3.

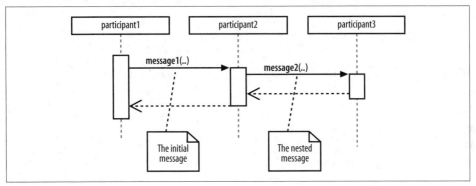

*Figure 8-3. Nested messages on sequence diagrams are easy to see; when the initial message, message1(..),is invoked on participant2, participant2 then invokes the nestedmessage2(..) on participant3*

Communication diagrams use their message numbering scheme to show the order of nested messages. If we say that the initial message is numbered `1.`, then any messages nested within the initial message begin with `1.`, adding a number after the decimal point for the ordering of the nested messages. If an initial message's number was `1.`, then the first nested message's number would be `1.1`. An example of this nested message ordering is shown in Figure 8-4.

## Messages Occurring at the Same Time

Communication diagrams have a simple answer to the problem of messages being invoked at the same time. Although sequence diagrams need complicated constructs, such as par fragments, communication diagrams take advantage of their number-based message ordering by adding a *number-and-letter* notation to indicate that a message happens at the same time as another message, shown in Figure 8-5.

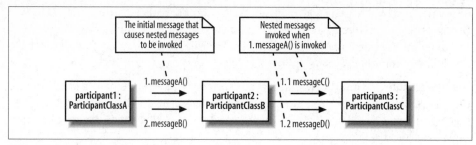

*Figure 8-4. messageA() directly leads to nested 1.1 messageC(), followed by nested messageD(), before message 2 is invoked*

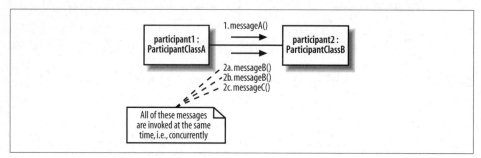

*Figure 8-5. Messages 2a. messageB(), 2b. messageB(), and 2c. messageC() are all invoked at the same time after 1. messageA() has been invoked*

## Invoking a Message Multiple Times

When describing the messages on a communication diagram, you likely will want to show that a message is invoked a number of times. This is similar to showing that your messages will be invoked in a for(..) loop if you are mapping your communication diagram's participants to software.

Although UML does not actually dictate how a communication diagram can show that a message is invoked a number of times, it does state that an asterisk should be used before a looping constraint is applied. This rather complicated statement means that the following example is a safe way to specify that something is going to happen 10 times:

```
*[i = 0 .. 9]
```

In the above looping constraint, i represents a counter that will count up from 0 to 9, doing whatever task is associated with it 10 times. Figure 8-6 shows how this looping constraint can be applied to a message on a communication diagram.

## Sending a Message Based on a Condition

Sometimes a message should be invoked only if a particular condition is evaluated to be true. For example, your system might have a message that should be invoked

---

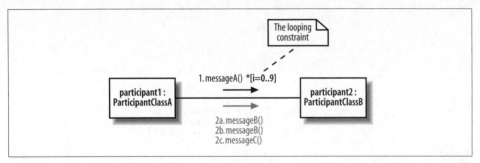

*Figure 8-6. The addition of a new looping constraint to 1. messageA( ) means that the message will be invoked 10 times before the next set of messages—2a, 2b, and 2c—can be invoked*

only if the previous message has executed correctly. Just as with sequence diagram fragments, communication diagram messages can have guards set to describe the conditions that need to be evaluated before a message is invoked.

A *guard condition* is made up of a logical Boolean statement. If the guard condition evaluates to true, the associated message will be invoked—otherwise, the message is skipped.

Figure 8-7 shows how a guard condition can be applied to one of three concurrently executing messages.

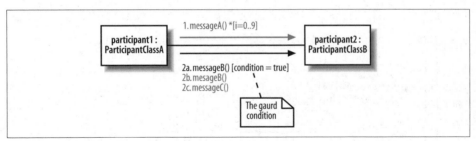

*Figure 8-7. 2a. messageB( ) will be invoked only at the same time as 2b. messageB( ) and messageC( ) if the expression condition == true is evaluated as true; if condition == true returns false, then 2a. messageB( ) is not invoked, but message 2b. messageB( ) and 2c. messageC( ) are*

## When a Participant Sends a Message to Itself

A participant talking to itself may sound strange at first, but if you think in terms of a software object making a call to one of its own methods, you might start to see why this form of communication is needed (and even common). Just as on sequence diagrams, a participant on a communication diagram can send a message to itself. All that is needed is a link from the participant to itself to enable the message to be invoked, as shown in Figure 8-8.

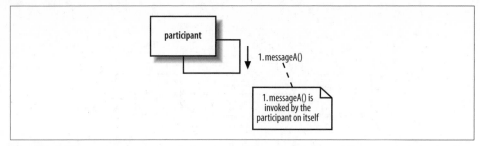

*Figure 8-8. The participant can invoke 1. messageA( ) on itself because it has a communication line to itself*

# Fleshing out an Interaction with a Communication Diagram

With the new communication diagram notation out of the way, it's now time to look at a practical example. We're going to take one of the sequence diagrams from Chapter 7 and show how its interactions can also be modeled on a communication diagram (see Figure 8-9).

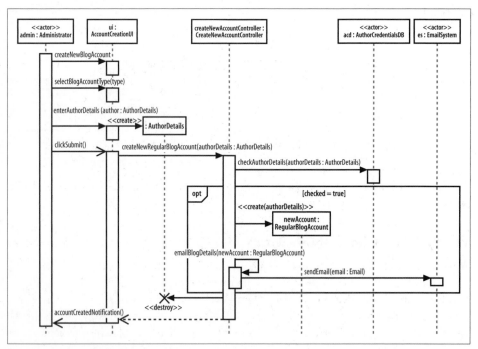

*Figure 8-9. This sequence diagram describes the interactions that take place in a CMS when a new regular blog account is created*

Don't be afraid to refer back to Chapter 7 to help you out with the notation shown on the sequence diagram. Sequence diagrams contain a lot of unique notation, and mastering it all can take some time! It isn't necessary to have a sequence diagram before you create a communication diagram. You can create communication diagrams or sequence diagrams for your interactions in whatever order you see fit.

The first step is to add the participants from Figure 8-9 to the communication diagram shown in Figure 8-10.

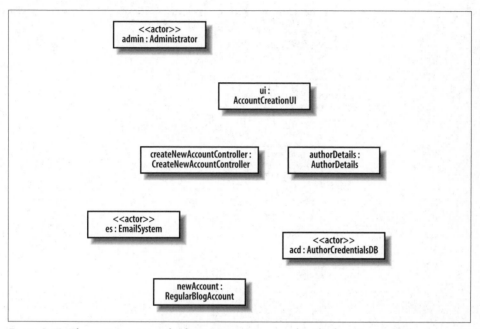

*Figure 8-10. The participants involved in an interaction are often the first pieces added to a communication diagram*

Next, the links between each of the participants are added so they can communicate with each other, as shown in Figure 8-11.

It's now time to add the messages that are sent between participants during the lifetime of the interaction, as shown on Figure 8-12. When adding messages to a communication diagram, it's usually best to start with the participant or event that kicks off the interaction.

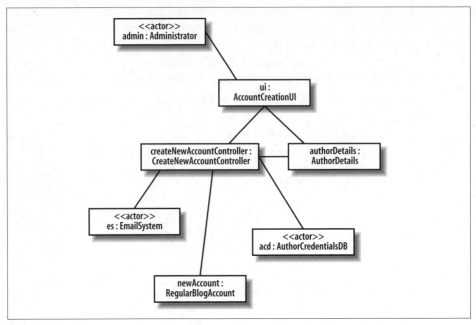

*Figure 8-11. By looking at the sequence diagram in Figure 8-9, the links required to support the message passing can be added to the communication diagram*

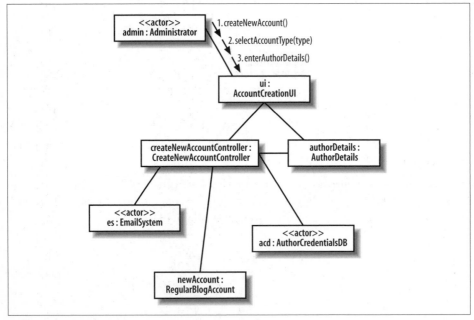

*Figure 8-12. The Administrator actor starts things off by passing three separate messages to the ui: AccountCreationUserInterface participant*

Once the initial message or messages are added to the communication diagram, things start to get more complicated. The 3. enterAuthorDetails( ) message triggers a nested creation message that is sent from the ui : AccountCreationUserInterface participant to create a new authorDetails : CustomerDetails participant. Nested messages get an additional decimal point based on the triggering message's number, as shown in Figure 8-13.

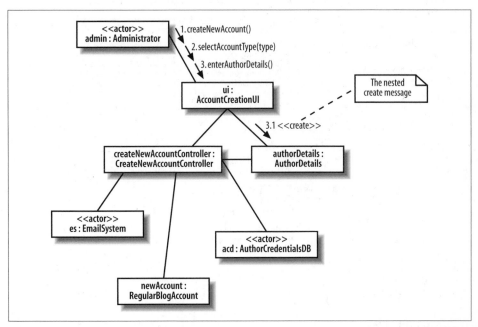

*Figure 8-13. When the <<create>> message is added to the communication diagram, its message order number is set to 3.1. to show that it is nested inside the 3. enterAuthorDetails( ) message*

With that small hurdle out of the way, the rest of the messages can be added to the communication diagram (see Figure 8-14).

# Communication Diagrams Versus Sequence Diagrams

Communication and sequence diagrams present such similar information that a comparison is almost inevitable. Setting personal preferences aside, what are the best reasons for picking a sequence diagram, a communication diagram, or even a combination of both to model a particular interaction?

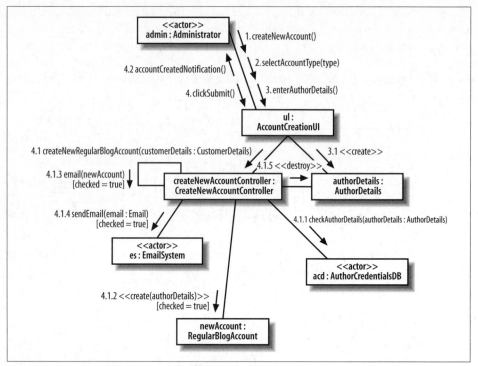

*Figure 8-14. The finished communication diagram shows the complete set of messages within the Create a new Regular Blog Account interaction according to those shown on the original sequence diagram shown in Figure 8-9*

## How the Fight Shapes Up

Figure 8-15 shows the two different representations of the same Create a new Regular Blog Account interaction.

## The Main Event

Beyond any arguments about personal preference, and using the interaction shown in Figure 8-15 as an example, Table 8-1 compares sequence diagrams and communication diagrams to help you decide which diagram is most useful for your modeling purposes.

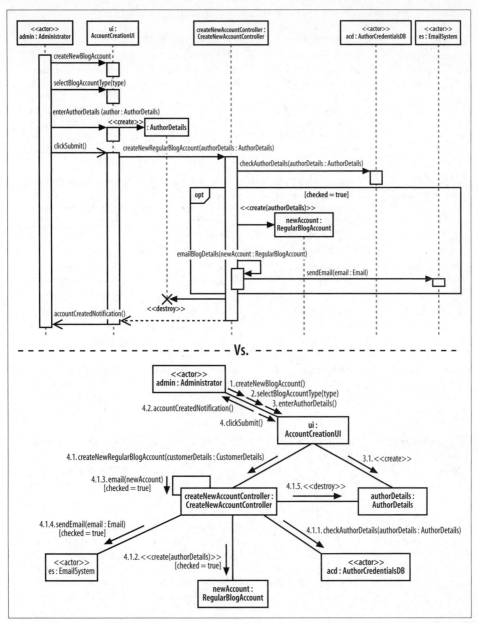

*Figure 8-15. The Create a new Regular Blog Account interaction can be modeled using a sequence diagram and a communication diagram*

*Table 8-1. Comparing sequence and communication diagrams*

| Feature | Sequence diagrams | Communication diagrams | The result |
|---|---|---|---|
| Shows participants effectively | Participants are mostly arranged along the top of page, unless the drop-box participant creation notation is used. It is easy to gather the participants involved in a particular interaction. | Participants as well as links are the focus, so they are shown clearly as rectangles. | **Communication diagrams** *barely* win. Although both types of diagram can show participants as effectively as each other, it can be argued that communication diagrams have the edge since participants are one of their main focuses. |
| Showing the links between participants | Links are implied. If a message is passed from one participant to another, then it is implied that a link must exist between those participants. | Explicitly shows the links between participants. In fact, this is the primary purpose of these types of diagram. | **Communication diagrams** win because they explicitly and clearly show the links between participants. |
| Showing message signatures | Message signatures can be fully described. | Message signatures can be fully described. | **Draw!** Both types of diagram can show messages as effectively as each other. |
| Supports parallel messages | With the introduction of sequence fragments, sequence diagrams are much better. | Shown using the number-letter notation on message sequences. | **Draw!** Both types of diagram show parallel messages equally well. |
| Supports asynchronous messages (fire and forget) | Achieved using the asynchronous arrow. | Communication diagrams have no concept of the asynchronous message since its focus is not on message ordering. | **Sequence diagrams** are a clear winner here because they explicitly support asynchronous messages. |
| Easy to read message ordering | This is a sequence diagram's forté. Sequence diagrams clearly show message ordering using the vertical placement of messages down the diagram's page. | Shown using the number-point-nested notation. | **Sequence diagrams** are a clear winner here since they really show off message ordering clearly and effectively. |
| Easy to create and maintain the diagram | Creating a sequence diagram is fairly simple. However, maintaining sequence diagrams can be a nightmare unless a helpful UML tool is being used. | Communication diagrams are simple enough to create; however, maintenance, especially if message numbering needs to be changed, still ideally needs the support of a helpful UML tool. | This is a difficult one to judge and is largely based on personal preference. However, **communication diagrams** do have the edge on the ease-of-maintenance stakes. |

OK, so the fight was a little biased and tongue-in-cheek in that the features assessed were already clear discriminators between communication and sequence diagrams. Although the results shown in Table 8-1 are not really surprising, it's worth stating once again that you should:

- Use sequence diagrams if you are mainly interested in the flow of messages throughout a particular interaction.
- Use communication diagrams if you are focusing on the links between the different participants involved in the interaction.

Perhaps the most important message to take away from this comparison is that although both types of diagram convey similar information, communication diagrams and sequence diagrams offer different benefits; therefore, the best approach, time willing, is to use both.

## What's Next?

You've seen sequence and communication diagrams, which are the two most commonly used types of interaction diagrams. Timing diagrams are a more specialized interaction diagram focusing on time constraints on interactions, which is particularly useful for expressing time constraints in real-time systems. Timing diagrams are covered in Chapter 9.

# Focusing on Interaction Timing: Timing Diagrams

*Timing diagrams* are, not surprisingly, all about timing. Whereas sequence diagrams (covered in Chapter 7) focus on message order and communication diagrams (see Chapter 8) show the links between participants, so far there has been no place on these interaction diagrams to model detailed timing information. You may have an interaction that must take no longer than 10 seconds to complete, or a message that should take no more than half the interaction's total time to return. If this type of information is important to an interaction that you are modeling, then timing diagrams are probably for you.

Interaction timing is most commonly associated with real-time or embedded systems, but it certainly is not limited to these domains. In fact, the need to capture accurate timing information about an interaction can be important regardless of the type of system being modeled.

In a timing diagram, each event has timing information associated with it that accurately describes when the event is invoked, how long it takes for another participant to receive the event, and how long the receiving participant is expected to be in a particular state. Although sequence diagrams and communication diagrams are very similar, timing diagrams add completely new information that is not easily expressed on any other form of UML interaction diagram. Not having a timing diagram for an interaction is like saying, "I know what events need to occur, but I'm not really worried about exactly when they happen or how quickly they will be worked on."

## What Do Timing Diagrams Look Like?

Timing diagrams will look strangely familiar to anyone with a little experience of the analysis of electronic circuit boards. This is because a timing diagram looks very similar to a plot that you'd expect to see on a logic analyzer. Don't worry if you've never seen a logic analyzer before, though; Figure 9-1 shows a typical display that you would expect to see on one of these devices.

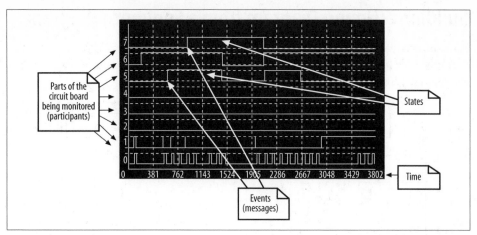

*Figure 9-1. All of the information on a logic analyzer is also shown on a timing diagram in the form of messages, participants, and states*

A *logic analyzer* captures a sequence of events as they occur on an electronic circuit board. A readout from a logic analyzer (such as the one shown in Figure 9-1) will typically show the time at which different parts of the circuit board are in particular states and the electronic signals that will trigger changes in those states.

Timing diagrams perform a similar job for the participants within your system. On a timing diagram, events are the logic analyzer's signals, and the states are the states that a participant is placed in when an event is received. The similarities between a timing diagram and a logic analyzer are apparent when you compare Figure 9-1 with Figure 9-2, which gives a sneak preview of how a complete timing diagram looks. This example was taken from *UML 2.0 in a Nutshell* (O'Reilly).

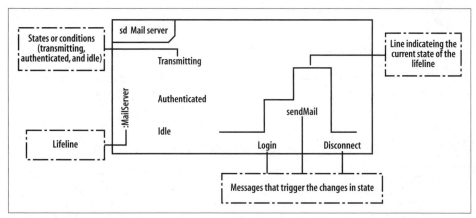

*Figure 9-2. Compare this simple yet complete timing diagram for a mail server with the logic analyzer in Figure 9-1*

# Building a Timing Diagram from a Sequence Diagram

Let's assemble a timing diagram from scratch. We're going to work from the same example used in the communication and sequence diagram chapters, the Create a new Regular Blog Account interaction, shown in Figure 9-3.

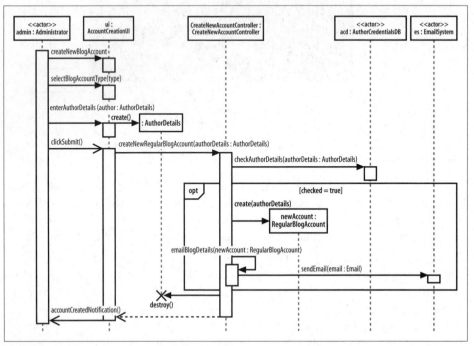

*Figure 9-3. A sequence diagram contains very little, if any, information about timing, and its main focus is the order of events within an interaction*

## Timing Constraints in System Requirements

The interaction shown in Figure 9-3 was originally the result of a requirement such as the one described in Requirement A.2.

---

### Requirement A.2

The content management system shall allow an administrator to create a new regular blog account, provided the personal details of the author are verified using the Author Credentials Database.

---

Now, let's extend the original requirement with some timing considerations so that we've got something to add by modeling the interaction in a timing diagram.

---

### Requirement A.2 (Updated)

The content management system shall allow an administrator to create a new regular blog account *within five seconds of the information being entered*, provided the personal details of the author are verified using the Author Credentials Database.

---

Requirement A.2 has been modified to include a timing constraint that dictates how long it should take for the system to accept, verify, and create a new account. Now that there is more information about the timing of Requirement A.2, there is enough justification to model the interaction that implements the requirement using a timing diagram.

# Applying Participants to a Timing Diagram

First, you need to create a timing diagram that incorporates all of the participants involved in the Create a new Regular Blog Account interaction, as shown in Figure 9-4.

The full participant names have been left out of Figure 9-4 to keep the diagram's size manageable, although you could equally have included the full <name>:<type> format for the title of a participant.

Another feature that is missing from Figure 9-4 is the participants that are created and destroyed within the life of the interaction: the :AuthorDetails and :RegularBlogAccount participants. Details of these participants have been left out because timing diagrams focus on timing in relation to state changes. Apart from being created and/or destroyed, the :AuthorDetails and :RegularBlogAccount participants do not have any complicated state changes; therefore, they are omitted because they would not add anything of interest to this particular diagram.

During system modeling activities, you will need to decide what should and should not be explicitly placed on a diagram. Ask yourself, "Is this detail important to understanding what I am modeling?" and "Does including this detail make anything clearer?" If the answer is yes to either of these questions, then it's best to include the detail in your diagram; otherwise, leave the additional detail out. This might sound like a fairly crude rule, but it can be extremely effective when you are trying to keep a diagram's clutter to a minimum.

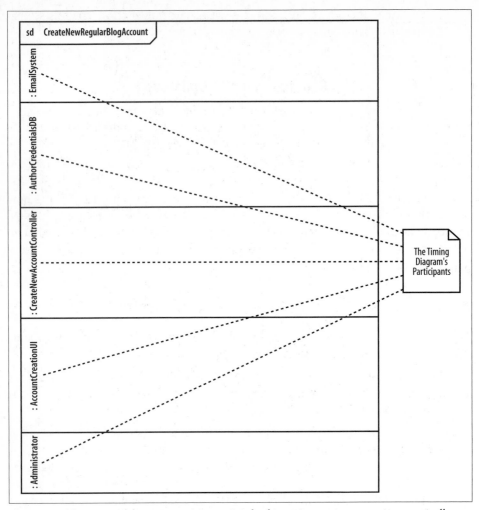

*Figure 9-4. The names of the main participants involved in an interaction are written vertically on the lefthand side of a timing diagram*

## States

During an interaction, a participant can exist in any number of states. A participant is said to be in a particular state when it receives an event (such as a message). The participant can then be said to be in that state until another event occurs (such as the return of that message). See the "Events and Messages" section later in this chapter for an explanation of how events and messages are applied to timing diagrams.

States on a timing diagram are placed next to their corresponding participant, as shown in Figure 9-5.

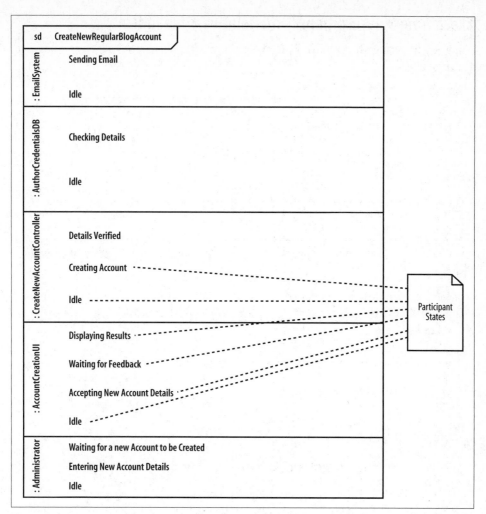

*Figure 9-5. States are written horizontally on a timing diagram and next to the participant that they are associated with*

# Time

For a type of diagram that is actually called a "timing" diagram, it might seem a little strange that we haven't yet mentioned time. So far, we've just been setting the stage, adding participants and the states that they can be put in, but to really model the information that's important to a timing diagram, it's now time to add time (pun intended).

## Exact Time Measurements and Relative Time Indicators

Time on a timing diagram runs from left to right across the page, as shown in Figure 9-6.

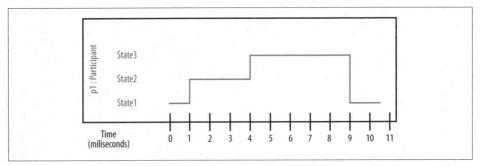

*Figure 9-6. Time measurements are placed on a timing diagram as a ruler along the bottom of the page*

Time measurements can be expressed in a number of different ways; you can have exact time measurements, as shown in Figure 9-6, or relative time indicators, as shown in Figure 9-7.

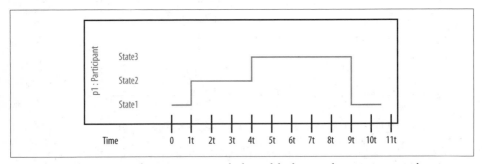

*Figure 9-7. Relative time indicators are particularly useful when you have timing considerations such as "ParticipantA will be in State1 for half of the time that ParticipantB is in State2"*

In a timing diagram, t represents a point in time that is of interest. You don't know exactly when it will happen because it may happen in response to a message or event, but t is a way to refer to that moment without knowing exactly when it is. With t as a reference, you can then specify time constraints relative to that point t.

Adding time to the diagram we've been putting together so far is tricky because we don't have any concrete timing information in the original requirement. See the "Timing Constraints in System Requirements" section earlier in this chapter if you need a quick reminder as to what the extended Requirement A.2 states.

However, we still need to apply the constraints mentioned in Requirement A.2, so some measure of relative time represented by t is shown in Figure 9-8.

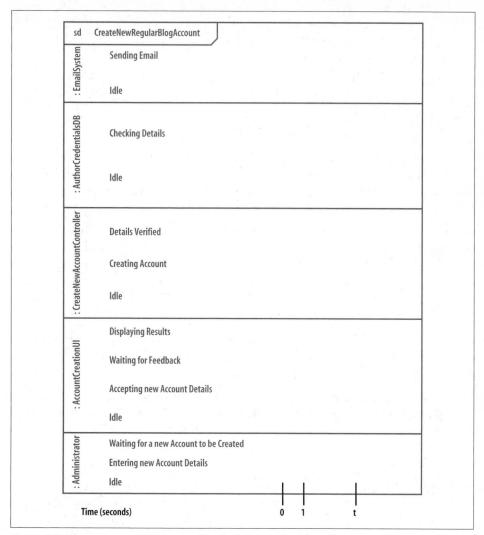

*Figure 9-8. The timing constraints are a blend of exact and relative timings*

In this figure, the initial stages of the interaction are simply measured as seconds, and the single t value represents a single second wherever it is mentioned on any further timing constraints on the diagram. See the "Timing Constraints" section later in this chapter for more on how the value t can be used on a timing diagram.

# A Participant's State-Line

Now that you have added time to the timing diagram (fancy that!), you can show what state a participant is in at any given time. If you take a look back at Figure 9-6 and Figure 9-7, you can already see how participant's current state is indicated: with a horizontal line that is called the *state-line*.

At any given time in the interaction, a participant's state-line is aligned with one of the participant's states (see Figure 9-9).

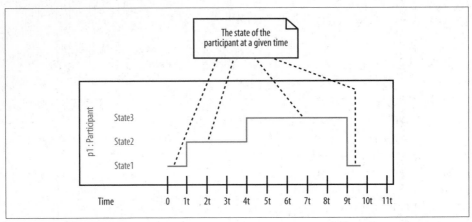

*Figure 9-9. In this example, p1:Participant's state-line indicates that it is in State1 for 1 unit of time, State2 for three units of time, and State3 for roughly five units of time (before returning to State1 at the end of the interaction)*

Figure 9-10 shows how the `Create a new Regular Blog Account` timing diagram is updated to show the state of each participant at a given time during the interaction.

 In practice, you would probably add both events and states to a timing diagram at the same time. We've split the two activities here simply because it makes it easier for you to see how the two pieces of notation are applied (without confusing one with the other).

That's all there is to showing that a participant is in a specific state at a given time. Now it's time to look at why a participant changes states in the first place, which leads us neatly to events and messages.

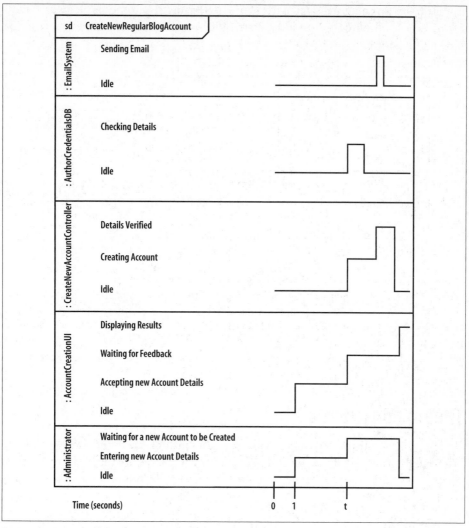

Figure 9-10. Each of the participants needs to have a corresponding state-line to indicate their state at any given point in time

# Events and Messages

Participants change state on a timing diagram in response to events. These events might be the invocation of a message or they might be something else, such as a message returning after it has been invoked. The distinction between messages and events is not as important on a timing diagram as it is on sequence diagrams. The important thing to remember is that whatever the event is, it is shown on a timing diagram to trigger a change in the state of a participant.

An event on a timing diagram is shown as an arrow from one participant's state-line—the event source—to another participant's state-line—the event receiver (as shown in Figure 9-11).

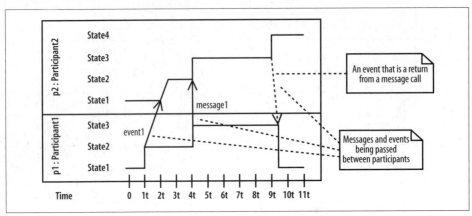

*Figure 9-11. Events on a timing diagram can even have their own durations, as shown by event1 taking 1 unit of time from invocation by p1:Participant1 and reception by p2:Participant2*

Adding events to the timing diagram is actually quite a simple task, because you have the sequence diagram from Figure 9-3 to refer to. The sequence diagram already shows the messages that are passed between participants, so you can simply add those messages to the timing diagram, as shown in Figure 9-12.

## Timing Constraints

Up until this point, you have really only been establishing the foundation of a timing diagram. Participants, states, time, and events and messages are the backdrop against which you can start to model the information that is really important to a timing diagram—timing constraints.

Timing constraints describe in detail how long a given portion of an interaction should take. They are usually applied to the amount of time that a participant should be in a particular state or how long an event should take to be invoked and received, as shown in Figure 9-13. By applying constraints to this timing diagram, the duration of event1 must be less than one value of the relative measure t, and p2: Participant2 should be in State4 for a maximum of five seconds.

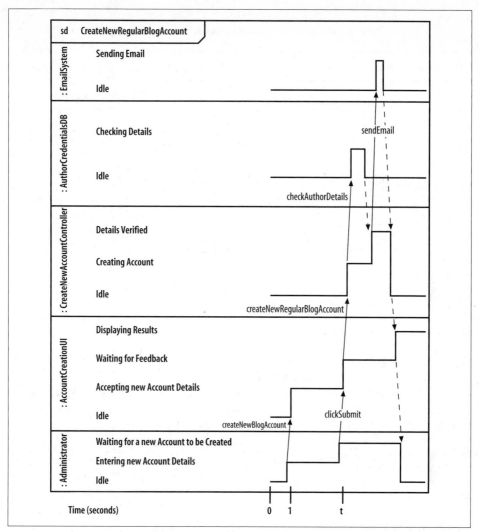

*Figure 9-12. Participant state changes make much more sense when you can see the events that cause them*

## Timing Constraint Formats

A timing constraint can be specified in a number of different ways, depending on the information your are trying to model. Table 9-1 shows some common examples of timing constraints.

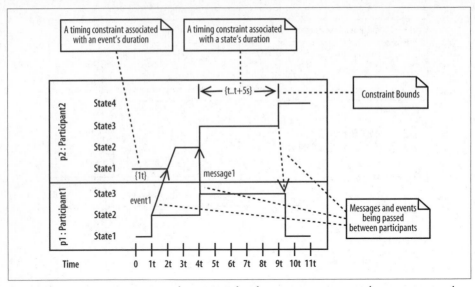

*Figure 9-13. Timing constraints can be associated with an event or a state and may or may not be accompanied by constraint boundary arrows*

*Table 9-1. Different ways of specifying a timing constraint*

| Timing Constraint | Description |
| --- | --- |
| {t..t+5s} | The duration of the event or state should be 5 seconds or less. |
| {<5s} | The duration of the event or state should be less than 5 seconds. This is a slightly less formal than {t..t+5s}, but an equivalent notation. |
| {>5s, <10s} | The duration of the event or state should be greater than 5 seconds, but less than 10 seconds. |
| {t} | The duration of the event or state should be equal to the value of t. This is a relative measure, where t could be any value of time. |
| {t..t*5} | The duration of the event or state should be the value of t multiplied 5 times. This is another relative measure (t could be any value of time). |

## Applying Timing Constraints to States and Events

At the beginning of this chapter, we extended Requirement A.2 to specify some timing considerations. Requirement A.2's timing considerations can now be added to the timing diagram as timing constraints. Figure 9-14 completes the Create a new Regular Blog Account timing diagram, capturing Requirement A.2's timing considerations by applying constraints to the relevant states.

As you can see from Figure 9-14, applying the 5 seconds per new regular blog account creation timing constraint is not a straightforward job since it affects several different nested interactions between participants. This is where the skill of the modeler comes into play on a timing diagram; you need to decide which events or states need to be allocated portions of the available five seconds so each participant can do its job (and get those allocations right).

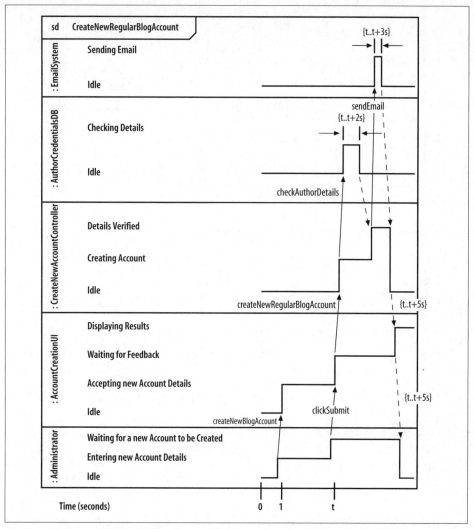

*Figure 9-14. From when the :Administrator clicks on submit until the point at which the system has created a new account, no more than five seconds have passed*

# Organizing Participants on a Timing Diagram

Where you arrange participants on a timing diagram does not at first appear to be very important. However, as you add more details to your diagram in the form of events and timing information, you'll soon discover that the place where a participant is located on the timing diagram can cause problems if you haven't thought about it carefully enough (see Figure 9-15).

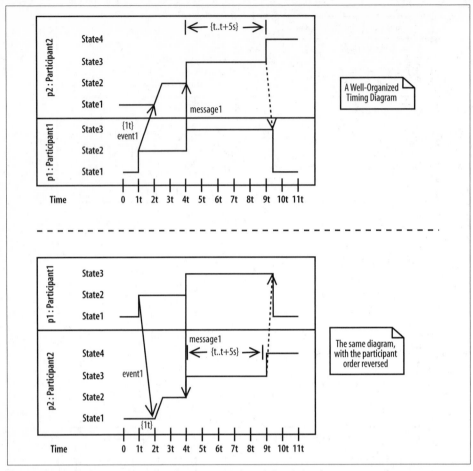

*Figure 9-15. The bottom diagram is harder to read, and details are beginning to obscure one another*

If you're lucky and you already have a sequence diagram for an interaction, then there is an easy rule of thumb to get you started when arranging participants for the first time on a timing diagram. Simply take the order of the participants as they appear across the top of the page on a sequence diagram and flip the list of participant names 90 degrees counterclockwise, as shown in Figure 9-16. If your sequence diagram is well-organized, then you should now have a good candidate order for placing the participants on your timing diagram.

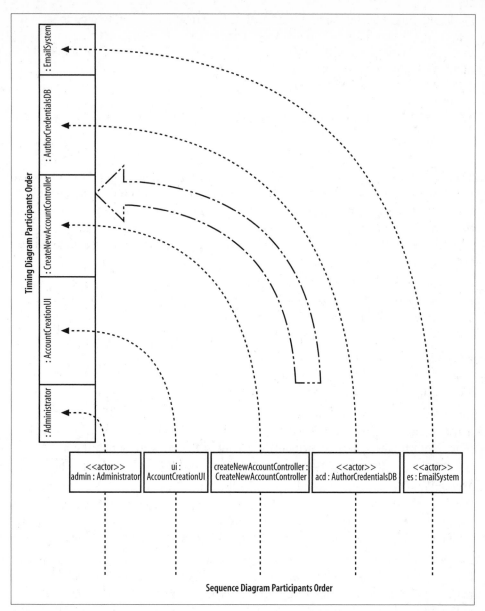

*Figure 9-16. Rotating a sequence diagram's major participants 90 degrees counterclockwise is an easy way to get an initial placement for your timing diagram's participants*

# An Alternate Notation

Real estate on a UML diagram is almost always at a premium. In previous versions of UML, sequence diagrams were known as being the hardest diagram to manage when modeling a complex interaction. Although timing diagrams are not going to steal the sequence diagram's crown in this respect, the regular timing diagram notation shown in this chapter so far doesn't scale particularly well when you need to model a large number of different states.

 Some of the problems with sequence diagrams have been alleviated with the inclusion of sequence fragments in UML 2.0; see Chapter 7.

The Create a new Regular Blog Account interaction's timing diagram, as shown in Figure 9-14, is actually a fairly simple example. However, you might already be beginning to grasp how large a timing diagram can get—at least vertically—for anything more than a trivial interaction that includes a small number of states. A good UML 2.0 tool will help you work with and manage large timing diagrams, but there is only so much a tool can really do.

The developers of UML 2.0 realized this problem and created an alternative, simpler notation for when you have an interaction that contains a large number of states, shown in Figure 9-17.

When you look closely at the alternative timing diagram notation, things are not dramatically different from the regular notation. The notation for participants and time hasn't changed at all. The big change between the regular timing diagram notation and the alternative is in how states and state changes are shown.

The regular timing diagram notation shows states as a list next to the relevant participant. A state-line is then needed to show what state a participant is in at a given time. Unfortunately, if a participant has many different states, then the amount of space needed to model a participant on the timing diagram will grow quickly.

The alternative notation fixes this problem by removing the vertical list of different states. It places a participant's states directly at the point in time when the participant is in that state. Therefore, the state-line is no longer needed, and all of the states for a particular participant can be placed in a single line across the diagram.

To show that a participant changes state because of an event, a cross is placed between the two states and the event that caused the state change is written next to the cross. Timing constraints can then be applied in much the same way as regular notations.

Bringing the subject of timing diagrams to a close, Figure 9-18 shows the alternate timing diagram notation in a practical setting: modeling the Create a new Regular Blog Account interaction.

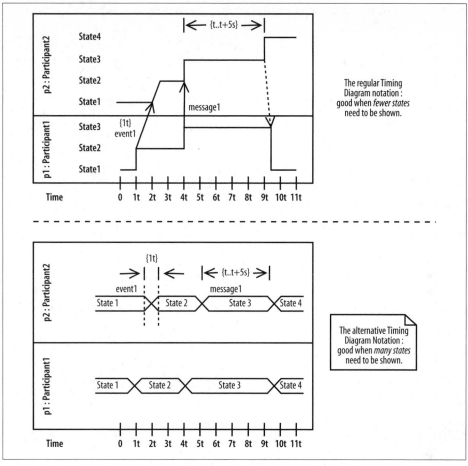

*Figure 9-17. The top diagram's notation should be familiar to you, but the diagram at the bottom uses the new alternative timing diagram notation*

## A Second Notation for Timing Diagrams

So, why have a second notation for timing diagrams? Luckily, there is an easy answer to this question: the regular timing diagram notation simply does not scale well when you have many participants that can be put in many different states during an interaction's lifetime. Just as the answer is quite simple, so is the rule of thumb you can use to help you decide which notation to adopt for a particular interaction. If a participant is placed in many different states during the course of the interaction, then it is worth considering using the alternative notation. Otherwise, use the regular notation since, at this point of writing, it is more widely recognized throughout the modeling community.

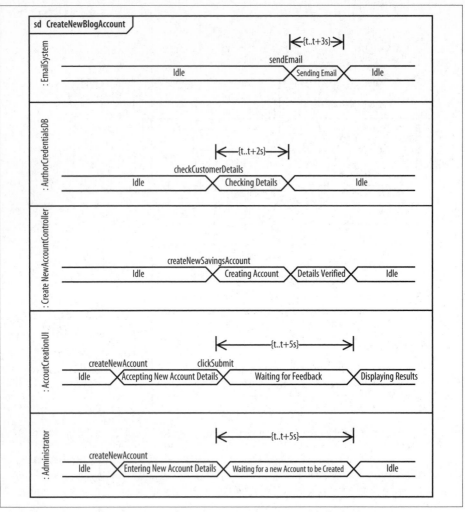

*Figure 9-18. Even though there are not many states in this interaction, you can begin to see how the alternate notation is more compact and manageable in a situation where there are many states per participant*

## What's Next?

The concept of an object's state is integral to timing diagrams since they show states of an object at particular times. State machine diagrams show in detail the states of an object and triggers that cause state changes. Both diagram types are very important to models of real-time and embedded systems. State machine diagrams are covered in Chapter 14.

# CHAPTER 10

# Completing the Interaction Picture: Interaction Overview Diagrams

Ever been asked to "look at the bigger picture"? Whether you are working on a new idea or modeling in UML, sometimes it helps to take a step back from the details to get a better feel for what you are doing and the context within which you are doing it. This is the job of interaction overview diagrams; they exist to give you that big picture perspective on your system's interactions.

*Interaction overview diagrams* provide a high-level view of how several interactions work together to implement a system concern, such as a use case. Sequence, communication, and timing diagrams focus on specific details concerning the messages that make up an interaction, but interaction overview diagrams tie together the different interactions into a single complete picture of the interactions that make up a particular system concern.

An interaction overview looks very much like an activity diagram (see Chapter 3) except that each of the actions are interactions within their own right. Think of each part of an interaction overview as a complete interaction in itself. If one interaction within the overview is most concerned with timing, then a timing diagram could be employed (see Chapter 9), while another interaction of the overview may need to focus on message ordering, and so a sequence diagram could be used (see Chapter 7). The interaction overview glues together separate interactions within your system in the notation that makes most sense to the particular interaction to show how they work together to implement a system concern.

## The Parts of an Interaction Overview Diagram

The best way to understand a interaction overview diagram notation is to think of it as an activity diagram, except instead of an action, a complete interaction is described by using its own diagram, as shown in Figure 10-1.

Any number of participants may be involved in the interactions that occur within the overview. To see which participants are involved across the entire overview, a *lifelines* subtitle is added to the diagram title, as shown in Figure 10-2.

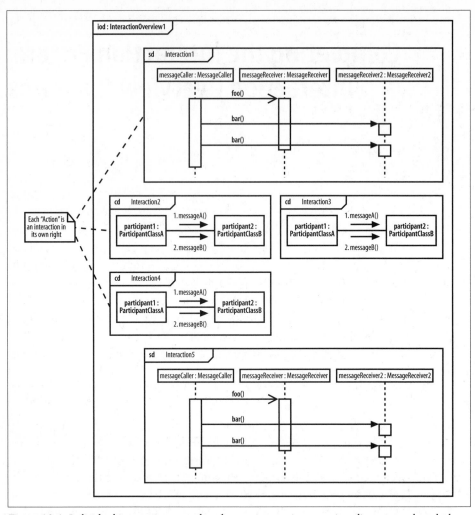

*Figure 10-1. Individual interactions are placed on an interaction overview diagram as though they were actions on an activity diagram*

*Figure 10-2. The lifelines subtitle shows the combined list of participants involved in the interactions within the overview*

Similar to an activity diagram, the interaction overview begins with an initial node and ends with a final node. Control flows between these two nodes and passes through each of the interactions in between. However, you are limited not to just a simple sequential flow between the interactions.

Just as control flow on an activity diagram can be subjected to decisions, parallel actions, and even loops, so can the control flow on an interaction diagram, as shown in Figure 10-3.

# Modeling a Use Case Using an Interaction Overview

That's all the new notation for interaction diagrams; now it's time to look at a practical example. To set the stage, we are going to develop an interaction overview diagram from scratch for the Create a New Regular Blog use case reusing parts from the interaction diagrams created in the previous chapters.

The big difference between the example in this chapter and the modeling in previous chapters is that with an interaction overview, we can pick and choose from the different interaction diagram types. By using an interaction overview approach, each part of the interaction is modeled using the techniques that are most effective for that part.

## Pulling Together the Interactions

First, we need to decide how the interaction overview will be broken down into the most effective diagrams for each of the individual interactions, as shown in Figure 10-4.

When modeling the Select Blog Account Type, Create Regular Blog Account, and Tidy Up Author Details interactions, message order is more important than any other factor. The relevant steps can be reused from the sequence diagrams modeled in Chapter 7, as shown in Figure 10-5.

For variety's sake, the Enter Author Details will be displayed as a communication diagram, as shown in Figure 10-6.

You could decide to represent the Enter Author Details interaction as a communication diagram simply because it is easier to understand, but there is so much similarity between sequence and communication diagrams that mixing the two on one interaction overview is not often seen; modelers tend to prefer one type of diagram or the other.

The Check Author Details interaction must enforce the timing constraint that its messages will all be executed within five seconds (see Chapter 9). The focus is on timing for this part of the overview and thanks to the fact that an interaction overview can contain any of the different types of interaction diagram, a timing diagram can be employed for the Check Author Details interaction, as shown in Figure 10-7.

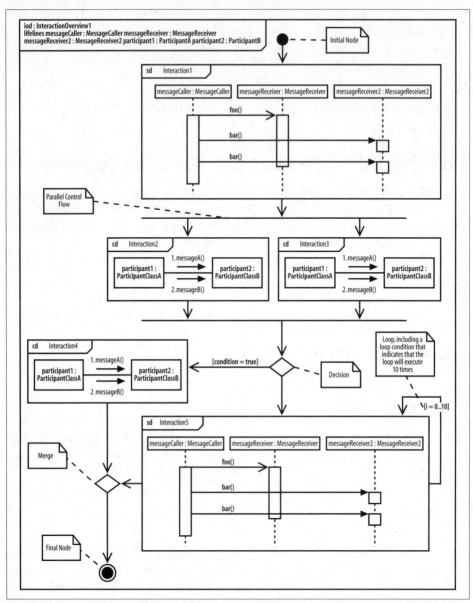

*Figure 10-3. Starting with the initial node, the control flow executes Interaction1, followed by Interactions 2 and 3 in parallel; Interaction4 will execute only if the condition is assessed as being true; otherwise, Interaction5 is executed 10 times in a loop before the control flow merges and the final node is reached*

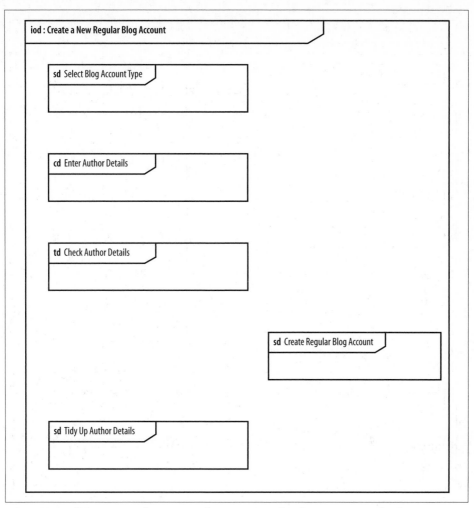

iod : Create a New Regular Blog Account

sd  Select Blog Account Type

cd  Enter Author Details

td  Check Author Details

sd  Create Regular Blog Account

sd  Tidy Up Author Details

*Figure 10-4. All three types of interaction diagram are used in this overview— sd indicates a sequence diagram, cd is for a communication diagram, and, not surprisingly, td stands for a timing diagram*

An interaction overview diagram can offer an ideal place to use the alternative timing diagram notation, as shown in Figure 10-7. Since interaction overviews can get pretty big, the alternative notation often works best since it makes good use of the space available.

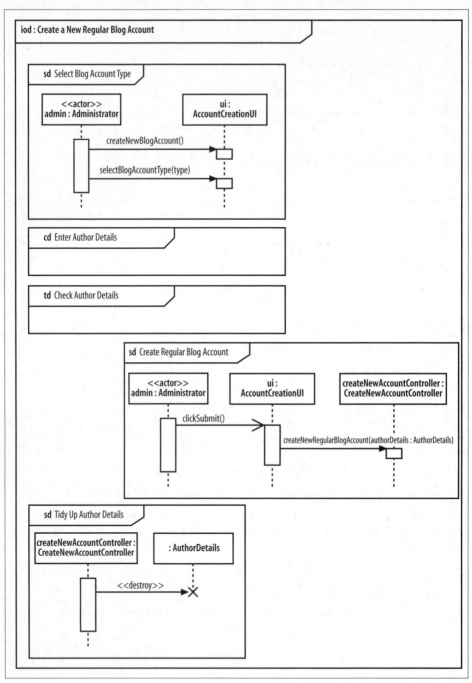

*Figure 10-5. Some interactions to are best modeled using sequence diagrams to focus on message ordering*

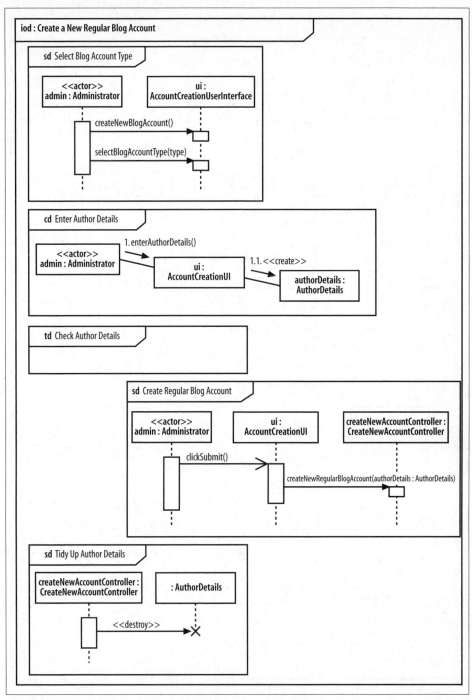

*Figure 10-6. Enter Author Details in a communication diagram*

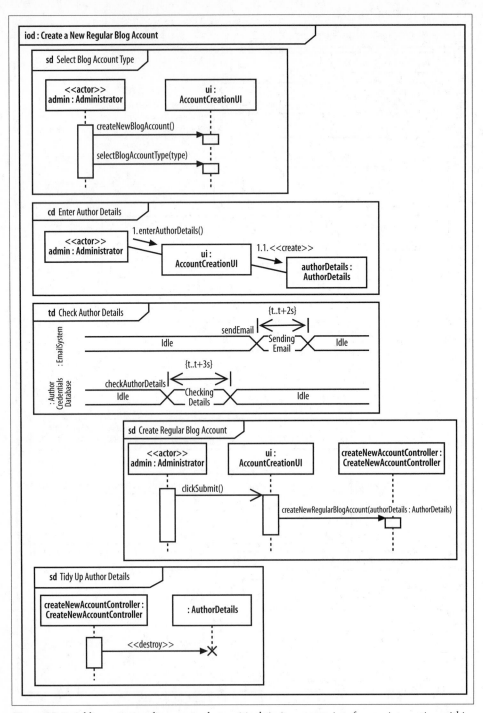

*Figure 10-7. Adding a timing diagram to show critical timing constraints for one interaction within the overview*

Now that all the interactions have been added to the interaction overview, all of the participants involved are known so we can add their names to the diagram's title, as shown in Figure 10-8.

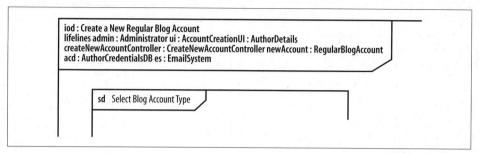

*Figure 10-8. Adding each of the participants involved in an interaction to the lifeline list in the interaction overview's title bar*

## Gluing the Interactions Together

The final piece of the puzzle in the Create a New Regular Blog Account interaction overview is the actual flow of control between each of the separate interaction diagrams, as shown in Figure 10-9.

The control flow in Figure 10-9 shows that each of the separate interactions are executed in order. The one deviation from the normal path occurs at the Create Regular Blog Account interaction, shown as a sequence diagram, which is executed only if the author details checked out during the Check Author Details interaction.

# What's Next?

Interaction overview diagrams glue together combinations of sequence diagrams, communication diagrams, and timing diagrams, showing the higher-level picture. At this point, you're done considering interaction diagrams, but you may want to back up and review any of the interaction diagram chapters if you weren't clear when to use which diagram type. Sequence diagrams were covered in Chapter 7; communication diagrams were described in Chapter 8; timing diagrams were covered in Chapter 9.

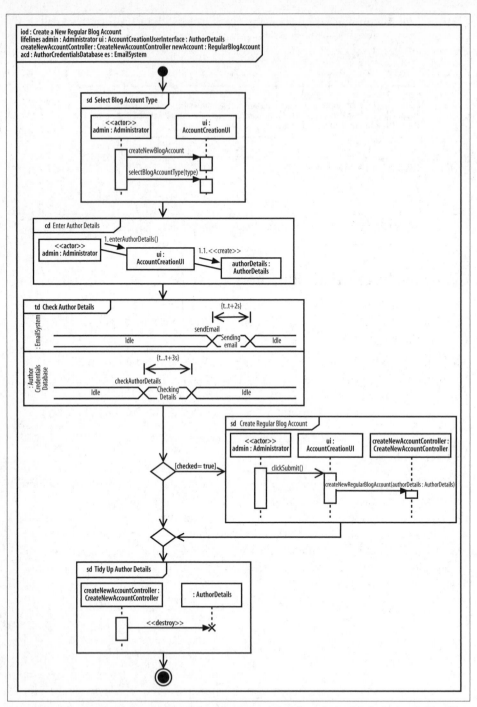

*Figure 10-9. Starting with an initial node and finishing with a final node, the flow of control is the thread that ties each of the interactions together*

# CHAPTER 11

# Modeling a Class's Internal Structure: Composite Structures

Sometimes the primary UML diagrams, such as class and sequence diagrams, aren't a perfect match for capturing certain details about your system. Composite structures help fill some of those gaps. Composite structures show how objects create a big picture. They model how objects work together inside a class, or how objects achieve a goal. Composite structures are fairly advanced, but they're good to have in your bag of tricks because they are perfectly suited for specific modeling situations, such as showing:

*Internal structures*
> Show the parts contained by a class and the relationships between the parts; this allows you to show context-sensitive relationships, or relationships that hold in the context of a containing class

*Ports*
> Show how a class is used on your system with ports

*Collaborations*
> Show design patterns in your software and, more generally, objects cooperating to achieve a goal

Composite structures provide a view of your system's parts and form part of the logical view of your system's model, as shown in Figure 11-1.

## Internal Structure

Chapter 5 introduced possession-related relationships between classes, including association ("has a") and composition ("contains a"). Composite structures offer an alternate way of showing these relationships; when you show the internal structure of a class, you draw the items it possesses directly inside the class. Relationships between items in a class's internal structure hold only in the context of the class, so you can think of them as context-sensitive relationships. To see why internal structures are useful, let's look at a relationship that a class diagram can't model.

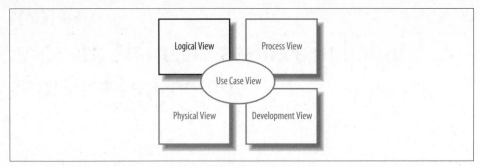

*Figure 11-1. The logical view captures the abstract descriptions of a system's parts, including composite structures*

## When Class Diagrams Won't Work

Figure 11-2 repeats a class diagram from Chapter 5, showing that `BlogEntry` contains objects of type `Introduction` and `MainBody` through composition.

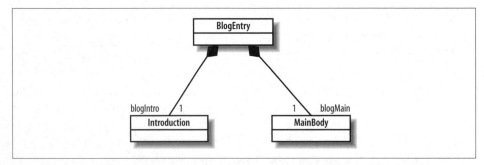

*Figure 11-2. Class diagram showing that BlogEntry contains Introduction and MainBody*

Suppose you want to update your diagrams to reflect that a blog entry's introduction has a reference to its main body because it's convenient for other objects to ask an `Introduction` object for the `MainBody` object it introduces. As a first pass, you modify the class diagram in Figure 11-2 by drawing an association between the `Introduction` and the `MainBody` classes, as shown in Figure 11-3.

But there's a problem. Figure 11-3 specifies that an object of type `Introduction` will have a reference to an object of type `MainBody`, but it can be any `MainBody` object—not just the one owned by the same instance of `BlogEntry`. That's because the association between `Introduction` and `MainBody` is defined for all instances of those types. Informally, `Introduction` doesn't concern itself with the composition relationship between `BlogEntry` and `MainBody`; as far as an `Introduction` object is concerned, all it has to do is associate with some `MainBody` object (but it doesn't care which one).

Because Figure 11-3 doesn't specify which `Introduction` and `MainBody` objects should be associated, the object diagram in Figure 11-4 conforms to the class diagram in Figure 11-3.

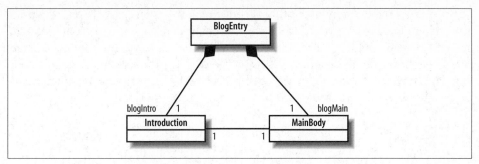

Figure 11-3. This first pass at showing that a blog entry's introduction introduces its main body doesn't quite work

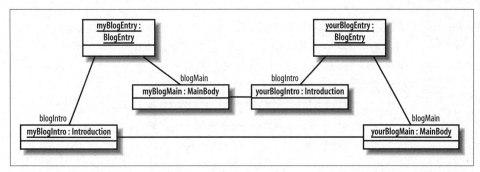

Figure 11-4. Unintended but valid object structure

According to the class diagram in Figure 11-3, it's perfectly legal for an introduction in one blog entry to introduce the main body of another. But what you meant to say is that the introduction introduces the main body that is contained by the same class that contains the introduction, as shown in Figure 11-5.

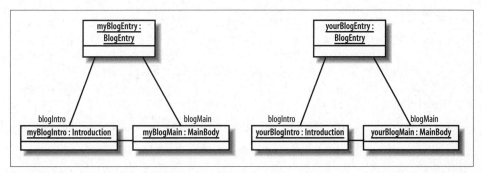

Figure 11-5. This was the intended object structure

It turns out that class diagrams are not good at expressing how items contained in a class relate to each other. This is where internal structure comes in: it allows you to specify relationships in the context of the class that contains them.

Right now, you may be thinking that this distinction is a bit fussy. If you're writing the code to implement these classes, you can make sure that the correct objects are linked up. You could also use a UML sequence diagram to show the objects' creation and how they get connected. But keep reading—the internal structure notation is a convenient and simple way to show relationships between contained items, especially when the contained items have complex relationships.

 This is just one example of how composite structures can model relationships that are hard to show in class diagrams. For a more thorough discussion, see *http://www.jot.fm/issues/issue_2004_11/column5*.

## Parts of a Class

Figure 11-6 shows the internal structure of `BlogEntry`. Its contained items are now drawn directly inside, instead of connected through filled diamond arrowheads.

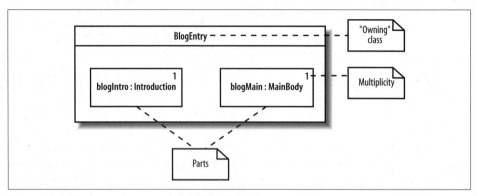

*Figure 11-6. The internal structure of the BlogEntry class*

When showing the internal structure of a class, you draw its *parts*, or items contained by composition, inside the containing class. Parts are specified by the role they play in the containing class, written as `<roleName> : <type>`. In Figure 11-6, the part of type `Introduction` has the role `blogIntro` and the part of type `MainBody` has the role `blogMain`. The *multiplicity*, or number of instances of that part, is written in the upper righthand corner of the part.

Figure 11-7 shows the internal structure diagram side by side with the class diagram from Figure 11-2, allowing you to see how the class names, roles, and multiplicities correspond.

"Part"—as in the parts contained by `BlogEntry`—sounds straightforward, but it's a subtle concept. A part is a *set of instances* that may exist in an instance of the containing class at runtime. If that's confusing, it may help to consider the example shown in Figure 11-8, in which the part with role `pic` has multiplicity of zero to three in the internal structure of `BlogEntry`.

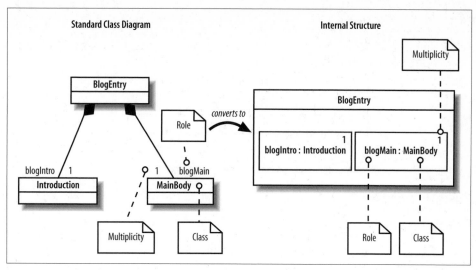

*Figure 11-7. How the internal structure of BlogEntry matches up to the class diagram*

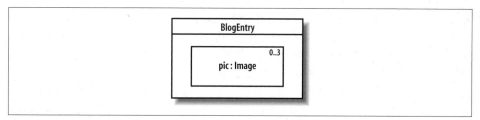

*Figure 11-8. In the internal structure of BlogEntry, the part with role pic has a multiplicity of zero to three*

In this case, if you run across an instance of BlogEntry at runtime, it will have anywhere from zero to three instances of type Image. It may contain one Image object, it may contain three Image objects, and so on, but with parts, you don't have to worry about such details. A part is a general way to describe these contained objects by the role they play, without specifying exactly which objects are present.

Because parts represent the objects that are owned by a single instance of the containing class, you can specify relationships between those specific parts and not arbitrary instances of the class types. This means you can specify that an introduction introduces the main body in the same blog entry it belongs to—in other words, the introduction doesn't introduce an arbitrary main body—and you do this with connectors.

## Connectors

You show relationships between parts by drawing a *connector* between the parts with the multiplicities specified at each end of the connector, as shown in Figure 11-9.

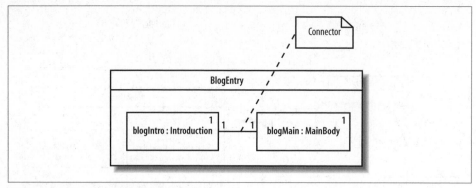

*Figure 11-9. Using connectors to link parts in the internal structure of a class*

 The notation for multiplicities on connectors is the same as multiplicities on associations, discussed in Chapter 4.

A *connector* is a link that enables communication between parts. A connector simply means that runtime instances of the parts can communicate. A connector can be a runtime instance of an association or a dynamic link established at runtime, such as an instance passed in as a parameter.

A connector applies only to the parts it's connected to—in Figure 11-9, that means only the set of instances that will exist in an instance of BlogEntry. You can now be certain that an introduction introduces the main body in the same blog entry as the introduction.

## Alternate Multiplicity Notations

Figure 11-4 showed the multiplicity by using a number in the upper right hand corner. You can also show multiplicity in brackets after the name and type, as shown in Figure 11-10.

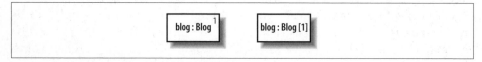

*Figure 11-10. Equivalent notations for multiplicity*

## Properties

In addition to showing parts, which are contained by composition, you can also show *properties*, which are referenced through association and therefore may be shared with other classes in the system.

Properties are drawn with a dashed outline, unlike parts, which are drawn with a solid outline. Figure 11-11 shows a class diagram in which Frame has an association with File, and then shows what File looks like as a property in the internal structure of Frame. Figure 11-11 models a merge tool GUI that displays the two files to compare in one panel and the merged file in another panel.

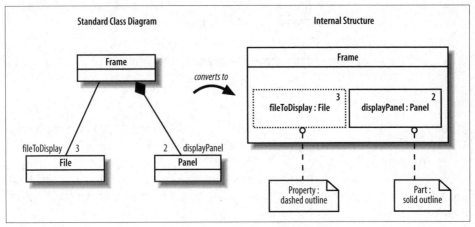

*Figure 11-11. Parts and properties in the internal structure of a class*

The notation for properties and parts is identical except for the dashed versus solid rectangle outlines: you specify roles, types, and multiplicity the same way. As with parts, properties can be connected to other properties or parts using connectors.

## Showing Complex Relationships Between Contained Items

Showing a class's internal structure is especially useful when its contained items relate to each other in unusual ways. Revisiting the merge tool example in Figure 11-11, suppose you want to explicitly model one panel displaying the two files being compared and the other panel displaying the merged file. You can do this by defining more detailed roles for files and panels to show how they relate to each other within a frame, as shown in Figure 11-12.

Figure 11-2 demonstrates that there can be parts (or properties) of the same type playing different roles. Internal structures help make these roles and their relationships explicit.

## Internal Structure Instances

Just as you can model instances of classes (introduced in Chapter 6), you can also show instances of classes possessing internal structure. This is essentially an object diagram for classes with internal structure. As in Chapter 6, this lets you show important examples of the objects that exist in your system at runtime.

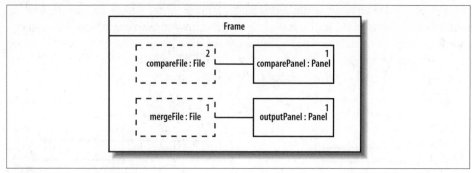

*Figure 11-12. A more detailed internal structure diagram that specifies how files and panels relate to each other within a frame*

If you're showing an instance of a class with internal structure, then you also show its parts and properties as instances. Specify instances of the parts and properties by writing the name followed by a slash, then the usual role and type, e.g., *{<name>} / <role> : <type>*. Since these are instances, however, they are now underlined. Figure 11-13 shows an example runtime instance of the internal structure diagram shown in Figure 11-12.

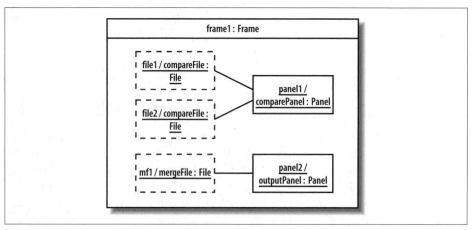

*Figure 11-13. An instance of Frame with instances of its contained parts*

As with object diagrams, showing instances of classes with internal structure allows you to show example configurations in your runtime system.

## Showing How a Class Is Used

The internal structure of a class focuses on the contents of a class; ports focus on the outside of a class, showing how a class is used by other classes.

A *port* is a point of interaction between a class and the outside world. It represents a distinct way of using a class, usually by different types of clients. For example, a Wiki class could have two distinct uses:

- Allowing users to view and edit the Wiki
- Providing maintenance utilities to administrators who want to perform actions such as rolling back the Wiki if incorrect content is provided

Each distinct use of a class is represented with a port, drawn as a small rectangle on the boundary of the class, as shown in Figure 11-14. Write a name next to the port to show the purpose of the port.

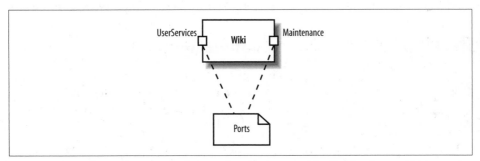

*Figure 11-14. A class with two ports showing that the class provides UserServices and Maintenance capabilities*

It's common for classes to have interfaces associated with ports. You can use ports to group related interfaces to show the services available at that port.

Recall from Chapter 5 that a class can realize an interface, and this relationship can be shown using the ball interface symbol. When a class realizes an interface, the interface is called a *provided interface* of the class. A provided interface can be used by other classes to access the class through the interface.

Similarly, classes can have *required interfaces*. A required interface is an interface that the class requires to function. More precisely, the class needs another class or component that realizes that interface so it can do its job. A required interface is shown with an open lollipop, or the socket symbol.

 Provided and required interfaces are used to promote loose coupling of classes and components. They are particularly important to components and so are discussed in more detail in component diagrams (see Chapter 12).

Suppose the Wiki class above implements the interfaces Updateable and Viewable, allowing other classes to update and view the Wiki through these interfaces. These interfaces are associated with the User Services port, so you can draw them extending out from the User Services port, as shown in Figure 11-15.

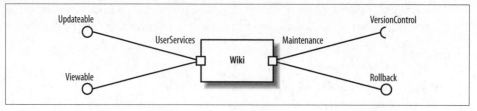

*Figure 11-15. Ports can be used to group "like" interfaces*

Figure 11-15 shows that the Maintenance port has a provided interface called Rollback, allowing administrators to roll back the Wiki. It additionally has a required interface called VersionControl, which is a service the Wiki uses for version control.

## Showing Patterns with Collaborations

Collaborations show objects working together, perhaps temporarily, to get something done. This may sound like object diagrams (see Chapter 6), but collaborations have a different focus: describing objects by the role they play in a scenario and providing a high-level textual description of what the objects are doing.

Collaborations are a good way to document *design patterns*, which are solutions to common problems in software design. Even if you've never heard of them, you've probably used some patterns without knowing it. Observer and Observable in the Java API are an implementation of the Observer design pattern—a way for an object to receive notification that another object changed.

 For more on design patterns and how they can improve your software design, check out *Design Patterns: Elements of Reusable Object Oriented Software* (Addison Wesley), or *Head First Design Patterns* (O'Reilly).

Let's consider a problem in the CMS design that can be solved with a design pattern, which we'll then model using collaborations. Suppose the CMS requires a content approval process: the author submits content, the reviewer may reject the content or pass it on to the editor, and the editor may reject or accept the content. You decide to implement this flow with the Chain of Responsibility (COR) design pattern. The COR design pattern allows an object to send a request without worrying about which object will ultimately handle the request. In the COR pattern, the *client* submits the request, and each *handler* in the chain decides whether to handle the request or to pass the request on to the next handler. In the content approval process, the author will play the role of client, while the reviewer and editor will each play the role of handler. The sequence diagram in Figure 11-16 illustrates this flow. Refer back to Chapter 7 for a refresher on sequence diagrams.

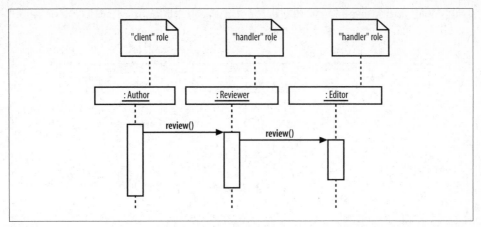

*Figure 11-16. Sequence diagram showing how the COR pattern is used in the content approval process*

There are two ways to model this pattern using collaborations. The first way uses a large dashed-lined oval with the collaboration participants drawn inside the oval. You name a participant by the role it plays in the collaboration and its class or interface type, written as *<role> : <type>* . The participants are linked together using connectors to show how they communicate. The name of the collaboration is written inside the oval above a dashed line. Figure 11-17 shows a `Chain of Responsibility` collaboration using the first notation. In this `COR` collaboration, the participant of type `Author` has the role `client`, and the other participants have the role `handler`.

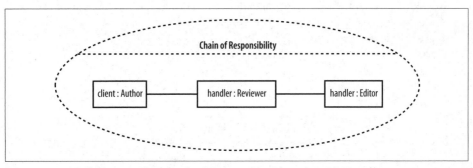

*Figure 11-17. Collaboration showing the COR pattern in the content approval process*

You can think of participants in a collaboration as placeholders for objects because at runtime, objects will fill those places (or play the roles). Connectors are temporary links; connectors mean that the runtime objects communicate during the collaboration, but the objects don't have to communicate outside the collaboration.

The second way to draw a collaboration is shown in Figure 11-18. In this notation, you show the class (or interface) rectangles of the participants, connecting each to a small collaboration oval. Write the participants' roles along the lines. This notation is useful for showing details of the class or interface, such as its operations.

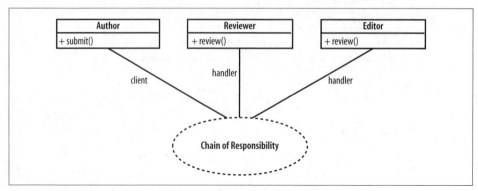

*Figure 11-18. Alternate representation of the COR design pattern*

Collaborations may not look particularly useful, but their strength is in their ability to express patterns that may not be obvious from other diagrams, such as class or sequence diagrams. Without collaborations, you'd have to come up with your own technique to describe what's going on, such as the attached notes in Figure 11-16.

Because collaborations are only temporary relationships, they have some interesting runtime properties that are best described with an everyday example of a collaboration. Suppose a company has monthly training sessions in which the topic changes every session, and in every session the resident expert on the topic performs the training. This is modeled as a Training collaboration that has participants with roles trainer and trainee, as shown in Figure 11-19.

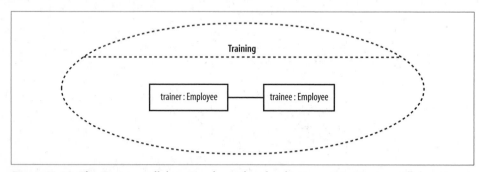

*Figure 11-19. This Training collaboration shows that the objects participating in a collaboration at runtime can interact with different collaborations in different ways*

Now let's turn to some objects that may play these roles at runtime. Ben is the XML expert, so during the XML training collaboration, Ben has the role of trainer, and his co-worker Paul has the role of trainee. However, Paul is the Java expert, so during the Java training collaboration, Paul has the role of trainer and Ben has the role of trainee. This training example illustrates the following points:

***An object isn't bound to its role in a collaboration; it can play different roles in different collaborations.*** Employee Ben and employee Paul remain the same objects; they're just playing different roles in different training collaborations.

***The objects in a collaboration aren't owned by the collaboration; they may exist before and after.*** Ben and Paul have a life outside of training.

***Even though objects in a collaboration are linked, they don't necessarily communicate outside the collaboration.*** Ben and Paul may not talk to each other unless they absolutely have to during the training sessions.

 The training collaboration also demonstrates that you can use collaborations to describe any type of object interaction that can be nicely summarized using a short phrase—not just design patterns.

This is a specialized UML notation because the oval simply draws attention to the existence of a pattern, describing it in brief, high-level terms. But collaborations are valuable for exactly that reason. Design patterns are about building a common vocabulary among developers for solving everyday problems, and collaborations help communicate that vocabulary. Collaborations don't show detailed interactions such as messages being passed between objects as sequence and communication diagrams do, but that can be a benefit when it comes to concisely expressing a well-known pattern.

## What's Next?

The concepts of ports and internal structure of a class, which are introduced in composite structures, are heavily reused for components in component diagrams. Component diagrams allow you to show the key components (or reusable parts) in your system. Components are typically major players in your architecture, using other classes to achieve their behavior, which is why internal structure is so important to components. Ports are often used to show the primary ways to use a component. Component diagrams are covered in Chapter 12.

# CHAPTER 12

# Managing and Reusing Your System's Parts: Component Diagrams

When designing a software system, it's rare to jump directly from requirements to defining the classes in your system. With all but the most trivial systems, it's helpful to plan out the high-level pieces of your system to establish the architecture and manage complexity and dependencies among the parts. Components are used to organize a system into manageable, reusable, and swappable pieces of software.

UML component diagrams model the components in your system and as such form part of the development view, as shown in Figure 12-1. The development view describes how your system's parts are organized into modules and components and is great at helping you manage layers within your system's architecture.

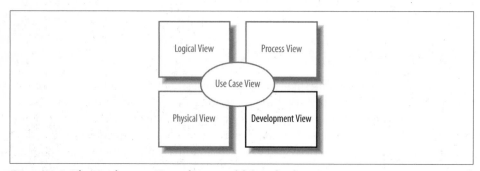

*Figure 12-1. The Development View of your model describes how your system's parts are organized into modules and components*

## What Is a Component?

A *component* is an encapsulated, reusable, and replaceable part of your software. You can think of components as building blocks: you combine them to fit together (possibly building successively larger components) to form your software. Because of this, components can range in size from relatively small, about the size of a class, up to a large subsystem.

Good candidates for components are items that perform a key functionality and will be used frequently throughout your system. Software, such as loggers, XML parsers, or online shopping carts, are components you may already be using. These happen to be examples of common third-party components, but the same principles apply to components you create yourself.

In your own system, you might create a component that provides services or access to data. For example, in a CMS you could have a conversion management component that converts blogs to different formats, such as RSS feeds. RSS feeds are commonly used to provide XML-formatted updates to online content (such as blogs).

In UML, a component can do the same things a class can do: generalize and associate with other classes and components, implement interfaces, have operations, and so on. Furthermore, as with composite structures (see Chapter 11), they can have ports and show internal structure. The main difference between a class and a component is that a component generally has bigger responsibilities than a class. For example, you might create a user information *class* that contains a user's contact information (her name and email address) and a user management *component* that allows user accounts to be created and checked for authenticity. Furthermore, it's common for a component to contain and use other classes or components to do its job.

Since components are major players in your software design, it's important that they are loosely coupled so that changes to a component do not affect the rest of your system. To promote loose coupling and encapsulation, components are accessed through interfaces. Recall from Chapter 5 that interfaces separate a behavior from its implementation. By allowing components to access each other through interfaces, you can reduce the chance that a change in one component will cause a ripple of breaks throughout your system. Refer back to Chapter 5 for a review of interfaces.

## A Basic Component in UML

A component is drawn as a rectangle with the <<component>> stereotype and an optional tabbed rectangle icon in the upper righthand corner. Figure 12-2 shows a ConversionManagement component used in the CMS that converts blogs to different formats and provides feeds such as RSS feeds.

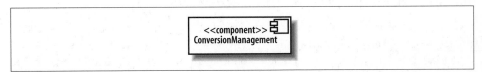

*Figure 12-2. The basic component symbol showing a ConversionManagement component*

In earlier versions of UML, the component symbol was a larger version of the tabbed rectangle icon, so don't be surprised if your UML tool still shows that symbol.

You can show that a component is actually a subsystem of a very large system by replacing <<component>> with <<subsystem>>, as shown in Figure 12-3. A *subsystem* is a secondary or subordinate system that's part of a larger system. UML considers a subsystem a special kind of component and is flexible about how you use this stereotype, but it's best to reserve it for the largest pieces in your overall system, such as a legacy system that provides data or a workflow engine in the CMS.

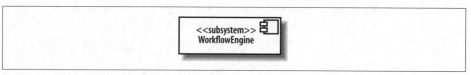

*Figure 12-3. You can substitute the <<subsystem>> stereotype to show the largest pieces of your system*

# Provided and Required Interfaces of a Component

Components need to be loosely coupled so that they can be changed without forcing changes on other parts of the system—this is where interfaces come in. Components interact with each other through provided and required interfaces to control dependencies between components and to make components swappable.

A *provided interface* of a component is an interface that the component realizes. Other components and classes interact with a component through its provided interfaces. A component's provided interface describes the services provided by the component.

A *required interface* of a component is an interface that the component needs to function. More precisely, the component needs another class or component that realizes that interface to function. But to stick with the goal of loose coupling, it accesses the class or component through the required interface. A required interface declares the services a component will need.

There are three standard ways to show provided and required interfaces in UML: ball and socket symbols, stereotype notation, and text listings.

## Ball and Socket Notation for Interfaces

You can show a provided interface of a component using the ball symbol introduced in Chapter 5. A required interface is shown using the counterpart of the ball—the socket symbol—drawn as a semicircle extending from a line. Write the name of the interface near the symbols.

Figure 12-4 shows that the ConversionManagement component provides the FeedProvider and DisplayConverter interfaces and requires the DataSource interface.

The ball and socket notation is the most common way to show a component's interfaces, compared with the following techniques.

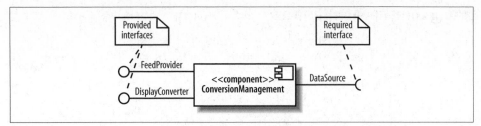

*Figure 12-4. The ball and socket notation for showing a component's provided and required interfaces*

## Stereotype Notation for Interfaces

You can also show a component's required and provided interfaces by drawing the interfaces with the stereotyped class notation (introduced in Chapter 5). If a component realizes an interface, draw a realization arrow from the component to the interface. If a component requires an interface, draw a dependency arrow from the component to the interface, as shown in Figure 12-5.

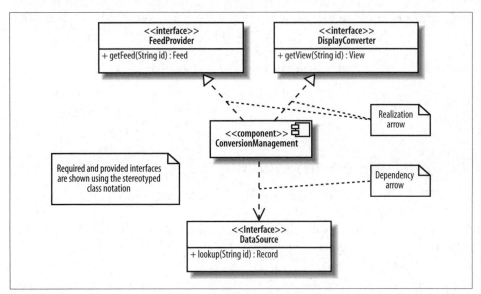

*Figure 12-5. The stereotyped class notation, showing operations of the required and provided interfaces*

This notation is helpful if you want to show the operations of interfaces. If not, it's best to use the ball and socket notation, since it shows the same information more compactly.

## Listing Component Interfaces

The most compact way of showing required and provided interfaces is to list them inside the component. Provided and required interfaces are listed separately, as shown in Figure 12-6.

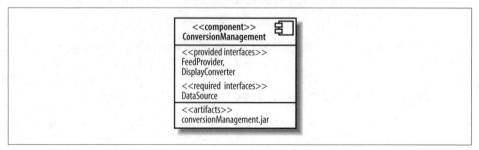

*Figure 12-6. Listing required and provided interfaces within the component is the most compact representation*

This notation additionally has an <<artifacts>> section listing the artifacts, or physical files, manifesting this component. Since artifacts are concerned with how your system is deployed, they are discussed in deployment diagrams (see Chapter 15). Listing the artifacts within the component is an alternative to the techniques shown in Chapter 15 for showing that artifacts manifest components.

Deciding when to use which notation for required and provided interfaces depends on what you're trying to communicate. This question can be answered more fully when examining components working together.

## Showing Components Working Together

If a component has a required interface, then it needs another class or component in the system to provide it. To show that a component with a required interface depends on another component that provides it, draw a dependency arrow from the dependent component's socket symbol to the providing component's ball symbol, as shown in Figure 12-7.

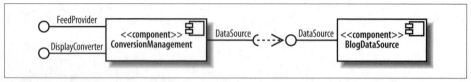

*Figure 12-7. The ConversionManagement component requires the DataSource interface, and the BlogDataSource component provides that interface*

As a presentation option for Figure 12-7, your UML tool may let you get away with snapping the ball and socket together (omitting the dependency arrow), as shown in

Figure 12-8. This is actually the assembly connector notation, which is introduced later in this chapter.

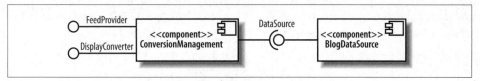

*Figure 12-8. Presentation option that snaps the ball and socket together*

You can also omit the interface and draw the dependency relationship directly between the components, as shown in Figure 12-9.

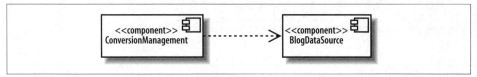

*Figure 12-9. You can draw dependency arrows directly between components to show a higher level view*

The second notation (omitting the interface, shown in Figure 12-9) is simpler than the first (including the interface, shown in Figure 12-7), so you may be tempted to use that as a shorthand, but keep in mind a few factors when choosing how to draw component dependencies.

Remember that interfaces help components stay loosely coupled, so they are an important factor in your component architecture. Showing the key components in your system and their interconnections through interfaces is a great way to describe the architecture of your system, and this is what the first notation is good at, as shown in Figure 12-10.

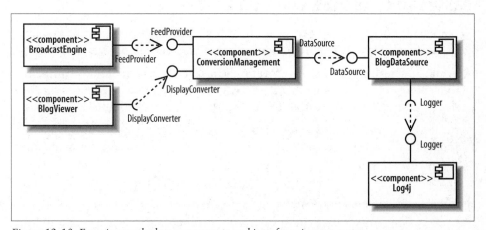

*Figure 12-10. Focusing on the key components and interfaces in your system*

The second notation is good at showing simplified higher level views of component dependencies. This can be useful for understanding a system's configuration management or deployment concerns because emphasizing component dependencies and listing the manifesting artifacts allows you to clearly see which components and related files are required during deployment, as shown in Figure 12-11.

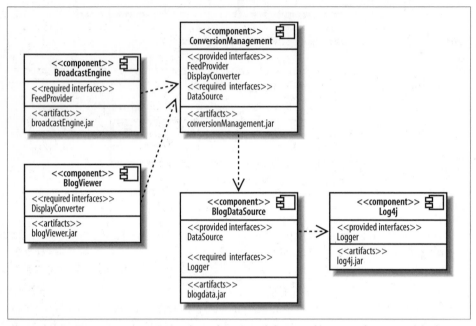

*Figure 12-11. Focusing on component dependencies and the manifesting artifacts is useful when you are trying control the configuration or deployment of your system*

## Classes That Realize a Component

A component often contains and uses other classes to implement its functionality. Such classes are said to *realize* a component—they help the component do its job.

You can show realizing classes by drawing them (and their relationships) inside the component. Figure 12-12 shows that the BlogDataSource component contains the Blog and Entry classes. It also shows the aggregation relationship between the two classes.

You can also show a component's realizing classes by drawing them outside the component with a dependency arrow from the realizing class to the component, as shown in Figure 12-13.

The final way to show realizing classes is to list them in a <<realizations>> compartment inside the component, as shown in Figure 12-14.

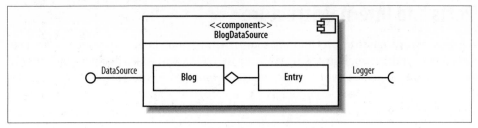

Figure 12-12. The Blog and Entry classes realize the BlogDataSource component

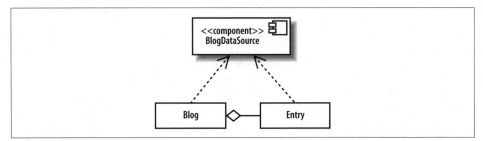

Figure 12-13. Alternate view, showing the realizing classes outside with the dependency relationship

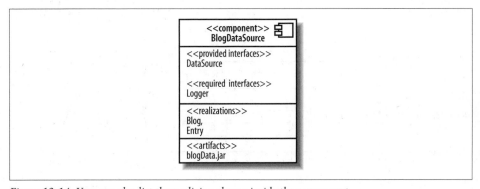

Figure 12-14. You can also list the realizing classes inside the component

How do you decide which notation to use to show the classes that realize a component? You may be limited by your UML tool, but if you have the choice, many modelers prefer the first notation (drawing the realizing classes inside) rather than drawing them outside since drawing them inside visually emphasizes that the classes make up a component to achieve its functionality. Listing the realizing classes may be helpful if you want something compact, but keep in mind that it can't show relationships between the realizing classes, whereas the first two notations can.

# Ports and Internal Structure

Chapter 11 introduced ports and internal structure of a class. Components can also have ports and internal structure. You can use ports to model distinct ways that a component can be used with related interfaces attached to the port. In Figure 12-15, the ConversionManagement component has a Formatting and a Data port, each with their associated interfaces.

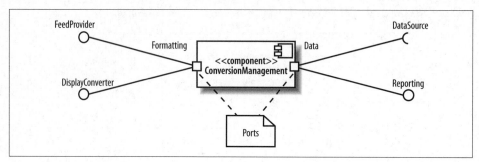

*Figure 12-15. Ports show unique uses of a component and group "like" interfaces*

You can show the internal structure of a component to model its parts, properties, and connectors (see Chapter 11 for a review of internal structure). Figure 12-16 shows the internal structure of a BlogDataSource component.

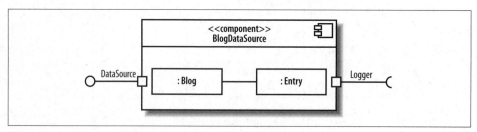

*Figure 12-16. Showing the internal structure of a component*

Components have their own unique constructs when showing ports and internal structure—called delegation connectors and assembly connectors. These are used to show how a component's interfaces match up with its internal parts and how the internal parts work together.

## Delegation Connectors

A component's provided interface can be realized by one of its internal parts. Similarly, a component's required interface can be required by one of its parts. In these cases, you can use *delegation connectors* to show that internal parts realize or use the component's interfaces.

Delegation connectors are drawn with arrows pointing in the "direction of traffic," connecting the port attached to the interface with the internal part. If the part realizes a provided interface, then the arrow points from the port to the internal part.

If the part uses a required interface, then the arrow points from the internal part to the port. Figure 12-17 shows the use of delegation connectors to connect interfaces with internal parts.

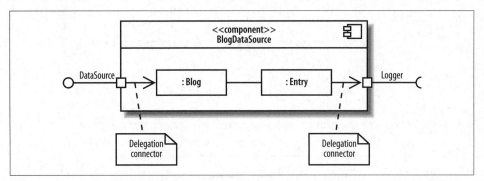

*Figure 12-17.  Delegation connectors show how interfaces correspond to internal parts: the Blog class realizes the DataSource interface and the Entry class requires the Logger interface*

You can think of the delegation connectors as follows: the port represents an opening into a component through which communications pass, and delegation connectors point in the direction of communication. So, a delegation connector pointing from a port to an internal part represents messages being passed to the part that will handle it.

If you're showing the interfaces of the internal parts, you can connect delegation connectors to the interface instead of directly to the part. This is commonly used when showing a component that contains other components. Figure 12-19 demonstrates this notation. The ConversionManagement component has a Controller and a BlogParser component. The ConversionManagement component provides the FeedProvider interface, but this is actually realized internally by the Controller part.

## Assembly Connectors

*Assembly connectors* show that a component requires an interface that another component provides. Assembly connectors snap together the ball and socket symbols that represent required and provided interfaces.

Figure 12-19 shows the assembly connector notation connecting the Controller component to the BlogParser component.

Assembly connectors are special kinds of connectors that are defined for use when showing composite structure of components. Notice that Controller and BlogParser

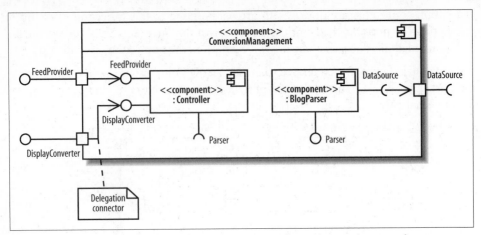

Figure 12-18. Delegation connectors can also connect interfaces of internal parts with ports

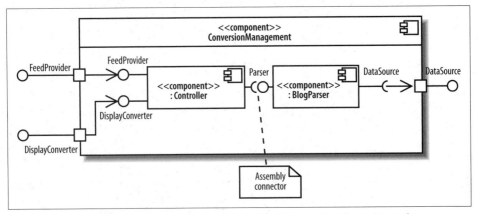

Figure 12-19. Assembly connectors show components working together through interfaces

use the roleName:className notation introduced in composite structures and help form the internal structure of ConversionManagement. But assembly connectors are also sometimes used as a presentation option for component dependency through interfaces in general, as shown earlier in Figure 12-8.

# Black-Box and White-Box Component Views

There are two views of components in UML: a black-box view and a white-box view. The *black-box view* shows how a component looks from the outside, including its required interfaces, its provided interfaces, and how it relates to other components. A black-box view specifies nothing about the internal implementation of a component. The *white-box view*, on the other hand, shows which classes, interfaces, and other components help a component achieve its functionality.

In this chapter, you've seen both black-box and white-box views. So, what's the difference in practical terms? A white-box view is one that shows parts inside a component, whereas a black-box view doesn't, as shown in Figure 12-20.

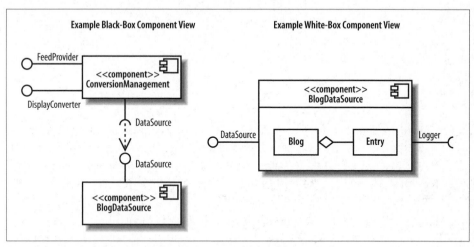

*Figure 12-20. Black-box component views are useful for showing the big picture of the components in your system, whereas white-box views focus on the inner workings of a component*

When modeling your system, it's best to use black-box views to focus on large-scale architectural concerns. Black-box views are good at showing the key components in your system and how they're connected. White-box views, on the other hand, are useful for showing how a component achieves its functionality through the classes it uses.

Black-box views usually contain more than one component, whereas in a white-box view, it's common to focus on the contents of one component.

# What's Next?

Now that you know how to model the components in your system, you may want to look at how your components are deployed to hardware in deployment diagrams. Deployment diagrams are covered in Chapter 15.

There is heavy overlap between certain topics in component diagrams and composite structures. The ability to have ports and internal structure is defined for classes in composite structures. Components inherit this capability and introduce some of their own features, such as delegation and assembly connectors. Refer back to Chapter 11 to refresh your memory about a class's internal structure and ports.

# CHAPTER 13

# Organizing Your Model: Packages

As a software program grows in complexity, it can easily contain hundreds of classes. If you're a programmer working with such a class library, how do you make sense of it? One way to impose structure is by organizing your classes into logically related groups. Classes concerned with an application's user interface can belong to one group, and utility classes can belong to another.

In UML, groups of classes are modeled with *packages*. Most object-oriented languages have an analog of UML packages to organize and avoid name collision among classes. For example, Java has *packages*, C# has *namespaces* (although Java packages, and C# namespaces differ significantly in other details). You can use UML packages to model these structures.

Package diagrams are often used to view dependencies among packages. Since a package can break if another package on which it depends changes, understanding dependencies between packages is vital to the stability of your software.

Packages can organize almost any UML element—not just classes. For example, packages are also commonly used to group use cases. Package diagrams form part of the development view, which is concerned with how your system's parts are organized into modules and packages, as shown in Figure 13-1.

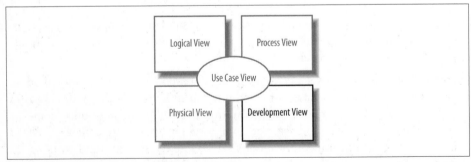

*Figure 13-1. The Development View describes how your system's parts are organized into modules, which are represented as packages in UML*

# Packages

Suppose that during the design of a CMS, you decide to keep classes related to security (for example, performing user authentication) grouped together. Figure 13-2
shows the security package and a few other packages from the CMS in UML. The
symbol for a package is a folder with a tab. The name of the package is written inside
the folder.

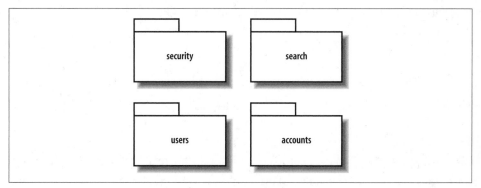

*Figure 13-2. Packages in a CMS; each package corresponds to a specific system concern*

## Contents of a Package

Packages organize UML elements, such as classes, and the contents of a package can
be drawn inside the package or outside the package attached by a line, as shown in
Figure 13-3. If you draw the elements inside the package, write the name of the package in the folder tab.

The notation shown in Figure 13-3 is used to model Java classes belonging to a Java
package. In Java, the package keyword at the beginning of a class specifies that a class
is in a package. Example 13-1 shows a Java code sample corresponding to the
Credentials class in Figure 13-3.

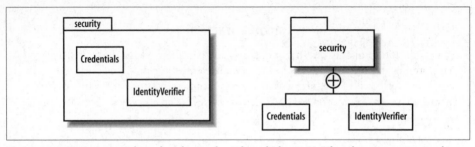

Figure 13-3. *Two ways to show that the Credentials and IdentityVerifier classes are contained in the security package*

Example 13-1. *The Credentials class is located in the security package in this Java implementation*

**package security;**

```
public class Credentials {
    ...
}
```

Packages can also contain other packages, as shown in Figure 13-4.

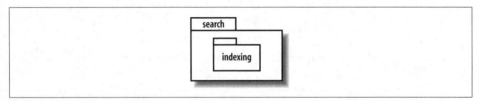

Figure 13-4. *A package that contains another package*

It's common to see deeply nested packages in enterprise applications. Java applications typically use the URL-in-reverse package naming convention (omitting the www part of the URL). For example, the ACME company with the URL *http://www.acme.com* would put all its packages under the acme package, which is under com, as shown in Figure 13-5.

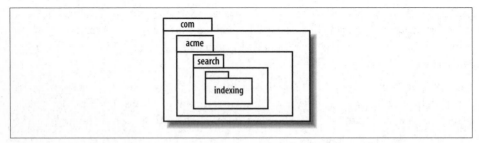

Figure 13-5. *Deeply nested packages are common in enterprise applications: the search and indexing packages are shown in a typical package structure for the ACME company*

Even at this point, these packages consume a lot of space, and if you want to show classes inside the indexing package, each package containing it would have to expand in size accordingly. Luckily, there's an alternate notation that can be easier to work with. You can "flatten" nested packages to write them as **packageA::packageB::packageC**, and so on. This converts Figure 13-5 into the less cluttered Figure 13-6.

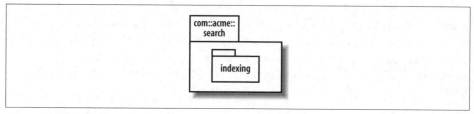

*Figure 13-6. Flattening nested packages*

## UML Tool Variation

Currently, a small amount of UML tools don't support the notations shown in Figure 13-3. However, almost all tools can show that a class belongs to a package using one of the notations shown in Figure 13-7. The notation to the far right is the standard UML namespace notation, discussed next in "Namespaces and Classes Referring to Each Other."

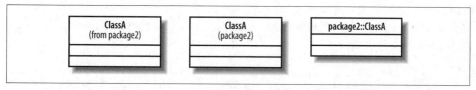

*Figure 13-7. Common ways UML tools show that a class belongs to a package*

To specify the package that a class belongs to, most UML tools allow you to enter the package name in a class specification dialog or manually drag the class into the package it belongs to in a tree display of the model elements.

# Namespaces and Classes Referring to Each Other

Breaking up your classes into packages introduces some bookkeeping. If you're a Java programmer, you may have encountered a related issue before. To use an ArrayList in a Java program, you have to specify that ArrayList is located in the java.util package. That is because Java packages define their own *namespaces*, or naming contexts. If an item is not in the current namespace, you have to specify where it is located.

Similarly, a UML package establishes a namespace. So, if an element in a package wants to use an element in a different package, it has to specify where the desired element is. To specify the context of a UML element, you provide the *fully-scoped name*, which includes the package name and the element name separated by double colons, as in ***packageName***::***className***. The fully-scoped name for the class Credentials belonging to the package security is security::Credentials. If you have two classes with the same name in different packages, using the fully-scoped name allows you to distinguish between them.

Elements in a namespace must have unique names. This means the security package cannot have two classes named Credentials, but there can be two classes called Credentials belonging to separate packages, for example security and utils. As discussed previously in "UML Tool Variation," your UML tool may display the classes in Figure 13-8 differently.

*Figure 13-8. Representing a class with its fully-scoped name: both the security and utils packages have a class named Credentials*

Why does this matter? To specify that a class has a relationship with another class, you may have to specify a namespace.

Classes in the same package are part of the same namespace, so they can refer to each other without using fully-scoped names. Since they are in the same package, IdentityVerifier can have an attribute of type Credentials and not have to specify the package (see Figure 13-9).

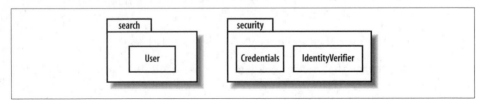

*Figure 13-9. Classes in different packages have to provide name scope*

On the other hand, a class outside the security package, such as User, would have to provide a scope when accessing Credentials, which it can do by using the fully-scoped name—security::Credentials. Later, in "Importing and Accessing Packages," you'll see that there are other ways to provide scope when accessing a class in a different package.

In Java, a fully-scoped name corresponds to specifying the Java package, e.g., security.Credentials instead of just Credentials.

In UML, elements in a nested package can refer to elements in the containing package without scoping the name, which in Figure 13-10 means that an element in indexing could refer to an element in search without using the fully-scoped name.

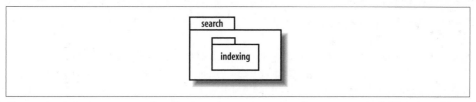

*Figure 13-10. In UML, a nested package implies namespace "inheritance," which doesn't apply in some implementation languages*

The implication that elements in nested packages have automatic access to elements in containing packages doesn't match with some implementation languages. For example, in Java, if a class in the indexing package uses a class in the search package, it has to provide a scope either by using its fully-qualified name or by importing the search package. Despite the fact that UML semantics of nested packages differ from Java packages, you could still use Figure 13-10 to model a package search. indexing in a Java system.

## Element Visibility

Elements in a package may have public or private visibility. Elements with *public visibility* are accessible outside the package. Elements with *private visibility* are available only to other elements inside the package. You can model public or private visibility in UML by writing a plus or minus symbol in front of the element's name, as shown in Figure 13-11.

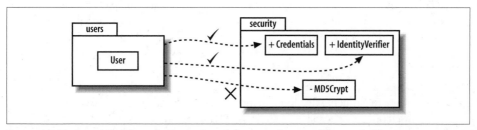

*Figure 13-11. Since MD5Crypt has private visibility, it isn't accessible outside the security package*

In Java, public and private visibility corresponds to a class being public or private to a Java package. A Java class is marked as public to a package by the public access modifier, as in:

```
public class Credentials {}
```

If the public keyword is absent, then the class is private to the package. Many UML tools don't offer the plus and minus symbols to show element visibility, so don't be surprised if yours doesn't.

## Package Dependency

The previous sections showed that sometimes a class in one package needs to use a class in another package. This causes a dependency between packages: if an element in package A uses an element in package B, then package A depends on package B, as shown in Figure 13-12.

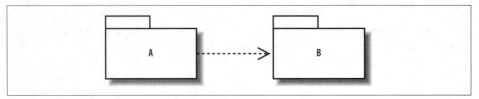

*Figure 13-12. Package A depends on package B*

### Packages in Your Software

Now that you've seen the basics of package diagrams, it's a good time to consider why you'd want to use packages in your software.

If you're creating a very small program (consisting of only a few classes), you might not bother organizing your classes into packages. As your program gets bigger and you add developers to the project, packages introduce structure and let you know who's working on what.

Code related to the graphical user interface (GUI) can belong to a gui package, code related to search capabilities can belong to a search package, and common utilities can belong to a util package. This makes it easier to find classes when looking through a complex API. For example, to locate a GUI dialog, you would know to look in the gui package.

Often, programmers work roughly undisturbed in their own or their group's package. Those working in gui generally don't change the search package and vice versa. Everyone may use common packages, such as the util package, but such commonly used packages are expected to be fairly stable since changes could affect everyone.Beyond organizing elements, packages can serve other useful functions. They can be used for access control: you can declare elements private to a package to prevent it from being used by other packages.

Packages can assist with organizing classes as deployment modules. For example, if you wanted to include search capability in some systems but not others, you could choose to include or exclude the search package in the build.

Understanding the dependencies among your packages is useful for analyzing the stability of your software, as discussed in "Managing Package Dependencies." In fact, the most common use of UML package diagrams is to give an overview of the core packages in your software and the dependencies among them, as shown in Figure 13-13.

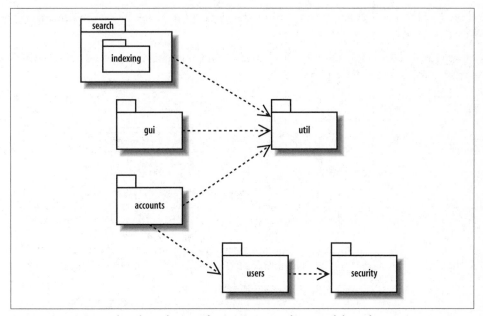

*Figure 13-13. A typical package diagram featuring core packages and dependencies*

"Managing Package Dependencies," later in this chapter, revisits package dependency diagrams, showing you how to use them to understand and improve the stability of your software.

# Importing and Accessing Packages

When a package *imports* another package, elements in the importing package can use elements in the imported package without having to use their fully scoped names. This feature is similar to a Java import, in which a class can import a package and use its contents without having to provide their package names.

In an import relationship, the imported package is referred to as the *target package*. To show the import relation, draw a dependency arrow from the importing package to the target package with the stereotype import (see Figure 13-14).

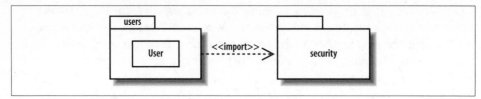

*Figure 13-14. The package users imports security, so classes in users may use public classes in security without having to specify the package name*

A package can also import a specific element in another package instead of the whole package, as shown in Figure 13-15.

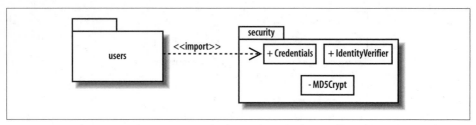

*Figure 13-15. The users package imports only the Credentials element from the security package*

When importing a package, only public elements of the target package are available in the importing namespace. For example, in Figure 13-16, elements in users can see Credentials and IdentityVerifier but not MD5Crypt.

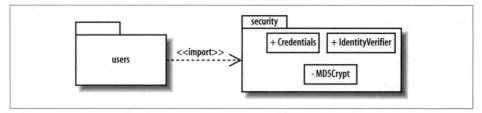

*Figure 13-16. Private visibility causes a class not to be seen even though its package is imported*

Not only do elements have visibility—the import relation itself has visibility. An import can be a *public import* or *private import* with public as the default. A public import means imported elements have public visibility inside the importing namespace; a private import means imported elements have private visibility inside the importing namespace. You show a private import with the stereotype access instead of import.

The difference between import and access arises when a package imports a package that imports or accesses others. Imported elements have public visibility in the importing package, so they get passed on with further imports, whereas accessed elements do not.

In Figure 13-17, package B imports C and accesses D, so B can see public elements in C and D. A imports B, so A can see public elements in B. A can also see public elements in C because C is publicly imported into B, but A cannot see anything in D because D is privately imported into B.

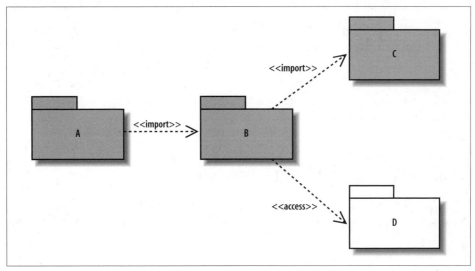

*Figure 13-17. Package A can see public elements in C but not D*

Import and access relationships can be used to model the programming world concepts of importing of classes into another namespace so that elements in the importing namespace may refer to elements in the target namespace without scoping the name. For example, the package relationships in Figure 13-14 could be used to model the Java code example in Example 13-2.

*Example 13-2. Because the User class imports the security package, it can refer to the Credentials class without using the fully qualified name security*

```
package users;

// importing all public elements in the security package
import security.*;

class User {
    Credentials credentials;
    ...
}
```

The element import in Figure 13-15 corresponds to the Java implementation shown in Example 13-3.

*Example 13-3. Only the Credentials class is imported from the security package*

```
package users;

// importing only the Credentials class
import security.Credentials;

class User {
    Credentials credentials;

    ...
}
```

Many modelers don't bother with specifying the import and access relationships, and instead show generic package dependencies, discussed earlier in "Package Dependency."

## Managing Package Dependencies

Having complicated dependencies among packages can lead to brittle software since changes in one package can cause its dependent packages to break. Figure 13-18 shows a dependency disaster: a change in any one package could ultimately affect every other package.

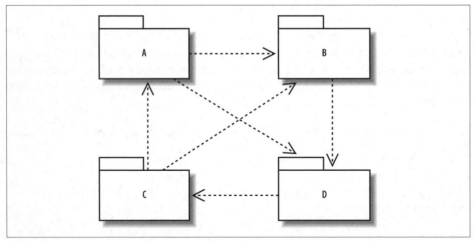

*Figure 13-18. Directly or indirectly, a change in any one package could affect every other package*

Robert C. Martin's *Agile Software Development* (Prentice Hall) establishes principles and metrics regarding dependencies between packages and deployment modules. A couple of these, such as avoiding cyclical package dependencies and depending in the "direction of stability," can be investigated by looking at package diagrams.

If you have cycles in your dependencies, you can break the cycles in different ways. You could factor out a new package that both packages can depend on or you could decide that all the classes really belong together anyway, as shown in Figure 13-19.

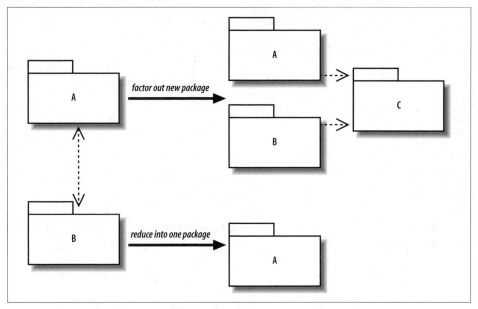

*Figure 13-19. Removing cycles in package dependencies*

Depending in the order of stability means that a package should depend only on packages more stable than itself. An unstable package depends on many other packages; a stable package depends on few packages. Studying package diagrams can help you spot potentially vulnerable designs resulting from the core packages of your system (such as those containing interfaces) depending on unstable packages.

## Using Packages to Organize Use Cases

Just as packages group classes of similar functionality, packages also group other UML elements such as use cases. Figure 13-20 shows some use case packages from a CMS.

Rolling up use cases into higher levels of your system can help organize your model, allowing you to see which actors interact with which portions of the system, as shown in Figure 13-21.

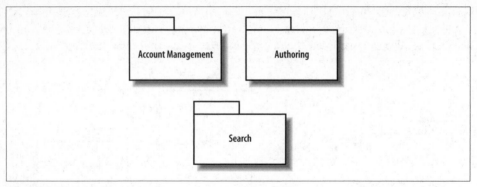

*Figure 13-20. Packaging major use case groups within a CMS*

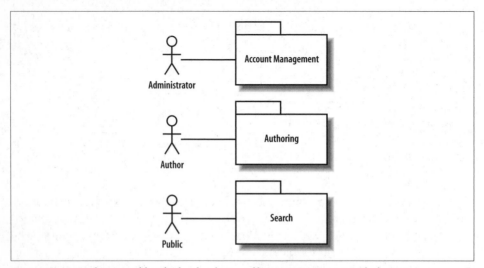

*Figure 13-21. Packages enable a higher level view of how actors interact with the system*

# What's Next?

Packages are used to group UML elements such as classes and use cases. You may want to review those chapters for more detail about showing the contents of a package. Class diagrams are covered in Chapter 4; use case diagrams are covered in Chapter 2.

One of the most important applications of package diagrams is to view dependencies in your system. Other important high-level system diagrams include component diagrams, which show the key software pieces, and deployment diagrams, which show how the pieces get deployed to hardware. Component diagrams are described in Chapter 12; deployment diagrams are covered in Chapter 15.

# CHAPTER 14

# Modeling an Object's State: State Machine Diagrams

Activity diagrams and interaction diagrams are useful for describing behavior, but there's still a missing piece. Sometimes the state of an object or system is an important factor in its behavior. For example, if the CMS required potential users to submit an application for an account, which could be approved or rejected, then the AccountApplication object may act differently depending on whether it is pending, accepted, or rejected.

In such situations, it's helpful to model states of an object and the events causing state changes—this is what state machine diagrams do best. Continuing the above example, the AccountApplication object could have the states pending, accepted, and rejected as possible values of an attribute, and change states upon events such as approve or reject. A state machine diagram allows you to model this behavior.

State machine diagrams are heavily used in special niches of software and hardware systems, including the following:

- Real-time/mission-critical systems, such as heart monitoring software
- Dedicated devices whose behavior is defined in terms of state, such as ATMs
- First-person shooter games, such as *Doom* or *Half-Life*

To reflect these common uses, this chapter will deviate from the CMS example used throughout the rest of this book.

Most of this chapter focuses on behavioral state machines, which can show states, transitions, and behavior (inside states and along transitions). There's another type of state machine called a *protocol state machine* that doesn't model behavior but is useful for modeling protocols such as network communication protocols. Protocol state machines are discussed briefly at the end of the chapter.

State machine diagrams are part of the logical model of your system, as shown in Figure 14-1.

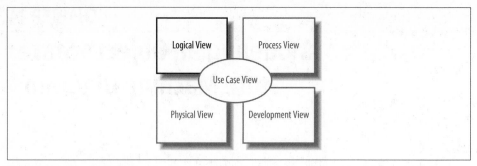

Figure 14-1. *The Logical View describes the abstract descriptions of a system's parts, including when and how those parts can be in different states using state machine diagrams*

State machine diagrams are often referred to informally as state diagrams. You may also have seen them referred to as a statechart diagrams in the past, since this diagram has undergone many name changes.

# Essentials

Let's look at the key elements of state diagrams using a simple example. Figure 14-2 shows a state diagram modeling a light. When you lift the light switch, the light turns on. When you lower the light switch, the light turns off.

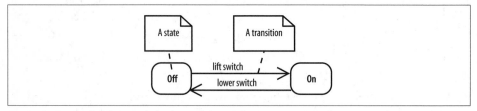

Figure 14-2. *The fundamental elements of a state diagram: states and transitions between states*

A state diagram consists of *states*, drawn as rounded rectangles, and *transitions*, drawn as arrows connecting the states. A transition represents a change of state, or how to get from one state to the next. A state is *active* when entered through a transition, and it becomes *inactive* when exited through a transition.

The event causing the state change, or *trigger*, is written along the transition arrow. The light in Figure 14-2 has two states: Off and On. It changes state when the lift switch or lower switch triggers occur.

If you haven't seen state diagrams before, it may help to view the states and transitions in table form, as shown in Table 14-1. In the left column are the states, and along the top row are triggers. The table is interpreted as follows: when the object is in a state and receives a trigger, the object moves to the resulting state specified in the cell. A dash (-) means that no transition happens or that the combination is impossible. Viewing states and transitions in table form can be helpful when getting up-to-speed, but don't depend on this too heavily; details of states and transitions can be more complex, and it will become easier to work with state diagrams.

*Table 14-1. Table view of light states and transitions—not UML notation*

| State/Trigger | Light switch lifted | Light switch lowered |
| --- | --- | --- |
| Off | On | - |
| On | - | Off |

State diagrams usually have an *initial pseudostate* and a *final state*, marking the start and end points of the state machine, respectively. An initial pseudostate is drawn with a filled circle, and a final state is drawn with two concentric circles with a filled inner circle, as shown in Figure 14-3.

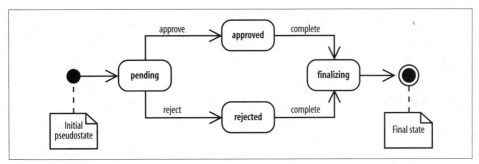

*Figure 14-3. Initial pseudostate and final states in an AccountApplication state diagram*

Pseudostates are special markers that direct the flow of traffic in a state diagram. As mentioned above, an initial pseudostate models the starting point of a state diagram. There are other pseudostates discussed later in "Advanced Pseudostates" that model complex transitions between states.

Now that you've seen the basic elements of state diagrams, let's look in detail at these elements.

# States

A *state* is a condition of being at a certain time. A state can be a passive quality, such as On and Off for the light object. A state can also be an active quality, or something that an object is doing. For example, a coffeemaker has the state Brewing during which it is brewing coffee. A state is drawn as a rounded rectangle with the name of the state in the center, as shown in Figure 14-4.

If the state is a "doing" state, you can write the behavior inside the state, as shown in Figure 14-5.

Figure 14-4. A rectangle with rounded corners and the name in the center is the most common way to draw a state

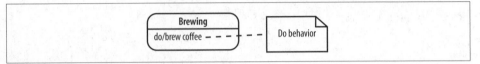

Figure 14-5. Showing the behavior details of a "doing" state

Do behavior, written as do/*behavior*, is behavior that happens as long as the state is active. For example, the coffeemaker in Figure 14-5 does the behavior brew coffee while in the Brewing state. Similarly, a CD player could have the behavior do/read disc while in the Playing state. Do behavior either completes on its own or is forced to complete when a trigger causes the state to exit, as discussed in "Transitions." Later in this chapter, you'll see additional ways to show details of a state, including entry and exit behavior, reactions to events within a state, and states within states.

# Transitions

A transition, shown with an arrow, represents a change of states from a *source state* to a *target state*. A *transition description*, written along the arrow, describes the circumstances causing the state change to occur.

The previous state diagrams in this chapter had fairly simple transition descriptions because they consisted only of triggers. For example, the light in Figure 14-2 changed state in response to the triggers lift switch and lower switch. But transition descriptions can be more complex. The full notation for transition descriptions is *trigger[guard] / behavior*, where each element is optional, as shown in Figure 14-6. This section defines each of these elements, and then in "Transition Variations" we'll show how these elements interact to model different types of state changes.

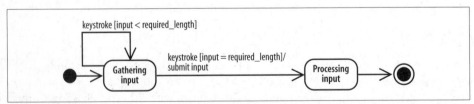

Figure 14-6. This input processing state diagram models features a trigger, guard, and transition behavior along one of its transitions

A *trigger* is an event that may cause a transition. In a system that processes user input, a keystroke trigger may cause the system to change states from Gathering input to Processing input.

In addition to triggers, transitions can also be prompted by the completion of internal behavior, as discussed later in this chapter.

A *guard* is a Boolean condition that permits or blocks the transition. When a guard is present, the transition is taken if the guard evaluates to true, but the transition is blocked if the guard is false. Continuing the user input example, after a keystroke trigger occurs, a guard can be used to block a transition if the input is less than the required length. Guards are commonly used to model a transition being blocked or a choice between transitions, as discussed next in "Transition Variations."

Transition *behavior* is an uninterruptible activity that executes while the transition takes place (if the transition is taken). For example, transition behavior could include submitting the user's input for processing while changing states from Gathering input to Processing input.

Figure 14-6 shows all three elements of a transition—trigger, guard, and transition behavior. When a keystroke occurs and the input is the required length, the transition from Gathering input to Processing input is taken. While the transition occurs, the transition behavior submit input is invoked. Figure 14-6 also shows that a state can transition to itself; this is known as a *self-transition*.

## Transition Variations

Figure 14-7 shows a state diagram for a CD player. Its transition descriptions feature an assortment of triggers, guards, and transition behavior. Let's break this diagram apart to see how combinations of guards and triggers can be used to model different types of state changes.

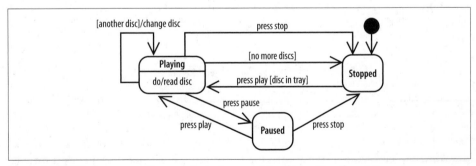

*Figure 14-7. CD player state diagram, featuring a variety of transition descriptions*

If a trigger is specified but no guard is, then the transition is taken when the trigger occurs. This is useful for modeling a state change in response to an event. In Figure 14-8, the CD player moves from the Playing state to Stopped when press stop occurs.

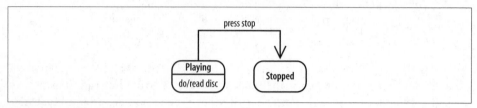

*Figure 14-8. The most common type of transition features only a trigger*

If a trigger and a guard are specified, then the transition is taken when the trigger occurs if the guard evaluates to true. Otherwise, the transition isn't taken. Combining a trigger and a guard is useful for modeling that a transition can be blocked depending on a condition. You can also use guards to model a choice between transitions, as you'll see later.

In Figure 14-9, the CD player moves from the Stopped state to Playing when press play occurs, but only if a disc is in the tray.

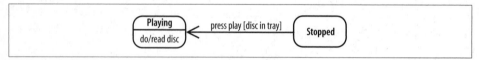

*Figure 14-9. A guard will block a transition if it evaluates to false*

If neither a trigger nor a guard are specified, then the transition is taken immediately after the source state's internal behavior (if any) is complete. This is useful for modeling a transition caused by completion of internal behavior. Figure 14-10 shows a triggerless, guardless transition leading from Playing to Stopped, which means that the CD player moves to the Stopped state as soon as it finishes reading the disc. (This transition is not seen in the full CD player state diagram in Figure 14-7, but is included to explain triggerless transitions, shown in Figure 14-11.)

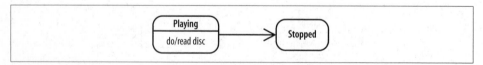

*Figure 14-10. In this example, a transition is caused by the completion of internal behavior*

Figure 14-9 showed the use of guards to block a transition. You can also use guards to show a choice between transitions: the transition whose guard evaluates to true is taken. In Figure 14-11, after the CD player is done reading the disc, it will either move to the Stopped state if there are no more discs or transition back to the Playing

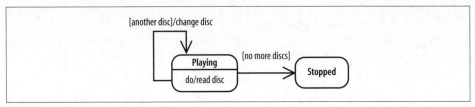

*Figure 14-11. Using guards to model a choice between paths*

state if there are more discs. Notice that if there are more discs, the transition includes transition behavior—changing the disc.

As a presentation option for choices, you can use a choice pseudostate, discussed later in "Advanced Pseudostates."

## States in Software

If you're a software developer, you're probably wondering when you'll ever need to model the operation of a CD player or coffeemaker. In software, state diagrams model an object's *life cycle*, or the states it goes through during its lifespan. Figure 14-12 shows the life cycle of an AccountApplication object as it passes from pending to approved or rejected and then to finalizing.

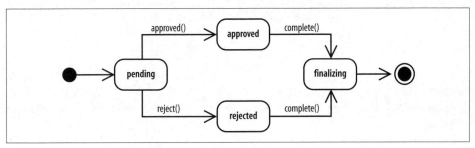

*Figure 14-12. The life cycle of an AccountApplication object*

State diagrams are useful for modeling an object that behaves differently depending on its state. Considering an AccountApplication object, calling the complete() method when the object is in the pending state wouldn't make sense if the finalizing state performs wrap-up behavior, such as creating the blog account if approved—it would first have to know whether the application was approved. State diagrams are an effective way to make this information explicit.

If an object has a simple life cycle, then it's not worth modeling its life cycle with a state diagram. For example, a ContactInformation object that stores an Author's contact information and doesn't change states other than being created and destroyed probably doesn't warrant a state diagram.

If you're wondering what an object's states would look like in code—
the `AccountApplication` class could have a status attribute and the
states shown in Figure 14-12 could be possible values of status. Transitions occur when methods on the `AccountApplication` object are
invoked. See Chapter 4 for a review of how an object's state is captured in its attributes.

State diagram are also heavily used in certain software niches, such as first-person
shooter (FPS) games. In FPS games, state machines are used to model game character states. For example, a game character, such as a troll, could have the states
`Neutral`, `Attack`, `Panic`, and `Die`, as shown in Figure 14-13. When the troll is in the
`Attack` state, he is performing behavior, such as unsheathing his sword or charging
his opponent (that's you). Triggers causing a state change include seeing an opponent or receiving a blow from the opponent.

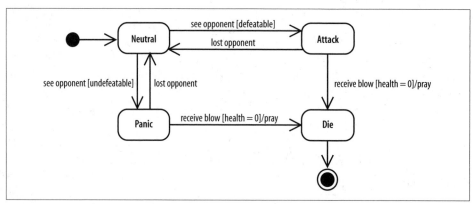

*Figure 14-13. State diagram modeling a troll in a FPS game; the troll's behavior is determined by
his state*

# Advanced State Behavior

You've seen the most common ways to model states. This section shows how to
model additional details of a state, including entry behavior, exit behavior, and reactions to events while in a state.

Figure 14-14 shows the detailed notation for a state: a large rounded rectangle with
separate compartments for *internal behavior* and *internal transitions*.

## Internal Behavior

*Internal* behavior is any behavior that happens while the object is in a state. You've
already seen do behavior, which is behavior that is ongoing while the state is active.
Internal behavior is a more general concept that also includes entry and exit behavior.

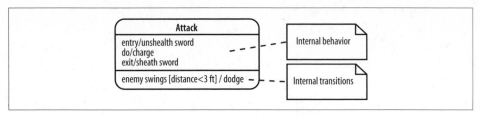

*Figure 14-14. Internal behavior and transitions of the Attack state*

Internal behavior is written as *label / behavior*. The label indicates when the behavior executes—in other words, events or circumstances causing the behavior. There are three special labels: entry, exit, and do.

Entry behavior happens as soon as the state becomes active and is written as entry/*behavior*. Exit behavior happens immediately before the state becomes inactive and is written as exit/*behavior*.

In Figure 14-15, unsheath sword is entry behavior and sheath sword is exit behavior. Unlike do behavior, entry and exit behaviors can't be interrupted.

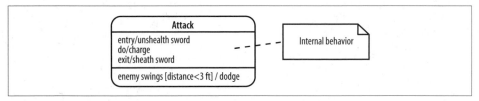

*Figure 14-15. The middle compartment shows internal behavior*

## Internal Transitions

An *internal* transition is a transition that causes a reaction within a state, but doesn't cause the object to change states. An internal transition is different from a self transition (see Figure 14-11) because self transitions cause entry and exit behavior to occur whereas internal transitions don't.

Internal transitions are written as *trigger [guard] / behavior*, and they are listed inside a state. In Figure 14-16, the Attack has an internal transition: when an opponent swings his weapon and is less than three feet away, the troll dodges.

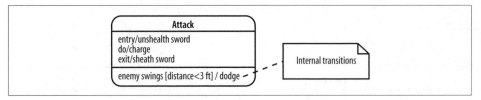

*Figure 14-16. The bottom compartment shows internal transitions*

Use internal transitions to model reactions to events that don't cause state changes. For example, you could use internal transitions to show that a pause-and-serve coffeemaker suspends dispensing the coffee when you remove the coffee pot but doesn't leave the Brewing state, as shown in Figure 14-17.

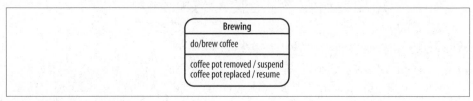

*Figure 14-17. An internal transition models a reaction while staying in the same state*

# Composite States

A key difference between UML state diagrams and other non-UML state diagrams you may be familiar with is that UML allows concurrent states, or being in multiple states at the same time. Composite states are what makes this possible.

Suppose the troll in the Neutral state is doing two things at the same time: Searching and Pacing. You can model two simultaneous states by using a composite state, as shown in Figure 14-18.

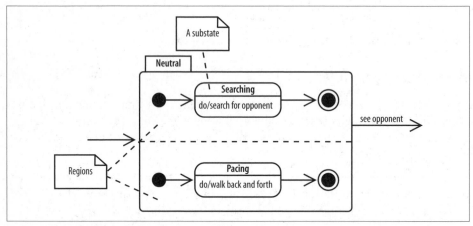

*Figure 14-18. Composite states contain one or more state diagrams; if they contain more than one state diagram, then the state diagrams execute in parallel*

A *composite state* is a state that contains one or more state diagrams. Each diagram belongs to a *region*, and regions are divided by a dotted line. A state in a region is referred to as a *substate* of the composite state.

Composite states work as follows: when the composite state becomes active, the initial pseudostate of each region becomes active, and the contained state diagrams begin executing. The contained state diagrams are interrupted if a trigger on the composite state occurs. In Figure 14-18, the substates will be halted when a trigger on the composite state—see opponent—occurs.

If substates have behavior that can run to completion, then the composite state is complete when every region's state diagram is complete.

# Advanced Pseudostates

You've already seen *initial* pseudostates, which mark the start of a state diagram. There are additional pseudostates that are useful for directing the flow of traffic between states.

A *choice* pseudostate is used to emphasize that a Boolean condition determines which transition is followed. A choice has guards on each of its outgoing transitions, and the transition that is followed depends on the guard. In Figure 14-19, the CD player will go back to the Playing state if another disc is available or will go to the Stopped state if there are no more discs. Notice that this is an alternate, and cleaner, way to model the transition choice in Figure 14-11.

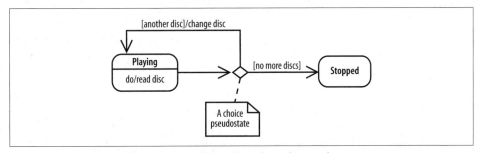

Figure 14-19. The path followed after a choice depends on the guard

 At least one of the guards following a choice must evaluate to true for your model to be well-formed. If more than one guard following a choice evaluates to true, then one of them is selected arbitrarily. If this situation doesn't make sense for your model, then it's a sign that you need to redefine your guards so that exactly one guard at a time evaluates to true.

*Fork* and *join* pseudostates show branching into concurrent states and then rejoining. For example, in Figure 14-20, the fork breaks the incoming transition into two transitions, allowing Searching and Pacing to happen simultaneously. The join then merges its two incoming transitions into one outgoing transition.

Figure 14-20 is an alternate way to model Figure 14-18. In Figure 14-18, forking and joining are implied by showing the initial pseudostates and final states.

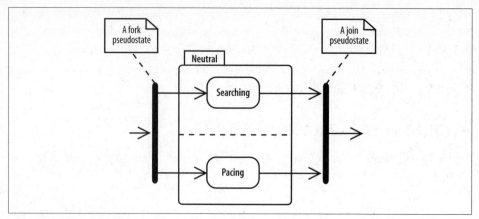

Figure 14-20. Forks and joins show concurrent states

# Signals

You can use special icons for transitions to draw attention to transitions and transition behavior. This is called a *transition-oriented* view.

In this view, a trigger is represented with a receive signal icon and transition behavior is represented with a send signal icon. Figure 14-21 shows how Figure 14-6 can be drawn in this alternate notation. It additionally uses the choice pseudostate introduced previously in "Advanced Pseudostates."

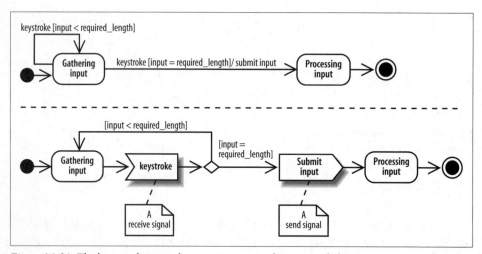

Figure 14-21. The bottom diagram draws transitions and transition behavior as receive and send signals

The main purpose of this notation is to visually emphasize sending and receiving signals. Although both diagrams say the same thing, the version with the signal icons focuses on the transitions and, in this case, makes the diagram more readable.

## Protocol State Machines

Protocol state machines are a special kind of state machine focusing on how a protocol, such as a communication protocol (e.g., TCP), works. The main difference between protocol state machines and behavioral state machines, which we've focused on previously, is that protocol state machines don't show behavior along transitions or inside states. Instead, they focus on showing a legal sequence of events and resulting states. Protocol state machines are drawn in a tabbed rectangle with the name of the state machine in the tab followed by {protocol}, as shown in Figure 14-22.

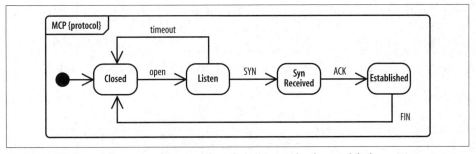

*Figure 14-22. Protocol state machine modeling the receiver side of a simplified communication protocol called My Communication Protocol (MCP)*

Because protocol state machines don't show behavior, you can't model what the system is doing in response—for example, if it's sending acknowledgements back. But it can be useful for showing how to work with an object or system, such as specifying a communication protocol or an expected call sequence for an object's operations.

## What's Next?

State diagrams show the states of an object and triggers causing a change of state. If you're interested in modeling object state changes in the context of a workflow, see activity diagrams, covered in Chapter 3.

If you want to show timing associated with state changes, then it's also worth checking out timing diagrams, covered in Chapter 9.

CHAPTER 15

# Modeling Your Deployed System: Deployment Diagrams

If you've been applying the UML techniques shown in earlier chapters of this book, then you've seen all but one view of your system. That missing piece is the *physical* view. The physical view is concerned with the physical elements of your system, such as executable software files and the hardware they run on.

UML *deployment diagrams* show the physical view of your system, bringing your software into the real world by showing how software gets assigned to hardware and how the pieces communicate (see Figure 15-1).

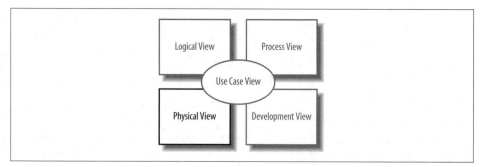

*Figure 15-1. Deployment diagrams focus on the Physical View of your system*

 The word *system* can mean different things to different people; in the context of deployment diagrams, it means the software you create and the hardware and software that allow your software to run.

## Deploying a Simple System

Let's start by showing a deployment diagram of a very simple system. In this simplest of cases, your software will be delivered as a single executable file that will reside on one computer.

To show computer hardware, you use a *node*, as shown in Figure 15-2.

*Figure 15-2. Use nodes to represent hardware in your system*

This system contains a single piece of hardware—a Desktop PC. It's labeled with the stereotype <<device>> to specify that this is a hardware node.

## One More Time…Model Levels

It must be about time to bring up modeling at the right level again. In Figure 15-2, the hardware node is specified as a Desktop PC. It's entirely up to you how much detail you want to give node names. You could be very precise with a name such as "64-bit Processor Intel Workstation," or very general with a name such as "Generic PC."

If you have specific hardware requirements for your system, you're likely to give your nodes very precise names. If your hardware requirements are undefined or insignificant, you might have vague node names. As with all other aspects of UML, it is important to make sure that you are modeling at the right level for *your* system.

Now, you need to model the software that runs on the hardware. Figure 15-3 shows a simple software artifact (see "Deployed Software: Artifacts," next), which in this case is just a JAR file named *3dpacman.jar*, containing a 3D-Pacman application.

*Figure 15-3. A physical software file such as a jar file is modeled with an artifact*

Finally, you need to put these two pieces together to complete the deployment diagram of your system. Draw the artifact inside the node to show that a software artifact is deployed to a hardware node. Figure 15-4 shows that *3dpacman.jar* runs on a Desktop PC.

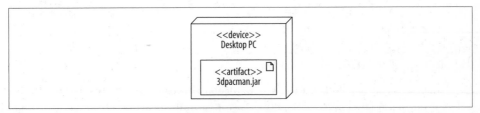

*Figure 15-4. Drawing an artifact inside a node shows that the artifact is deployed to the node*

But is it really complete? Don't you need to model the Java Virtual Machine (JVM) because without it, your code wouldn't execute? What about the operating system; isn't that important? The answer, unfortunately, is possibly.

Your deployment diagrams should contain details about your system that are important to your audience. If it is important to show the hardware, firmware, operating system, runtime environments, or even device drivers of your system, then you should include these in your deployment diagram. As the rest of this chapter will show, deployment diagram notation can be used to model all of these types of things. If there's a feature of your system that's not important, then it's not worth adding it to your diagram since it could easily clutter up or distract from those features of your design that *are* important.

# Deployed Software: Artifacts

The previous section showed a sneak preview of some of the notation that can be used to show the software and hardware in a deployed system. The *3dpacman.jar* software was deployed to a single hardware node. In UML, that JAR file is called an artifact.

*Artifacts* are physical files that execute or are used by your software. Common artifacts you'll encounter include:

- Executable files, such as *.exe* or *.jar* files
- Library files, such as *.dlls* (or support *.jar* files)
- Source files, such as *.java* or *.cpp* files
- Configuration files that are used by your software at runtime, commonly in formats such as *.xml*, *.properties*, or *.txt*

An artifact is shown as a rectangle with the stereotype <<artifact>>, or the document icon in the upper right hand corner, or both, as shown in Figure 15-5. For the rest of the book, an artifact will be shown with both the stereotype <<artifact>> and the document icon.

*Figure 15-5. Equivalent representations of a 3dpacman.jar artifact*

## Deploying an Artifact to a Node

An artifact is *deployed* to a node, which means that the artifact resides on (or is installed on) the node. Figure 15-6 shows the *3dpacman.jar* artifact from the previous example deployed to a Desktop PC hardware node by drawing the artifact symbol inside the node.

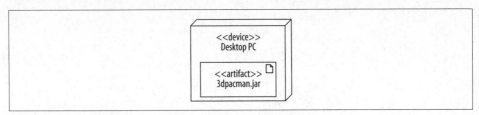

*Figure 15-6. The 3dpacman.jar artifact deployed to a Desktop PC node*

You can model that an artifact is deployed to a node in two other ways. You can also draw a dependency arrow from the artifact to the target node with the stereotype <<deploy>>, as shown in Figure 15-7.

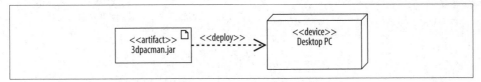

*Figure 15-7. An alternate way to model the relationship deployment*

When you're pressed for space, you might want to represent the deployment by simply listing the artifact's name inside the target node, as shown in Figure 15-8.

*Figure 15-8. A compact way to show deployment is to write the name of the artifact inside the node*

All of these methods show the same deployment relationship, so here are some guidelines for picking a notation.

Listing the artifacts (without the artifact symbol) can really save space if you have a lot of artifacts, as in Figure 15-9. Imagine how big the diagram would get if you drew the artifact symbol for each artifact.

But be careful; by listing your artifacts, you cannot show dependencies between artifacts. If you want to show that an artifact uses another artifact, you have to draw the artifact symbols and a dependency arrow connecting the artifacts, as shown in Figure 15-10.

## Tying Software to Artifacts

When designing software, you break it up into cohesive groups of functionality, such as components or packages, which eventually get compiled into one or more files—or artifacts. In UML-speak, if an artifact is the physical actualization of a

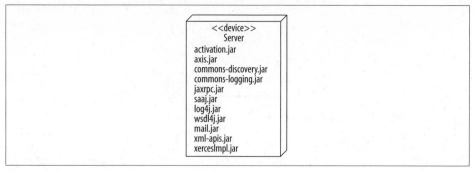

*Figure 15-9. Listing artifact names inside a node saves a lot of space compared to drawing an artifact symbol for each artifact*

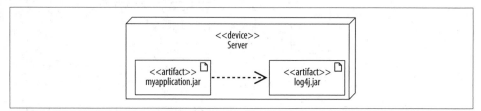

*Figure 15-10. A deployment notation that uses artifact symbols (instead of listing artifact names) allows you to show artifact dependencies*

component, then the artifact *manifests* that component. An artifact can manifest not just components but any packageable element, such as packages and classes.

The manifest relationship is shown with a dependency arrow from the artifact to the component with the stereotype <<manifest>>, as shown in Figure 15-11.

*Figure 15-11. The artifact mycomponent.jar manifests the component MyComponent*

Since artifacts can then be assigned to nodes, the manifest relationship provides the missing link in modeling how your software components are mapped to hardware. However, linking a component to an artifact to a node can result in a cluttered diagram, so it's common to show the manifest relationships separate from the deployment relationships, even if they're on the same deployment diagram.

 You can also show the manifest relationship in component diagrams by listing the artifacts manifesting a component within the component symbol, as discussed in Chapter 12.

If you're familiar with earlier versions of UML, you may be tempted to model a component running on hardware by drawing the component symbol inside the node. As of UML 2.0, artifacts have nudged components toward a more conceptual interpretation, and now artifacts represent physical files.

However, many UML tools aren't fully up to date with the UML 2.0 standard, so your tool may still use the earlier notation.

## What Is a Node?

You've already seen that you can use nodes to show hardware in your deployment diagram, but nodes don't have to be hardware. Certain types of software—software that provides an environment within which other software components can be executed—are nodes as well.

A *node* is a hardware or software resource that can host software or related files. You can think of a software node as an application context; generally not part of the software you developed, but a third-party environment that provides services to your software.

The following items are reasonably common examples of hardware nodes:

- Server
- Desktop PC
- Disk drives

The following items are examples of execution environment nodes:

- Operating system
- J2EE container
- Web server
- Application server

 Software items such as library files, property files, and executable files that cannot host software are *not* nodes—they are artifacts (see "Deployed Software: Artifacts," earlier in the chapter).

## Hardware and Execution Environment Nodes

A node is drawn as a cube with its type written inside, as shown in Figure 15-12. The stereotype <<device>> emphasizes that it's a hardware node.

Figure 15-13 shows an Application Server node. Those familiar with enterprise software development will recognize this as a type of execution environment since it's a software environment that provides services to your application. The stereotype <<executionEnvironment>> emphasizes that this node is an execution environment.

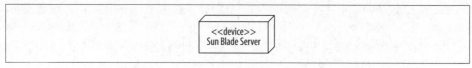

Figure 15-12. A Sun Blade Server hardware node marked with the stereotype <<device>>

Figure 15-13. An Application Server node marked with the stereotype <<executionEnvironment>>

Execution environments do not exist on their own—they run on hardware. For example, an operating system needs computer hardware to run on. You show that an execution environment resides on a particular device by placing the nodes inside one another, nesting them as shown in Figure 15-14.

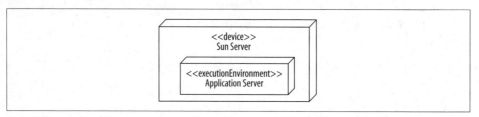

Figure 15-14. An Application Server node is shown nested in a Sun Server node, meaning that the Application Server runs on Sun Server hardware.

It's not strictly necessary in UML 2.0 to distinguish device nodes from execution environment nodes, but it's a good habit to get into because it can clarify your model.

 Want more variety? If you're using a profile (discussed in Appendix B), you can apply node stereotypes that are more relevant to your domain, such as <<J2EE Container>>. These new node types can be specified in your profile as a special kind of execution environment.

## Showing Node Instances

There are times when your diagram includes two nodes of the same type, but you want to draw attention to the fact that they are actually different instances. You can show an instance of a node by using the name : type notation as shown in Figure 15-15.

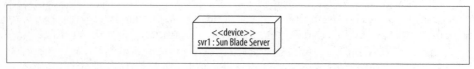

Figure 15-15. Showing the name and type of a node; an instance of a Sun Blade Server named svr1

Figure 15-16 shows how two nodes of the same type can be modeled. The nodes in this example, svr1 and svr2, are assigned different types of traffic from a load balancer (a common situation in enterprise systems).

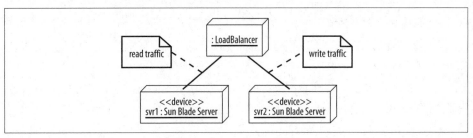

*Figure 15-16. One node gets read traffic and the other gets write traffic*

# Communication Between Nodes

To get its job done, a node may need to communicate with other nodes. For example, a client application running on a desktop PC may retrieve data from a server using TCP/IP.

*Communication paths* are used to show that nodes communicate with each other at runtime. A communication path is drawn as a solid line connecting two nodes. The type of communication is shown by adding a stereotype to the path. Figure 15-17 shows two nodes—a desktop PC and a server—that communicate using TCP/IP.

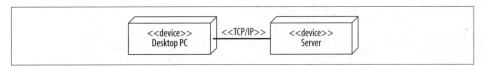

*Figure 15-17. A Desktop PC and Server communicate via TCP/IP*

You can also show communication paths between execution environment nodes. For example, you could model a web server communicating with an EJB container through RMI, as shown in Figure 15-18. This is more precise than showing an RMI communication path at the device node level because the execution environment nodes "speak" RMI. However, some modelers draw the communication paths at the outermost node level because it can make the diagram less cluttered.

Assigning a stereotype to a communication path can sometimes be tricky. RMI is layered using a TCP/IP transport layer. So, should you assign an <<RMI>> or a <<TCP/IP>> stereotype? As a rule of thumb, your communication stereotype should be as high-level as possible because it communicates more about your system. In this case, <<RMI>> is the right choice; it is higher level, and it tells the reader that you're using

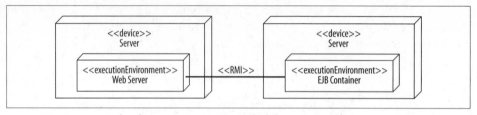

*Figure 15-18. You can also show communication paths between execution environment nodes*

a Java implementation. However, as with all UML modeling, you should tailor the diagram to your audience.

 Communication paths show that the nodes are capable of communicating with each other and are not intended to show individual messages, such as messages in a sequence diagram.

As of UML 2.0, stereotypes are supposed to be specified in a profile, so in theory, you should use only the stereotypes that your profile provides. However, even if you're not using a profile, your UML tool may allow you to make up any stereotype. Since stereotypes are a good way to show the types of communication in a system, feel free to make your own if necessary and if your tool allows. But if you do, try to keep them consistent. For example, don't create two stereotypes <<RMI>> and <<Remote Method Invocation>>, which are the same type of communication.

# Deployment Specifications

Installing software is rarely as easy as dropping a file on a machine; often you have to specify configuration parameters before your software can execute. A *deployment specification* is a special artifact specifying how another artifact is deployed to a node. It provides information that allows another artifact to run successfully in its environment.

Deployment specifications are drawn as a rectangle with the stereotype <<deployment spec>>. There are two ways to tie a deployment specification to the deployment it describes:

- Draw a dependency arrow from the deployment specification to the artifact, nesting both of these in the target node.
- Attach the deployment specification to the deployment arrow, as shown in Figure 15-19.

The *deploy.wsdd* file, shown in Figure 15-19, is the standard deployment descriptor file that specifies how a web service is deployed to the Axis web service engine. This file states which class executes the web service and which methods on the class can be called. You can list these properties in the deployment specification using the name

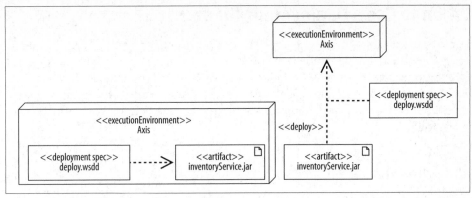

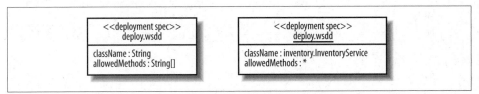

*Figure 15-19. Equivalent ways of tying a deployment specification to the deployment it describes*

: type notation. Figure 15-20 shows the *deploy.wsdd* deployment specification with the properties className and allowedMethods.

*Figure 15-20. Showing the properties of a deployment specification: the notation on the right shows an instance populated with values*

The symbol on the right shows an *instance* of a deployment specification populated with values. Use this notation if you want to show the actual property values instead of just the types.

> This chapter has only briefly mentioned instances of elements in deployment diagrams, but you can model instances of nodes, artifacts, and deployment specifications. In deployment diagrams, many modelers don't bother to specify that an element is an instance if the intent is clear. However, if you want to specify property values of a deployment specification (as on the right side of Figure 15-20), then this is a rare situation where a UML tool may force you to use the instance notation.
>
> Currently, many UML tools don't support the deployment specification symbol. If yours is one of them, you can attach a note containing similar information.

You don't need to list every property in a deployment specification—only properties you consider important to the deployment. For example, *deploy.wsdd* may contain other properties such as allowed roles, but if you're not using that property or it's insignificant (i.e., it's the same for all your web services), then leave it out.

# When to Use a Deployment Diagram

Deployment diagrams are useful at all stages of the design process. When you begin designing a system, you probably know only basic information about the physical layout. For example, if you're building a web application, you may not have decided which hardware to use and probably don't know what your software artifacts are called. But you want to communicate important characteristics of your system, such as the following:

- Your architecture includes a web server, application server, and database.
- Clients can access your application through a browser or through a richer GUI interface.
- The web server is protected with a firewall.

Even at this early stage you can use deployment diagrams to model these characteristics. Figure 15-21 shows a rough sketch of your system. The node names don't have to be precise, and you don't have to specify the communication protocols.

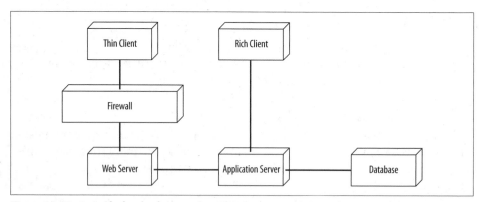

*Figure 15-21. A rough sketch of your web application*

Deployment diagrams are also useful in later stages of software development. Figure 15-22 shows a detailed deployment diagram specifying a J2EE implementation of the system.

Figure 15-22 is more specific about the hardware types, the communication protocols, and the allocation of software artifacts to nodes. A detailed deployment diagram, such as Figure 15-22, could be used be used as a blueprint for how to install your system.

You can revisit your deployment diagrams throughout the design of your system to refine the rough initial sketches, adding detail as you decide which technologies, communication protocols, and software artifacts will be used. These refined deployment diagrams allow you to express the current view of the physical system layout with the system's stakeholders.

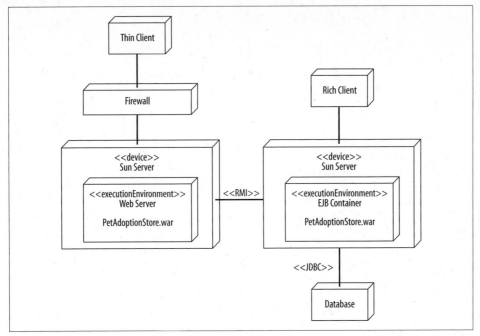

*Figure 15-22. You can provide any amount of detail about the physical design of your system*

# What's Next?

You've finished learning the fundamental UML concepts, but read on to the appendixes for an overview of some advanced modeling techniques. The appendices introduce you to the Object Constraint Language (OCL), which is a rigorous way to show constraints in your diagrams, and Profiles, which allow you to define and use a custom UML vocabulary. It's helpful to review these appendices to get a feel for extra precision you can add to your model and extra capabilities that result from that precision. The Object Constraint Language is covered in Appendix A; UML profiles are described in Appendix B.

# Object Constraint Language

Chapter 5 introduced writing constraints in your class diagrams using OCL. You don't have to use OCL to express constraints—you can use your favorite programming language syntax or even natural language. This appendix discusses the advantages of OCL and provides more details about how to more use OCL.

Recall from Chapter 5 that a constraint is written in curly braces after the element it constrains or displayed in an attached note. Figure A-1 shows different ways of specifying that the attribute `rating` has to be non-negative.

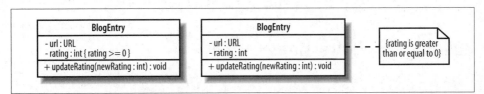

*Figure A-1. Different ways of attaching and expressing a constraint*

Figure A-1 shows that the words expressing a constraint can vary. Constraints can be written in natural language, such as:

```
rating is greater than or equal to zero
```

Constraints can also look like a programming language expression, such as:

```
rating >= 0
```

Because natural language can be ambiguous (and long-winded!), many modelers use syntax similar to their preferred programming language: notice that `rating >= 0` looks like a Java or C expression.

Constraints can get more complicated; for example, they can specify that a value isn't null. This means you have a lot of options for expressing constraints, so how do you decide which notion to use? Such an expression may look different in different programming languages. If constraints are expressed in a standard and predictable way, not only can you easily understand the constraint, but also automated tools can understand the constraint. This allows automatic checking of constraints in your diagrams and in the code generated from the diagrams.

Because of this, the Object Management Group (OMG, the group behind UML) was convinced that a single formal constraint language was needed, but the language had specific requirements. The language had to allow values to be checked but not changed—in other words, it had to be an *expression language*. The language had to be general enough that you could use it to express constraints in your UML diagrams regardless of your target implementation language. And finally, the language had to be simple enough that people would actually use it, which is not true of many formal languages.

OCL, developed at IBM for business modeling, had all of these features, and so it was a perfect match. So, OCL was chosen to work alongside UML to provide a formal yet easy-to-understand language for specifying constraints.

You don't *have* to use OCL. In general, modelers decide to use OCL depending on a combination of factors, including how extensively they model and how important they consider design by contract (discussed later). If these factors apply to you, OCL is worth considering because automated constraint checking allows greater integrity of your model.

In UML diagrams, OCL is primarily used to write constraints in class diagrams and guard conditions in state and activity diagrams.

# Building OCL Expressions

Figure A-2 shows a class diagram with a few OCL expressions, including:

*Simple number comparison*
    baseCost >= 0.0

*More complicated number comparison*
    totalCost = baseCost * (1+getTaxRate())

*String comparison*
    status <> 'Unpaid'

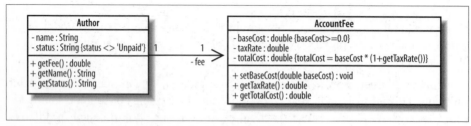

*Figure A-2. Example OCL constraints of varying complexity*

Unlike many languages, such as Java, in OCL the = operator is used to check whether two items are equal, not to assign a value.

OCL expressions consist of model elements, constants, and operators. Model elements include class attributes, operations, and members though association. The OCL expressions in Figure A-2 use the model elements baseCost, totalCost, and getTaxRate( ). (Later sections contain OCL expressions with members through association.)

Constants are unchanging values of one of the predefined OCL types. In Figure A-2, constants include 0.0 of type Real and 'Unpaid' of type String. Operators combine model elements and constants to form an expression. In Figure A-2, operators include <>, +, and =.

The following sections discuss the basics of OCL types and operators and then show how to combine these into expressions you can use in your UML models.

## Types

OCL has four built-in types: Boolean, Integer, Real, and String. Table A-1 shows examples of these four types. These examples are typical constants you could encounter in OCL expressions.

*Table A-1. Built-in OCL types*

| Type | Examples |
| --- | --- |
| Boolean | true; false |
| Integer | 1; 6,664; -200 |
| Real | 2.7181828; 10.5 |
| String | "Hello, World." |

## Operators

OCL has the basic arithmetic, logic, and comparison operators. OCL also has more advanced functions such as returning the maximum of two values and concatenating Strings. OCL is a typed language, so the operator has to make sense for its values. For example, you can't take the sum of an Integer and a Boolean. Table A-2 shows commonly used operators in OCL expressions.

*Table A-2. Commonly used operators in OCL expressions*

| Group | Operators | Used with types | Example OCL expression |
|---|---|---|---|
| Arithmetic | `+, -, *, /` | Integer, Real | baseCost + tax |
| Additional Arithmetic | `abs(), max(), min()` | Integer, Real | score1.max(score2) |
| Comparison | `<, <=, >, >=` | Integer, Real | rate > .75 |
| Equality | `=, <>` | All | age = 65<br>title <> 'CEO' |
| Boolean | `and, or, xor, not` | Boolean | isMale and (age >= 65) |
| String | `concat(), size(), substring(), toInteger(), toReal()` | String | title.substring(1,3) |

Operators in the groups Comparison, Equality, and Boolean all return results of type Boolean. For example, `age = 65` evaluates to true or false. The other operators in Table A-2 return the same type with which they're used. For example, if `baseCost` and `tax` are Real, then `baseCost + tax` will also be Real.

Figure A-2 shows that `getTaxRate()` returns a double (this model was written with Java types), but the table in Table A-2 mentions that the operator + is defined on Reals and Integers. That's perfectly fine; when building an OCL expression, you can match your types to the closest OCL type.

 OCL can also express operations on collections, such as unions of sets. For a more complete list of OCL expressions, see *UML 2.0 in a Nutshell* (O'Reilly).

# Pulling It Together

So far you've seen the building blocks of OCL expressions. Now let's combine them to build a sample OCL expression.

```
totalCost = baseCost * (1+getTaxRate())
```

This OCL expression is taken from Figure A-2. It contains the following building blocks of an OCL expression:

*Model elements*
  `totalCost`, `baseCost`, and `getTaxRate()`

*Constant*
  1

*Operators*
  `=`, `*`, and `+`

The above expression actually consists of several OCL expressions, which are in turn combined by operators. For example, 1+getTaxRate( ) evaluates to a Real, which is then multiplied with baseCost. That resulting value is checked for equality with totalCost using the = operator. You can combine model elements, constants, and expressions according to their type, but the combined expression must be type Boolean. This is because we're focusing on using OCL to express constraints and guards, which must evaluate to true or false.

Another commonly used constraint is to specify that an object isn't null. To specify that an object isn't null, you have to use the OCL's notation for sets and operations on sets. Figure A-3 shows how to check that Author's member through association fee isn't null using the expression:

```
self.fee->notEmpty( )
```

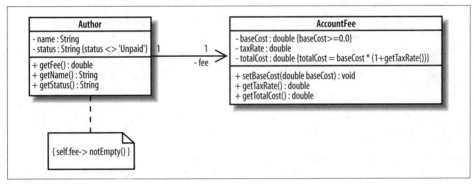

*Figure A-3. Constraining that a member isn't null*

Notice the reference to self in the OCL expression in Figure A-3. Because it is attached to Author, self refers to objects of type Author. The self keyword is commonly used when you set a context in an OCL expression, as shown in the following section.

# Context

Figure A-2 defined OCL expressions on the elements they constrain, while Figure A-3 defined an OCL expression on the containing class. You can write an OCL expression at different areas in your diagram. How you write the OCL expression depends on the *context*, or where you are in the diagram.

Figure A-4 shows how to check that baseCost of AccountFee is greater than or equal to 0 at different reference points in the diagram. The first diagram shows this constraint in the context of baseCost, the second shows this constraint at AccountFee, and the third shows this constraint at Author.

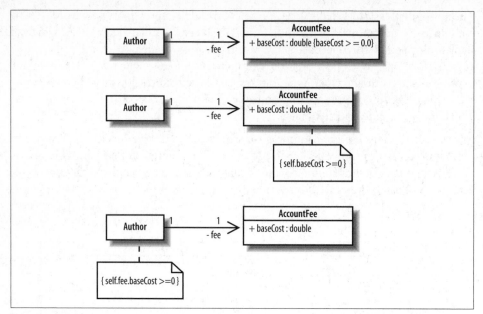

*Figure A-4. The way you write a constraint depends on your reference point in the diagram*

If your reference point is baseCost, e.g., by writing a constraint in curly braces after baseCost, then you write:

```
baseCost >= 0.0
```

If you're referring to the AccountFee class, e.g., by attaching a note to the AccountFee class, then you write:

```
self.baseCost >= 0.0
```

Finally, if you're referring to the Author class, e.g., by attaching a note to the Author class, then you write:

```
self.fee.baseCost >= 0.0
```

You can also write OCL constraints that aren't physically attached to model elements. For example, your UML tool may provide a text editor for entering constraints. If you do this, write the context explicitly. If the context is the AccountFee class, then you write:

```
Context AccountFee
inv: self.baseCost >= 0.0
```

The inv keyword indicates that the constraint is an *invariant*, or a condition that must always be true. When specifying the context, you also specify the type of constraint it is. Constraint types are discussed in "Types of Constraints," next.

# Types of Constraints

There are three types of constraints:

*Invariants*
> An *invariant* is a constraint that must always be true—otherwise the system is in an invalid state. Invariants are defined on class attributes. For example, in Figure A-4, the baseCost attribute of AccountFee must always be greater than or equal to zero.

*Preconditions*
> A *precondition* is a constraint that is defined on a method and is checked before the method executes. Preconditions are frequently used to validate input parameters to a method.

*Postconditions*
> A *postcondition* is also defined on a method and is checked after the method executes. Postconditions are frequently used to describe how values were changed by a method.

Previous examples in this chapter focused on invariants, but all three constraint types can be expressed in your UML diagrams or related documentation. The following examples will show how to provide preconditions and postconditions for the method incrementRating. The reference class diagram is shown in Figure A-5.

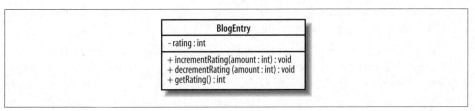

*Figure A-5. We'll provide preconditions and postconditions for the incrementRating method*

Suppose incrementRating will increment the value rating by the value amount. We want to first specify a precondition that amount is less than a maximum legal amount, say 100, and a postcondition ensuring that rating has been incremented by amount. To write these preconditions and postconditions, you first specify the context and then the constraints.

```
context BlogEntry::incrementRating(amount: int) : void
pre: amount <= 100
post: rating = rating@pre + amount
```

Notice the @pre directive: rating@pre is the value of rating before the method executes. You can use the @pre notation on methods too:

```
context BlogEntry::incrementRating(amount: int) : void
pre: amount <= 100
post: getRating( ) = getRating@pre( ) + amount
```

Invariants, preconditions, and postconditions are part of an approach known as "Design by Contract," developed by Bertrand Meyer. "Design by Contract" attempts to make more reliable code by establishing a contract between a class and its clients. A class's contract tells its clients that if they call its methods with valid values, then they will receive a valid value in response. A contract also establishes invariants on a class, meaning that the class's attributes will never violate certain constraints.

If you're wondering why you haven't encountered invariants, preconditions, and postconditions in your code, note that support for Design by Contract differs per programming language. "Design by Contract" is built into the Eiffel programming language, which was also developed by Bertrand Meyer. Eiffel has keywords for invariants, preconditions, and postconditions, and an exception is thrown if any of these constraints are violated. With other languages, you have to either implement constraint handing yourself or use a package such as iContract for Java. iContract is a preprocessor with doc-style tags to specify invariants, preconditions, and postconditions. iContract also throws an exception if a constraint is violated.

## OCL Automation

The real power of OCL comes from tools that can use the OCL constraints from your UML model to perform constraint checking for you. While at the moment there is wide variation in tool maturity and level of integration, the ultimate goal is to enhance integration of your UML model with the runtime behavior of your system. This has the benefit of allowing you to catch errors early and saving on debugging time.

Some UML tools focus on placing the OCL constraints from your diagrams into generated code so that the constraints can be checked at runtime (although at the moment, these may only be proposed or partial implementations). Example approaches include generating assert statements directly in your code to allow constraint checking, or embellishing your code with Java annotations or doc-style tags containing OCL constraints, which can then be used by standard OCL tools that can check constraints at runtime. For example, the open source UML tool ArgoUML inserts OCL constraints into generated Java code as doc-style tags. With doc or annotations in your code, you can take advantage of OCL tools (such as ocl4java or the Dresden OCL Toolkit) that perform code enhancement to provide you runtime feedback about constraint violations in your executed code.

Stay on the lookout for developments in this area; as MDA and Executable UML (introduced in Chapter 1) become increasingly central to UML, you can expect even more of these capabilities to be integrated with modeling tools.

# Adapting UML: Profiles

This book has used Java code examples to demonstrate UML concepts, but the UML model elements shown apply to almost any object-oriented system, regardless of the language (e.g., Java, C++, or Smalltalk), platform you're targeting (e.g., J2EE or .NET), or domain you're working with (e.g., medical or aerospace).

Object-oriented systems share many common characteristics structurally and behaviorally: they have classes, interactions among classes, and so on. But when it comes to platforms and domains, object-oriented systems often have many differences in terminology. For example, the J2EE platform has EJBs, JARs, and JSPs, whereas the .NET platform has ADOs, assemblies, and ASPs.

When you create your UML model, it is helpful if you label your model elements with the terminology specific to the environment or platform you've chosen. In other words, wouldn't it be great to be able to specify that a component is in fact going to be an EJB, instead of just calling it a component?

Trying to make UML target every possible platform or domain would be a losing battle and not really in the spirit of a general purpose modeling language. The group behind UML, the Object Management Group (OMG), realized this and built a mechanism by which UML can be adapted and tailored to meet your own specific needs. That mechanism was the profile.

## What Is a Profile?

*Profiles* are a lightweight way to adapt UML to a particular platform—J2EE, .NET, etc.—or domain—medical, financial, aerospace, etc. Profiles are made up of stereotypes, tagged values, and a set of constraints. They capture a vocabulary commonly used across a domain or platform and allow that vocabulary to be applied to your model's elements to make them more meaningful.

Even better, code generation tools can use profiles to generate artifacts specific to a platform or environment. A component labeled with an EJB stereotype could be converted to the classes and interfaces it takes to implement an EJB.

In earlier versions of UML, you could make up stereotypes on the fly. This led to confusion about when to use stereotypes and modelers were left to informally standardize and reuse a common set of stereotypes. UML 2.0 fixed this problem by declaring that stereotypes and tagged values (see "Tagged Values" later in this chapter) should be created in a profile.

## Stereotypes

*Stereotypes* signify that an element has a special use or intent. Stereotypes are most often shown by specifying the name of the stereotype between two guillemots, as in <<stereotype_name>>; you can substitute angle brackets if you don't have guillemots available on your system, as shown in Figure B-1.

*Figure B-1. An artifact with a JAR stereotype applied to it; this is an example of a stereotype you might see in a J2EE profile*

If a stereotype has an icon associated with it, you may also display the element with its icon. UML tools generally allow you to switch between these display options. Figure B-2 shows the standard JAR stereotype display notation as well as an example JAR icon.

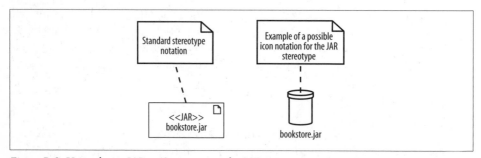

*Figure B-2. Using the <<JAR>> Stereotype and a JAR icon*

There is no limit to the number of stereotypes that can be applied to a particular element, as shown in Figure B-3.

*Figure B-3. The bookstore.jar has both the JAR and file stereotype applied to it*

# Tagged Values

Stereotypes may have one or more associated tagged values. Tagged values provide extra information that is associated with the stereotype.

A tagged value is shown in a note that is attached to the stereotyped element, as shown in Figure B-4.

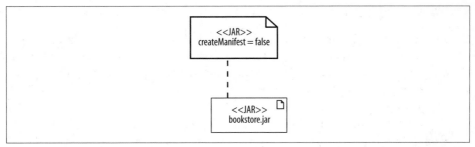

*Figure B-4. This tagged value, attached in a note, specifies whether a manifest should be created for the JAR file*

If multiple stereotypes have been applied to the same element then you split any tagged values for those stereotypes in their corresponding note, shown in Figure B-5.

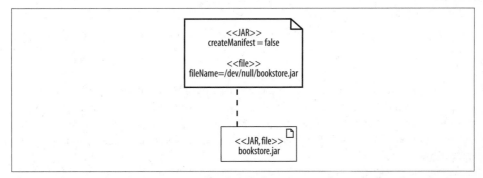

*Figure B-5. Applying multiple stereotypes, each with their own set of tagged values*

# Constraints

Unlike stereotypes and tagged values, constraints don't correspond to symbols that you use in your UML models. Constraints are also specified in the profile definition, but they impose rules or restrictions on model elements. An example of a constraint is shown in "Creating a Profile."

An introduction to constraints outside the context of profiles can be found in Chapter 5.

# Creating a Profile

Usually you will simply use an existing profile that is built into your UML tool or one provided by a standard source such as the OMG. However, if you find that there simply is no standard profile available, then many UML tools will allow you to create your own.

Be careful when creating your own profiles. The real power of profiles only comes when they are standardized and in common use, discussed in "Why Bother with Profiles?" later on in this chapter.

Your UML tool may allow you to create a profile using a simple text entry dialog; for example, it may ask you for the name of the stereotype and ask you to choose what type of element it can be applied to. However, the behind-the-scenes graphical model of a profile looks like the one shown in Figure B-6.

Stereotypes defined in the profile are themselves given the standard stereotype <<stereotype>>. Two new stereotypes are declared in Figure B-6: WebService and Exposed.

To show that the WebService stereotype can be applied to classes an *extension* arrow points from WebService to Class. The extension arrow has a solid arrowhead and it connects the new stereotype to the element type that it can be applied to. The extension arrow is also used to show that the Exposed stereotype can be applied to operations.

If the stereotype has tagged values, they are listed in a compartment below the stereotype name. The WebService stereotype has two tagged values: service and encoding. The possible values of these tagged values are shown in the enumerations ServiceStyle and EncodingStyle.

Finally, any applicable constraints on the use of the WebService and Exposed stereotypes are specified in notes. The Exposed stereotype has a constraint, in curly braces,

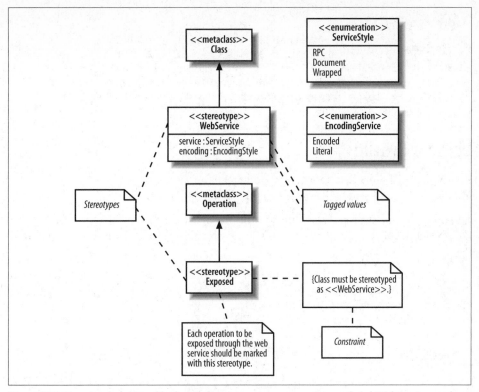

*Figure B-6. Creating a new profile that contains two stereotypes, Exposed and WebService, and some associated tagged values and constraints*

that specifies that it can be applied only to operations of classes that are themselves stereotyped as a WebService.

# Working with the Meta-Model

At this point, you may be thinking that the model in Figure B-6 looks similar to the other UML models you've seen in this book. However, it contains some striking differences: the WebService stereotype is related to the element Class for one, and the *extension* arrow is different from the previous relationships you've seen for another. Normally, you would never explicitly refer to Class in your UML models because it is a UML meta-model element.

The term meta-model was introduced in Chapter 1. *Meta-models* define rules about how the UML elements work, e.g., a class can have a subclass or a class can be associated with any number of other classes. When you are modeling a profile you are working with the meta-model, customizing the regular UML's rules for a particular context.

This customization of UML for your particular context may sound dangerous at first, almost like you are making up your own language! This is actually not the case, profiles are a safe and controlled way of customizing UML, but should be used only when you really need them (see "Why Bother with Profiles?"). They can be a powerful way of making your model mean much more than it would do with standard UML alone.

## Using a Profile

The model in Figure B-6 shows how to create the Web Service profile. To actually use the profile, you *apply* the profile to the package that will use it.

To apply a profile to a package, draw a dashed arrow from the package that will use the profile to the profile, with the <<apply>> stereotype along the arrow as shown in Figure B-7.

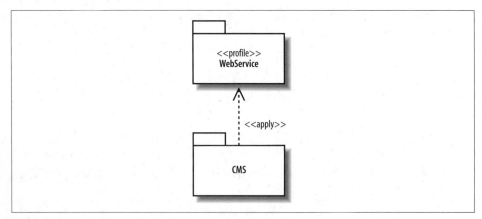

*Figure B-7. Applying the Web Service profile to the CMS package allows you to use the Web Service profile in your CMS model*

Not all UML tools use this method for applying a profile to your model. For example, it may let you specify which profile to apply to a package using a dialog box.

Now that you've applied the profile, you may use the profile in your CMS model, as shown in Figure B-8.

In Figure B-8, the BlogFeedService is marked with the WebService stereotype. Its single method is marked with the Exposed stereotype, allowing it to be exposed through the web service. The tagged values for the WebService stereotype are attached in a note, populated with values from the enumerations.

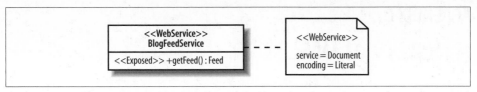

*Figure B-8. Applying elements of the Web Service profile to the BlogFeedService class in the CMS package*

The constraint from the Web Service profile isn't explicitly seen in this model, but it is used because the Exposed stereotype on the getFeed() operation is contained in a class that uses the WebService stereotype.

# Why Bother with Profiles?

The real power of a profile comes when it is used by many people interested in that platform or domain. Not only does it introduce a common vocabulary, but also it allows you to leverage tools that generate source code and other artifacts based on the profile. For example, a tool could convert a model that uses our Web Service profile into a deployable web service. Such a tool could generate the implementation class and populate a deployment descriptor file with the service type and encoding values, keeping the model and code in sync. As another example, the Omondo Eclipse IDE plugin provides a J2EE profile which, when applied to your model, allows automatic generation of the medley of classes required to implement an EJB (prior to EJB 3.0) and even deploys them to the application server.

The OMG maintains some common profiles, such as profiles for CORBA and testing. The testing profile, for example, describes mappings to JUnit—a widely-used Java unit testing framework.

# A History of UML

UML has not always been the de facto modeling language that it is today. In fact, not so long ago, everyone involved in complex system modeling was using a plethora of different modeling languages—some formal, some informal—and each had its own associated development approach.

Nowhere was the problem more apparent than in software modeling. Object orientation had just become a fully recognized technique for developing software, and it did not take long for new modeling methods to start incorporating this revolutionary technique into their practices.

Unfortunately, even though object-oriented software modeling was seen as a good thing, the mess of different and conflicting approaches to modeling cancelled out a lot of the advantages that modeling promised. If you were designing using one modeling language and another member of your group was using another modeling language, the advantages of communicating designs to each other were completely lost. Software and system groups were forced to pick a modeling language, knowing that their choice was potentially a dangerous decision that could exclude other groups from easily joining the design effort.

This time of confusion and chaos in the software modeling world is now rather dramatically referred to as the "method wars." Three of the primary protagonists in these method wars were Grady Booch, Ivar Jacobson, and James Rumbaugh. Each of these innovators had their own software development methods and a modeling language with their own distinct notation. More importantly, they also headed up their own community of users that evangelized their approach to software modeling. It was these three approaches to software development and their associated languages and notation that were to form the basis of UML.

# Take One Part OOAD...

Grady Booch's approach was named Object-Oriented Analysis and Design (OOAD), or less formally, the Booch method. These grand titles encompassed a method that included a modeling language constructed of diagrams to show classes, state, state transitions, interactions, modules, and processes.

This formidable collection of diagrams was probably best known for its class notations, which were depicted as clouds and a selection of arrows with simple names such as *has a* that could be used to specify different types of inter-class relationships, as shown in Figure C-1.

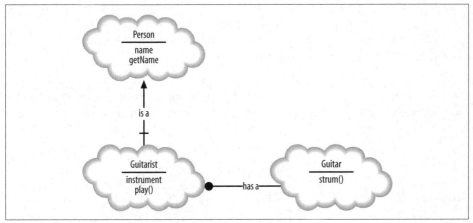

*Figure C-1. A cloud OOAD notation describes classes and the relationships between them*

The cloud notational style and the simple naming of Booch's inter-class relationship arrows worked themselves into the hearts of adopters to such a degree that even to this day, they reminisce about the clouds. In fact the use of either the cloud notation or the rectangle notation for classes prompted some of the most vehement, and useless, arguments during the inception of UML.

# ...with a Sprinkling of OOSE...

Ivar Jacobson and his Object-Oriented Software Engineering (OOSE) approach is probably best known for the revolutionary technique of mapping requirements to object-oriented software designs, called *use cases*. There was a definite focus in OOSE to accurately capture and model the problem domain, and use cases were a key technique in achieving this as part of a requirements model.

OOSE was not just about requirements, though; it also had corresponding models for analysis and design. The analysis model in OOSE was one in which object relationships could be modeled. It drew distinctions between entity objects that contain data, control objects that control other objects, and interface objects that interact with users or other external systems. UML has inherited these types of objects, and they are particularly popular on sequence diagrams (see Chapter 7).

The design model allowed you to describe how the system behaves using state transition and interaction diagrams, which—although the notation has changed—are still present to some extent in UML today. Communication diagrams are covered in Chapter 8; state machine diagrams are covered in Chapter 14.

To complete the picture, the OOSE also specified implementation and test models. An implementation model captured how use cases were mapped to the underlying system implementation and the test model closed the loop by showing how use cases could drive the development of a system's tests.

Despite all of these various models, use cases are the thing that OOSE will be most noted for; see Figure C-2 for an example. UML has gone through various iterations over the years, but of all the UML constructs, use cases is the one technique that's remained unchanged.

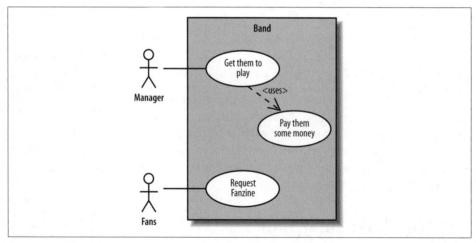

Figure C-2. The OOSE use case notation describes three use cases within a system and the two outside influences—actors—that interact with those use cases

# ...Add a Dash of OMT...

If Booch's OOAD brought class modeling and Jacobson's OOSE gave us use cases, state transitions, and interaction modeling, then James Rumbaugh added his object modeling technique (OMT). Although Booch's class and object diagrams were well loved by his adopters (those clouds again), it was the class and object diagram notation from OMT that most influenced what was to come. The OMT's notation for its object view was arguably simpler to draw, even if its interclass relationships were not as intuitive as Booch's (see Figure C-3).

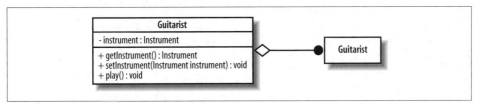

*Figure C-3. This diagram is easy to read, even for a novice developer*

That is not to say that object and class diagram notation was all that OMT added to the mix. The OMT also had notation for diagrams showing the dynamic qualities of software, namely sequence diagrams.

# ...and Bake for 10 to 15 Years

It is not an understatement to say that the modeling world was in a mess (it was a war, after all!). The mere suggestion of a unified approach to modeling was likely to bring passionate objections as modeling practitioners protected their skills, tools, and—most importantly—approaches.

But it was time for a change. In early 1996, Ivar Jacobson gave Richard Mark Soley a call at home, late at night as always, and confirmed that the time was ripe to standardize on a modeling language and bring an end to the modeling method wars. At this point, the modeling tools market was worth about $30 million worldwide total, split among several vendors. The largest vendor was Rational Software Corporation, but even at this point Rational was only a $25 million company—small fish compared to software behemoths such as Microsoft and IBM.

As a first step, Soley and Jacobson made a list all of the major methodologists and invited them to come to an Object Management Group (OMG) meeting to explore the possibility of developing a standard. Little did they know just how important and successful that meeting would be. The OMG was traditionally a standards body that specifically targeted distributed systems; however, in an act of excellent foresight, the group organized its first meeting targeted at creating a standard modeling language Hosted by Tandem Computer in San Jose, California, almost every major methodologist or representative of every major methodologist made it to that meeting. According to legend, the organizers were very careful to leave all the windows open so that the room would not explode with the number of egos—it was a very impressive assembly. Early on, it was realized that the most difficult facet of the meeting probably would be finding the right person to chair it. They needed somebody who would be recognized as a methodologist, who was also sufficiently impartial and focused, and who could actually guide the meeting towards a useful conclusion.

Mary Loomis was that person. Back then, Mary was a research director at Hewlett-Packard, and she was on the team at General Electric that had developed the OMT methodology. Mary was the perfect person to keep all those egos in check. Very quickly, Mary managed to get all the gurus in the room to actually make progress toward an agreement. The goal was not a technical discussion about which technologies to use, or whether to draw a class as a box or a cloud, but to determine *how* to develop a Unified Modeling Language.

This is what the OMG brought into the mix. The OMG excelled at getting direct competitors to agree on issues, which was the most important aspect of getting to a Unified Modeling Language. Participants agreed that:

- It was time for a standard.
- They would attempt to use the OMG standards process to develop that standard.

These two simple goals were really an amazing achievement. At that point in time, the OMG had used only its standards process to develop specific distributed object computing standards, such as CORBA and its services. The OMG had *never* created anything like development standards, which is what a UML specification would have to be. Without a doubt, managing a community as passionate as the methodologists and, on top of that, building a successful standard that everyone could sign up for was new and hazardous territory for the OMG.

But the OMG was in the middle of a transition. During part of that transition, it recognized that one of the group's biggest strengths was its standards process itself and not any specific technology. Following its process, the OMG developed and sent a requirements document to the industry that described precisely what was needed of a standard modeling language. It was then up to industry to send in their own ideas for how they could meet those requirements.

By the middle of 1997, the OMG had received what was to be an acceptable single joint proposal for a standard modeling language. Written by 21 different companies, this joint proposal was the product of a merger between each of those company's own proposals. The whole process came to an end in September 1997 when the OMG published a specification for a standard modeling language, but there was a slight problem with its preferred name. The OMG had decided to name the standard modeling language the Unified Modeling Language, but UML as a name was already owned by one of the companies that had agreed to the original joint proposal—Rational Software Corporation.

Rational Software employed Jacobson, Booch, and Rumbaugh—collectively known as the three amigos—and had already given a huge amount of input into the development of the OMG's standard, as well as continuing on with research toward their own joint specification for a modeling language. The Rational modeling language brought together the three amigos' considerably popular methodologies and toolsets, but unfortunately it too had also been called the Unified Modeling Language.

It was crunch time; would the industry slip back into confusion with both the OMG and Rational's UML, or would the OMG have to find a new name entirely and thereby lose any name recognition that the UML brand had already gained? As it happens, there was a particularly happy ending to this story. To solve the naming nightmare, the OMG achieved something that was nothing short of a coup.

The OMG were able to convince Rational, even though there was already some considerable marketing value to the UML brand, to donate at no charge both the UML name and the cube logo (see Figure C-4). This way, the OMG could go ahead with a truly open standard modeling language, which could officially be named UML.

Figure C-4. The UML cube logo

For a couple of years afterward, people thought that only Rational was involved in the development of the UML specification, largely because the UML name and logo originated with Rational, and Rational Rose was the most popular modeling tool at the time. In fact, some companies did not want the standard modeling language to be called UML because they believed the public would continue to associate the UML name with Rational. Those fears have proved largely unfounded over time, and now more than 90 percent of practitioners recognize that UML is a standard owned and managed by the OMG.

UML has undergone several revisions as it evolves to accommodate various new industry advances and best-practice techniques. The original input from Jacobson, Booch, and Rumbaugh, although still very important, now happily works alongside the other full set of possible UML 2.0 diagrams, as shown in Figure C-5.

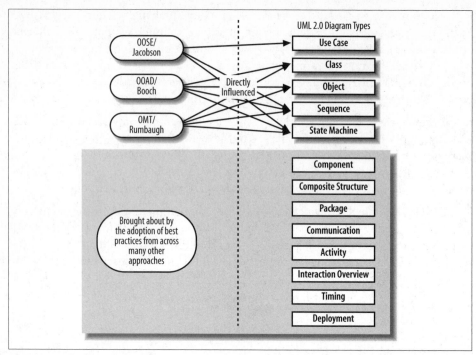

*Figure C-5. Building on the best practices of the past, UML draws on OOSE, OOAD, and OMT as well as a plethora of other techniques to create the best toolset for modeling systems*

Systems development techniques, particularly software systems, are in a vibrant state of flux most of the time. This means that any unified approach to modeling software must be flexible and open to new approaches to still be of practical use; however, with UML, there is finally a common language for expressing your models.

*Special thanks to Richard Mark Soley for all the first-hand anecdotes and explanations about how the OMG process worked and why it was ideal for standardizing UML.*

# Index

We'd like to hear your suggestions for improving our indexes. Send email to *index@oreilly.com*.

internal structures, Composite Structure diagram showing, 174–180
interruption regions, 58
invariants, 91
iterative methods of software development, 14

## J

Java 5 Tiger: A Developer's Notebook (O'Reilly), 107
Java in a Nutshell, 5th Edition (O'Reilly), 117
Java Threads (O'Reilly), 117
join pseudostates, 221
joins, Activity diagram, 50

## K

Krutchen, Philippe ("Architectural Blueprints—The "4+1"View Model of Software Architecture"), 15
Krutchen's 4+1 view model, 14–15

## L

<<library>> stereotype, 18
life cycle of object, 217
lifelines
    in Interaction Overview diagram, 163
    in Sequence diagram, 109, 123
lines
    activation bars for active participants, 113
    arrowed lines (edges), 45
    between actors and use cases (communication lines), 26
    between classes (associations), 85
    between nodes (communication paths), 231
    between objects (links), 103
    between participants (communication links), 132
    lifelines for participants, 109, 123, 163
    lightning bolt line (interruption regions), 58
    state-lines for participants, 152
    (see also diagram notations)
links
    between objects, 103
    communication links, 132, 137, 142
lists, templates used for, 99, 106

logic analyzer, Timing diagram compared to, 144
logical view, 15
loop fragment, 129

## M

<<manifest>> stereotype, 227
Martin, Robert C. (Agile Software Development), 208
MDAs (Model Driven Architectures), 10
merges, Activity diagram, 46, 48–50
messages
    diagrams showing, 142
    in Communication diagram, 132, 137
        invoked conditionally, 134
        invoked multiple times, 134
        nested, 133, 139
        sent by participant to itself, 135
        simultaneous, 133
    in Sequence diagram, 111
        arrows used by, 114–119
        asynchronous, 116–117, 124, 142
        for participant creation and destruction, 118
        nested, 114
        return messages, 118
        signature for, 112
        synchronous messages, 115
    in Timing diagram, 153
meta-models, 2, 249
methods (see operations)
minus symbol (-), private visibility, 71, 203
Model Driven Architictures (MDAs), 10
modeling language, 2
    formal languages as, 8
    informal languages as, 5–8
    software code as, 3–5
    (see also UML)
models, 1
    diagrams as views of, 12
    sharing between machines, 10
    views of, 14–16
multiple inheritance (generalization), 90
multiple processes, forks representing, 51
multiple threads, forks representing, 51
multiplicity
    of attributes, 74
    on connectors, 177

physical view, 15, 224
pictures as modeling language, 6
PIMs (Platform Independent Models), 10
pins, 54
Platform Independent Models (PIMs), 10
Platform Specific Models (PSMs), 10
plus symbol (+)
    public visibility, 68, 203
ports
    for classes, 173, 180
    for components, 194
postconditions, 92
preconditions, 92
private import, 206
private visibility, 71, 203
process view, 15, 43
processes, forks representing, 51
profiles, 232, 245
    as meta-models, 249
    constraints in, 248
    creating, 248
    reasons to use, 251
    standard, 248, 251
    stereotypes in, 246
    using, 250
programming language, UML used as, 13
properties
    in Composite Structure diagram, 178
    of attributes, 75
    (see also attributes)
protected visibility, 69
protocol state machines, 211, 223
provided interfaces
    of classes, 181
    of components, 188
pseudostates, 213
PSMs (Platform Specific Models), 10
public import, 206
public interface of class, 68
public visibility, 68, 203
publications
    Agile Software Development (Prentice
        Hall), 208
    Design Patterns: Elements of Reusable
        Object-Oriented Software
        (Addison-Wesley), 90, 95, 182
    Head First Design Patterns (O'Reilly), 82,
        182
    Java 5 Tiger: A Developer's Notebook
        (O'Reilly), 107

    Java in a Nutshell, 5th Edition
        (O'Reilly), 117
    Java Threads (O'Reilly), 117
    UML 2.0 in a Nutshell (O'Reilly), 145

# R

readOnly property of attributes, 75
realization relationship, 97
<<realizations>> stereotype, 192
receive signals, 56, 57
recurring time events, Activity diagram, 52
ref fragment, 127, 129
region fragment, 130
region of states, 220
relative time indicators, 150
required interfaces
    of classes, 181
    of components, 188
requirements (see system requirements)
return messages, 118
return type of operation, 78
reusability, 5
reuse
    <<include>> relationships for, 33
    components for, 186
    generalization for, 89

# S

scalability of UML, 3
self-transition, 215
send signals, 56
Sequence diagram, 11, 109
    activation bars in, 113
    compared to Communication
        diagram, 131, 139–143
    creating from use case, 120–126
    creating Timing diagram from, 146
    events in, 111
    fragments in, 126–130
    in logical view, 15
    incorporating into Interaction Overview
        diagram, 165
    messages (signals) in, 111
    participants in, 109, 122
    time in, 110
    when to create, 62, 82, 100, 107
    when to use, 143
sequence fragments, 126–130
<<service>> stereotype, 18
shall requirements, 22

shapes (see diagram notations)
should requirements, 22
signals
    between participants, 56
    between transitions, 222
    starting an activity, 57
    (see also messages)
Singleton design pattern, 82
sketch, UML used as, 13
software code
    as artifact in Deployment diagram, 226
    as modeling language, 3–5
    nodes hosting, 229
    package dependencies and, 208
    packages used in, 204
    reuse of
        <<include>> relationships for, 33
        components for, 186
        generalization for, 89
    states in, 217
    UML model as detailed as, 13
software development process
    methods of, 14
    UML as part of, 13
source state, 214
<<source>> stereotype, 18
standard for UML, 3
standard profiles, 248, 251
standard stereotypes, 17
State Machine diagram, 12, 211–213
    final state of, 213
    guards in, 215
    in logical view, 15
    initial pseudostate of, 213
    pseudostates in, 213, 221
    states in, 213
    transition-oriented view of, 222
    transitions in, 214–217
    triggers in, 215
    when not to use, 217
    when to use, 211, 217
states, 212, 213
    active and inactive, 212
    composite states, 220
    in software, 217
    internal behavior of, 218
    internal transitions of, 219
    notation for, 212
    regions of, 220
    source state, 214
    substates, 220

target state, 214
static classes or class elements, 79–82
stereotypes, 16–18
    creating new stereotypes, 232
    for interfaces, 96, 189
    icons associated with, 246
    in profiles, 246
    notation for, 16, 17, 246
    profiles for, 232
    standard, list of, 17
    tagged values for, 18
    (see also specific stereotypes)
substates, 220
<<subsystem>> stereotype, 18, 188
subsystems, 188
swimlanes (see partitions, Activity diagram)
symbols (see diagram notations)
synchronous messages, 115
system boundaries, 27
system clock, as tricky actor, 23
system requirements
    associated with use case, 28
    defining, 22
    shall requirements, 22
    should requirements, 22
    (see also use cases)

## T

tagged values, 18
target package, 205
target state, 214
templates, 83, 99
    binding, 105–107
    for lists, 99, 106
threads
    asynchronous messages used for, 116
    forks representing, 51
tightly coupled classes, 83, 90
tilde (~), package visibility, 70
time events, Activity diagram, 51
time, in Sequence diagram, 110
Timing diagram, 11, 144
    alternate notation for, 159
    complexity of, 159
    creating from Sequence diagram, 146
    events in, 153
        alternate notation for, 160
    in logical view, 15
    incorporated into Interaction Overview
        diagram, 165
    messages in, 153

## About the Authors

**Russ Miles** is a software engineer for General Dynamics UK, where he works with Java and Distributed Systems, although his passion at the moment is Aspect Orientation and AspectJ, in particular. To ensure that he has as little spare time as possible, Russ contributes to various open source projects while working on books for O'Reilly. He is currently studying at Oxford University in England for an MSc in software engineering.

**Kim Hamilton** is a senior software engineer at a major aerospace corporation, where she has designed and implemented a variety of systems, including web applications and distributed systems. Kim has a Master's in applied math and computer science from Cornell University.

## Colophon

The animal appearing on the cover *of Learning UML 2.0* is a gorilla (*Gorilla gorilla*). Despite its reputation for aggression, the gorilla is generally shy and inoffensive, rising to an erect position and beating its chest only when provoked or threatened. This behavior is meant to intimidate intruders rather than harm them. However, if the family group is attacked, male gorillas will risk death to protect their young. Gorillas are the largest and most powerful of the apes, with females weighing up to 200 pounds and males up to 400 pounds.

Gorillas are socially flexible, meaning their social structure is not set in stone. Troops can number as many as 30 individuals but are more often comprised of 6 or 7, including one silverback (mature male), a few females, and their young. In her lifetime, a female gorilla gives birth to about three offspring, which remain in her care until they are three or four years old. Offspring stay with their troop until they reach sexual maturity—about nine years old—at which time they generally start or join another troop.

Populations of gorillas are decreasing due to human encroachment and hunting. Scientists estimate that there are roughly 50,000 gorillas left in the wild in Africa, most of which are western lowland gorillas—only about 600 are mountain gorillas. Most countries have passed laws protecting gorillas, but enforcement is difficult in remote jungles where people survive by hunting. Tourism now generates a great deal of money in Rwanda, Uganda, and Zaire, which helps protect gorillas as well as other species.

The cover image is from *Lydekker's Royal History*. The cover font is Adobe ITC Garamond. The text font is Linotype Birka; the heading font is Adobe Myriad Condensed; and the code font is LucasFont's TheSans Mono Condensed.

# Better than e-books

Buy *Learning UML 2.0* and access the
digital edition FREE on Safari for 45 days.

Go to www.oreilly.com/go/safarienabled
and type in coupon code QUJE-7LDL-GS9E-MXKA-5UAM

**Search**
thousands of
top tech books

**Download**
whole chapters

**Cut and Paste**
code examples

**Find**
answers fast

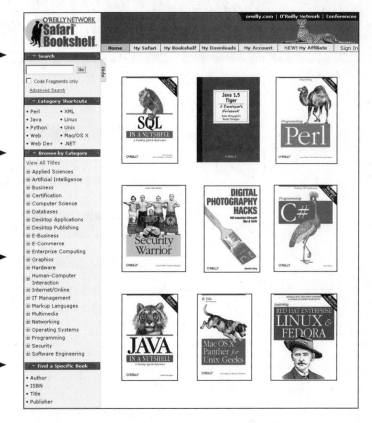

Search Safari! The premier electronic reference
library for programmers and IT professionals.